Recording And Production Techniques

Printed in the United Kingdom by MPG Books, Bodmin

Published by SMT, an imprint of Sanctuary Publishing Limited, Sanctuary House,
45-53 Sinclair Road, London W14 0NS, United Kingdom

www.sanctuarypublishing.com

ISBN: 1-86074-443-5

Recording And Production Techniques

Paul White

smt

CONTENTS

INTRODUCTION

A great deal of mystery surrounds the art of the professional record producer and studio engineer, for it is now recognised that, in some cases, their contribution to a record can be equal to that of the artist. Indeed, some producers have assumed a Svengali-like role, taking command of all stages of a project, from songwriting to final mix, and it's not unknown for the artist to make only a minor musical contribution. Examples of this are rare and come to our attention only because of the publicity they attract, but they serve to demonstrate the enormous influence that can be exercised by the producer. However, the true role of producer is really to do whatever it takes to come up with a commercially viable record, and that requires everything from musical knowledge to people-management skills.

The backgrounds and experiences of producers vary widely: some producers are competent engineers while others come from a musical background and rely solely on the studio engineer to interpret their needs. As you will discover, it is the diversity of backgrounds and approaches that makes record production such a lively and involving subject.

The aim of this book is to explain the role of the producer and his relationship with the artist, recording engineer and record company, but I also won't be neglecting the engineering side of things because, in the case of the project studio, the engineer and producer are often the same person. I'll also be covering techniques that can be used to create specific sounds and musical effects as well as trying to answer some common questions. Equally valuable, you'll find information on liaising with clients and planning sessions, all aspects of which are covered, from setting up to the final mix.

After the chapters devoted to the mixing process, you'll find a section addressing the little-understood area of post-production, which includes album compilation, audio sweetening, remixing and editing, as well as the final steps in producing a professional recorded product.

In addition to my own experience, much of the information has been distilled from long conversations with top producers and engineers worldwide and is applicable to a wide range of musical styles and disciplines. Wherever possible, information is provided that is relevant to working with analogue tape, digital tape, tapeless recording hardware and sequencers. This revised version also looks at the technical and artistic implications of surround sound and some of the creative possibilities opened up by the plug-in revolution.

1 A LITTLE HISTORY

When you consider the flamboyant personalities and rock 'n' roll lifestyles that have been associated with the music business over the past two or three decades, it might come as quite a surprise to learn that, in the early days of recording, the whole process was very formal – and, by modern standards, rather basic. The first records ever made were recorded in mono, with very simple mixing techniques used to record what was, in effect, a live performance.

The only tools at the engineer's disposal in these early days were level faders; the first mixers had no EQ, so if the engineer wanted a different sound, he had to achieve it either by selecting a different mic or by changing the mic position. If a more ambient sound was needed, the only way of achieving this was to use a 'live' room; consequently, many improvised techniques of adding reverb to a mix, such as using reverberant chambers or even concrete stairwells, were pioneered during this period.

It was also quite common for studios to build dedicated echo rooms in their basements. These were essentially large, reflective rooms with angled surfaces, often tiled. A loudspeaker and microphone would be set up in the room, then any sound needing treatment would be fed into the room. The signal picked up by the mic would be added back into the mix, in much the same way as we now add digital effects using the effects-return channels on a multitrack console or a sequencer's virtual mixer.

Company Producers

In those early days, engineers and producers were usually full-time employees of the record company, which also often owned the studio. Because of this arrangement, the same people would work on a wide range of musical styles covering classical, jazz, pop, ballads and so forth, which is why many of the 'old-school' engineers and producers are so versatile. In those days, efficiency was the prime objective and, because of the live way of working, whole albums were regularly completed in single four-hour sessions – for example, The Beatles' album *Please Please Me* was apparently recorded in one 13-hour day! Engineers wearing white lab coats remained on one side of the control-room glass with the artists on the other. Rarely, if ever, was an artist allowed into the control room during a session!

What we now call record production was originally often split between two people: the musical director and the producer. This is a close parallel to the way in which things are still done in the film industry – the producer looks after the business side and the director concentrates on artistic considerations. The musical director would be responsible for the musical arrangements, the quality of the musical performance and the sound and mix of the final recording. In turn, he would be under pressure from the producer to work quickly while spending as little money as possible! In the days when all non-pop backing music was provided by orchestras, a little wasted time could add up to a lot of money, and even today this is an area of concern. One major consideration is that orchestras tend not to be booked by the minute but in blocks of half an hour or so, depending on the country in which they're working and the rules of the particular union to which they belong. This means that 'just one more take' can take you into the next block of time, which can add hundreds or even thousands of pounds to the cost of a session.

Low Tech

Mono recording technology later evolved into stereo and mono shellac records gave way to vinyl stereo records. Back in the studio, working directly to stereo was soon followed by four-track recording, which allowed singers to overdub their parts rather than tie up a live band or orchestra for every take. Basic EQ and pan pots were added to the mixing consoles and the plate reverb was developed to eliminate the need for a 'live' room. It was with this fairly basic technology that many of the classic pop records of the early '60s were made (although many of the early Phil Spector-produced hits were recorded in mono). During this decade, the only real effects unit was the tape echo, although guitar amps were being built with integral electronic tremolo and spring reverb. A little later in the decade, these were joined by the fuzz box and the wah-wah pedal.

During the early days of pop recording, improvisation was a vital ingredient to achieving a distinctive commercial sound, and with no hi-tech processing (and no samplers or polyphonic synths) to help, this involved a lot of experimentation. Rooms with interesting acoustics were pressed into service, while double-tracking was taken to extremes by some producers, who would hire in several guitar players, for example, to play identical parts. This was apparently one of Phil Spector's favourite recording methods, and whatever else you think of it, it certainly pushed mic technique to the limit.

Flanging

When the flanging effect was first discovered, it had to be created manually by recording the same piece of music onto two tape recorders, which would then be started simultaneously. Getting a reasonable degree of synchronisation using this method was a bit hit and miss, but by applying slight hand pressure onto the tape reels of first one and then the other machine, the two machines could be made to drift in and out of sync, resulting in some frequencies being cancelled and others being added, or *comb filtering*. The change in comb-filter frequencies as the delay between the two machines varied gave rise to the characteristic whooshing sound used on so many psychedelic records. At the time, this effect could be added only after the recording – there was no way to achieve it live. Nevertheless, it became very popular in the late '60s and early '70s and was used by everyone from Jimi Hendrix ('Gypsy Eyes') to The Beatles and The Small Faces ('Itchycoo Park').

Changing Roles

As the way in which pop songs were composed started to change (ie with pop songs starting to be written by the artists themselves, who often had little or no musical training), the role of producer and musical director gradually merged, and if a producer lacked the specialised musical knowledge needed to arrange songs, he would hire in an arranger. Even so, the producer was still very much tied to his record company, and the relationship between George Martin and The Beatles was probably the greatest incentive to challenge the status quo. All the world knew just what an influence George Martin had on The Beatles, and few doubt that he was a key figure in ensuring their continued success. This relationship inspired many producers to go freelance, which gave them the opportunity to negotiate royalties, or 'points', with the artist's management, at the same time allowing producers to specialise. Prior to this, the 'tied' producer had to make the best of any job that came his way, regardless of its musical style. And regardless of the commercial success of a record, the producer still received only his basic salary.

Things were changing, though, and it was also at around this time that recording engineers were allowed to turn up for work without a tie! Rigidly defined morning and afternoon recording sessions also became more flexible, with some musicians being allowed to record during the night. Also at this time, musicians were even managing to get into the control room! I've interviewed a number of old-school producers, and it seems that, early on, the studio regime was so rigid that you weren't even allowed to try experimental mic techniques – everything had to be done strictly by the book, with scheduled breaks and fixed session lengths.

Fortunately for creativity, the whole system gradually became more flexible and less formal, with freelance studios springing up to accommodate the growing number of projects. No longer was it set in stone that an artist had to record at his or her record company's studio with the company engineer and in-house producer. The more forward-thinking record companies recognised that certain projects could benefit from being handled by producers who favoured a certain musical style or who had a good track record in producing hit records. Inevitably, these producers built up relationships with engineers with whom they found it easy to work, and so the freelance engineer was created. Now a musical act could benefit from working in the most appropriate studio with a sympathetic producer and an engineer who knew the producer's requirements. Similarly, a good producer would also be able to call on a circle of suitable session players.

This slackening of the old regime was a double-edged sword. On the positive side, it did allow the right people to work together and some great records were made, but in the late '60s and early '70s, when the music business still made a lot of money, this freedom was frequently abused. Aside from the stories of all-night recording sessions consisting of sex, drugs and very little rock 'n' roll, work was seldom approached with any sense of economy. Bands would book studios for months on end and actually write the songs in there! Artist mismanagement was rife, and many young bands didn't realise that, at the end of the day, it was their own money that was being wasted.

Record Advances

Much of this waste of resources and time was down to a basic misunderstanding of what a record company advance really is. It isn't just free spending money! When a company signs a band, they generally make available a sum of money for the band to live on and to enable them to go into the studio and make a record. All of the studio expenses and any other cash advanced is ultimately deducted from the artists' royalties once the record starts to sell. If the record doesn't sell, then it's the record company, not the artist, who loses out. However, in the past it was quite common for bands to have a hit single and then find that they received none of the proceeds from it because their share had all been frittered away in recording time, chauffeured cars and expensive catering. In other words, a record

company advance should be considered as an unsecured, interest-free loan, which is repaid when the artist's records begin to sell.

Over the past decade or two, the music business has suffered a considerable decline, partly because consumers now have interests other than collecting records and partly – so the record companies argue – because of unauthorised copying of CDs and cassettes. The truth probably goes deeper than that; the original '60s music generation are now middle aged, with enough money to buy records but with little chance to hear any music that might appeal to them, while on the other hand the younger listeners seem more interested in what the artist looks like than what they sound like, hence the prevalence of boy and girl bands.

It could be that the national obsession with the Top 40 and pop stars created on TV programmes has served only to alienate a great many potential record buyers, and while we may feel that it's up to record companies and record producers to redress this situation, there seems little sign that the companies intend to change their marketing tactics. Of course, there's always the possibility of promoting music independently via the internet, and one day, when everyone has 'wide-pipe', high-bandwidth internet access, maybe that will become viable, but at the moment the traditional means of selling records prevails.

MP Free?

One aspect of the .mp3 sound-file format (which the record companies usually regard as a threat, due its ease of transmission over the internet) that hasn't been taken as seriously as I feel it should is the ability to get over ten hours of music on a CD-ROM, along with text data, such as information about the artists and details of where to order the record. If this space were used to promote selected tracks or segments of new releases (categorised by musical style, of course), the record companies could afford to give these away free in the major record stores and it would enable them to market effectively a much wider choice of material without the need for conventional, expensive advertising. Even if the artists themselves paid for the production of the CD-ROMs on a *pro rata* basis, the cost would be incredibly low, given the current cost of

CD/CD-ROM mass production (based on over 500 one-minute segments per disc). Correctly formatted .mp3 CD-ROMs will play in all modern computers and even some DVD players. If this does happen, I suspect that it will be an enterprising independent record company that does it first.

2 TODAY'S PRODUCER

Today's producer requires a significantly different range of skills to those of his '60s counterpart, although the underlying objectives of bringing in a commercially successful project at the right budget will still be at the top of his list. Today, a producer must have a flair for music (although he doesn't have to be a musician), he must have the right contacts, he must be able to plan finances and – not to be underestimated – it is essential that he can handle people. He also needs an ear for what will sell and must have more than a passing familiarity with modern music-production technology, such as sequencing, virtual instruments and popular commercial systems such as Pro Tools. Even if he can't use any of these systems proficiently, he still needs to know what they are capable of and what they can realistically achieve.

Many producers come from a musical rather than an engineering background and have made their contacts during their years in the business, although in dance music it's not uncommon for producers and even remix engineers to have started out as DJs, with no traditional musical skills but with a good ear for what audiences want. The more traditional producer will probably have worked in studios and, during that time, will have made contact with engineers, record-company staff and other musicians who may be able to contribute to future sessions.

Job Description

Of the producers I have spoken to over the past few years, nearly every one has adopted a different approach to the subject, so there is no absolute definition or job specification. Some are competent recording engineers while others need a house engineer on hand to do virtually everything for them. Some are trained musicians while others are DJs. Some may only fine-tune the arrangements presented by the artists while others may rewrite the whole thing and even replace band members with session musicians. The only bottom line is results, and different producers have different ways of getting from A to B. The important thing, after all, is getting to B and still showing a profit!

There is one point, however, on which most producers seem to agree, and that is that the ability to handle people in a stressful environment is very near the top of the list of qualities that a producer needs. Working against the clock in an expensive recording studio can be very stressful, especially when things aren't going well, and the producer must shoulder the responsibility for ensuring that a creative atmosphere is maintained.

Musical Style

A great many record producers build a reputation for working in a particular style, but the more astute among them have realised that styles change, and if you allow yourself to get pigeon-holed, you run the risk of becoming out of fashion and hence out of work. Even so, it's only natural for producers to relate better to some styles of music than to others, and even the most broad-based producers tend to have pet areas in which they particularly like to work. The main thing is to appreciate the risks and take care to ensure that you don't get left out in the cold when styles change, as they inevitably will. This may be a particularly apt warning in these times when dance music is so successful, but the production techniques are so different to traditional pop work that a dance-only producer might be hard pushed to find work in any other area. Having said that, most European pop trends tend to be based on a watering-down of dance music styles, so I don't foresee any sudden changes.

Project Planning

At one time, records were invariably made in the studio belonging to the record company with in-house engineering staff. In recent years, however, alternative working methods have evolved, which have meant advantages both creatively and for the recording budget. After spending some time talking to the artists and their record company, a producer will typically listen to demos of their material and pick out the tracks that he thinks are most suitable for the album/single. This is done in consultation with the artist, but the producer has to be happy with the final selection. A lot depends on the band and on their track record and standing in the business, and a top band with a proven chart track record will certainly have more say over which of their songs are chosen and how those songs are recorded, while a new band or artist is likely to have rather less influence.

Even at this stage, it's important for the producer to develop a comfortable rapport with the artist. They will be working very closely together, so it's essential to build a mutual trust and respect, as friction can easily occur when the going gets tough. The emphasis is on teamwork, and the producer is there to function as team leader. If both parties are constantly pulling in opposite directions, the project will almost certainly turn out badly, so it may be wise to walk away from offers that show signs of ending up this way. Your reputation is only as good as your last record, so you don't need to take any unnecessary risks.

In addition to working closely with the artist, the producer will know how to get hold of the right session musicians and (if necessary) sequencer programmers, as well as any necessary hire equipment. Adhering to both budget and deadlines is the producer's responsibility, and this usually extends to selecting an appropriate mastering engineer for the project.

The Engineer

Recording engineers come from a variety of backgrounds, although most appear to have had some connection with music prior to getting into recording, often playing in bands. Traditionally, the aspiring recording engineer started out in a commercial studio, making tea and maintaining the tape-filing system while picking up what he could about recording from the resident engineer. He'd then work on a few pet projects during studio downtime, help out on sessions and, eventually, be in the right place at the right time to control a session of his own. Most of the tales I've been told include stories of ludicrously long working hours, poverty pay and an almost total lack of sleep. Even so, most successful producers have a right-place-at-the-right-time story and recognise this event as the turning points in their careers.

Over the years, I've answered countless enquiries from people who want to get into record production or studio engineering. Unfortunately, a lot more people want to do the job than there are vacancies available, and the old 'tea boy' entry into the business can no longer be relied upon. There are so many engineers around that studios can afford to demand some level of experience from would-be applicants; the trick is to gain experience without actually doing the job.

Recording Courses

Recording courses are available in several guises, from cheap-and-cheerful weekend introductory sessions run in budget studios to full-time courses at recognised educational establishments. There's no doubt that these courses can help to get you started, but they offer no guarantee of a job. Likewise, you can run a home studio and learn a great deal about recording that way, but this still doesn't guarantee you the job of your dreams. However, all experience is useful, and if it makes you better equipped than the next candidate, then it has to be worth it.

But being able to physically do the job is only the first prerequisite – you also need the right attitude. Engineering can be a very stressful job, and, like the record producer, you have to be able to work with often highly strung musicians in a confined, potentially stressful environment for long periods. You have to be able to think on your feet and anticipate problems, and you have to accept that nobody is going to suggest that you take a tea break, let alone half an hour off for something as trivial as a meal! If anything goes wrong in a studio, it's always seen as the engineer's fault, whether this is justified or not, so you need to be broad shouldered as well as possessing infinite stamina. On top of all this, you need to be able to maintain a strong focus, because one mistake in the middle of a recording session can be disastrous.

An engineer doesn't have to be a record producer, but even so, a good engineer will anticipate a producer's demands so that, when the producer wants to try out a little vocal compression or reverb, the engineer will already have them patched in with suitable settings in place. Some producers are really not deserving of the title, and the bulk of the creative work then falls to the engineer, who may also be a musician and end up playing and arranging most of the keyboard parts. In many such cases, the engineer receives little credit for his creative input – it's still the producer's name that ends up on the record sleeve, and stories abound of engineers who have asked for their creative input to be acknowledged only to find that the client has asked for them to be taken off the job. But then, nobody said that the world of music was fair!

Why Be A Recording Engineer?

You might well ask why anyone becomes a recording engineer because the work is arduous, not at all well paid and very often demands that you work anti-social hours, in terms of both the number of hours worked and the time of night you eventually get to finish work. I can't even pretend to answer the question, but there seems to be an endless stream of people waiting to take their place in that smoke-filled sweat-box that is the working recording-studio control room. I've done a lot of engineering over the past 20 years, but I've never been in the position of having to do it full time, all the time, so I still enjoy it. I wouldn't want to do it full time, but that doesn't mean that you won't enjoy it.

If you're determined to be a recording engineer, you have to be persistent – if you can't take banging your head against closed doors, you probably don't have the resilience for the job, anyway. Also, be aware that the world of audio is changing, so making records isn't the whole story any more – indeed, it's just a small part of the story. The whole multimedia market is opening up, with jobs now becoming available in internet audio, games soundtracks, TV and film sound and, of course, mastering, both for traditional stereo and the newer surround-sound formats. If you over-specialise, then unless you're close to the top in your field, you may find yourself qualified for a job that no longer exists. The key phrase is *transferable skills*, so learn everything you can and don't take your eye off the ball.

3 PLANNING A SESSION

The planning for a recording project starts as soon as the artists meet the producer. In some circumstances, the artists themselves will be in a position to choose the producer with which they work, but it's more often the case that the record company will choose the producer because of his or her track record with certain musical styles, especially where the band or artist is inexperienced. In some cases, artists are brought in to help produce other artists, either because of mutual interest or because the record company want the producer to impose an element of his own musical style, and indeed many of today's top producers originally played in bands or were solo artists in their own rights. Establishing a rapport with the artists is the first step towards establishing confidence, as is an exploration of the artists' own ideas as to how their material should be handled.

Some acts readily accept that they need the guidance of an experienced producer, but as musicians tend to be pretty self-opinionated people, it's also possible that they will resent the imposition of a third party who has the final say over their material. A good producer will tackle this problem at once by exploring the artists' own ideas and only then suggesting possible changes, rather than taking a hard line by dictating the way in which he intends things to be. Again, people management is pretty much top of the list of essential skills.

The Demo

As previously mentioned, most producers will start out by listening to the artists' own demos of the songs short-listed for the project, possibly by the record company's A&R department (often referred to as the 'um and ah department' because they can never seem to make up their minds about anything). Some producers like to copy the demo and then edit it to explore alternative arrangements, something that's very easy with a computer sequencer or editing package. The edited demos are then played back to the musicians before proceeding, often with some suggestions about further changes. Taking this pre-production procedure even further, some musician/producers might want to program their subsequent ideas for the final song into a sequencer and present various options to the artists.

An experienced producer might draw the artists' attention to sections that don't work particularly well and then elicit their ideas as to how the problem can be rectified. With any luck, the artists can be subtly coaxed until they draw the conclusions that the producer has already come to – it's much easier if the artists think that the ideas have come from them, as this means they're less likely to resist them!

Session Players

A more sensitive issue arises when band members have to be supplemented or even replaced by session musicians. This has to be handled extremely carefully in order to avoid damaging fragile egos, and it helps if the redundant band members can play at least some part in the recording. For example, the drummer who has been replaced by a drum machine might sit in on the rhythm programming and, in addition, may be asked to play a few live fills or hi-hat parts – it all depends on the producer and on his personal approach to the job.

Some producers may want to use MIDI sequencing extensively, in which case the preliminary programming will be done next, and the artists may play little part in this, especially if they are solo singers or part of a vocal ensemble rather than traditional band members. While vocal artists are usually OK with this (provided that they like what's being done), players can easily feel insecure in such circumstances, so it helps to get them as involved as is practical and to solicit their approval when things are changed. Even getting the drummer to record some of his own drum sounds into a sampler can be enough. The secret is to make everyone feel involved.

The Budget

Once the preliminary ground has been covered, the next step depends on the producer's approach and on the available budget. It can be artistically fruitful to allow a band to experiment as they go along, but when it comes to bringing a project in on time and to budget, the producer with a positive plan is likely to be more successful. In any event, a producer with definite ideas can't afford to give too much leeway, as he will have a pretty good idea at this stage of how the finished product should sound.

There are producers who like to be more open-ended, but a sensible approach is to do any experimental work in a low-budget facility or home studio and then move into the more costly facility once all uncertainties have been taken care of. If most of a project can be undertaken in a musician's home studio or programming suite, it can be completed at a much lower cost than if it takes place entirely within a traditional studio recording.

SMPTE And Sequencing

Whether MIDI is being used or not, if the project (or part of the project) is being recorded on traditional analogue multitrack tape (and a huge number still are), it's probably safest to stripe it with SMPTE (Society of Motion Picture and Television Engineers) time code so that a sequencer or computer audio system may be sync'd up later, if the need arises. SMPTE is also needed to facilitate automated mixing from an analogue source, although the majority of digital recorders either output SMPTE or MTC as standard without needing to take up a track. SMPTE code should normally be striped to

the tape at the prevailing TV frame rate, which is 30fps (frames per second) in the USA and 25fps in Europe. The other frame rate of 24fps is used exclusively for film work, and so-called 'drop-frame' SMPTE should be avoided unless the project specifies it.

Even if the majority of the musical parts are to be sequenced at the mixing stage, it helps to put a rough stereo mix of the sequenced backing onto tape, as this will allow the artists to work on their overdubs without having to worry about loading sequences. Strangely enough, although the prevailing wisdom is that sequencing MIDI parts directly into the mix is the right way to go, a surprising number of professional producers still like to record their sequenced instruments to tape. When asked why, they tend to reply that they feel more comfortable having something concrete on tape rather than relying on the vagaries of software. Additionally, they may profess to like what analogue tape does to the sound. They might also comment that making a commitment at this stage saves procrastination later on, but actually, provided that the time-code track stays intact, it's still possible to lock up the sequencer and change a sound or melody line right up to the final mix. Perhaps this approach gives the best of both worlds, in that the producer feels that a commitment has been made and yet he still has the complete flexibility accorded by the sequencer if he has to revert to the original sequence.

Where software-based digital-recording systems are being used, the available number of tracks tends to be much greater than with hardware, and certainly greater than with analogue tape, so recording sequenced parts as audio tracks is less of an extravagance.

There's another very valid reason for recording sequenced parts as audio tracks, and that is that the available synths, drum machines and samplers might not have sufficient polyphony to cope with the entire performance in one take. In this instance, the sequence must be played through with some parts muted and the different sections recorded to tape in several passes. This might involve adding effects as the sounds go to tape, simply because several different instrumental or percussion sounds may have to share the same tape tracks. The same applies if any instruments have been hired in specially for the session.

Before leaving the subject of sequencing for the moment, it's the producer's responsibility to ensure that back-up disks are made of any working material and that proper notes are kept to describe sounds, effects and so on. The producer also has to decide whether to work with the available instruments or whether to hire in extra equipment.

Vocals

The best time to record vocals depends on which producer you ask! Some like to get the main vocal down as soon as the bare bones of the musical backing have been recorded, their justification for this being that it allows any further instrumentation to be fitted in around the vocal line. In any event, it helps to get a guide vocal down first for the same reason – and it also helps the other players to navigate their way through the song. Often, the singer gives his or her best performance when recording the guide track, because there is less pressure to get it dead right. A good producer will keep the guide vocal until the end of the session just in case.

In home recording, the conventional practice is to record a vocal part all the way through and then run through it again, dropping in any phrases that weren't up to scratch. Some professionals work in this way, too, but they're more likely to record several complete takes on separate tracks from which the producer will compile one good, composite vocal track. The best phrases will then be bounced down onto a new track, and if the desk is fitted with mute automation, this process is very simple, even when using tape-based recording systems. If no mute automation is available, the different phrases must be 'brought up' manually, using either the channel Mute buttons or the channel faders. Good notes are essential in order to keep track of the wanted phrases during this process.

Comping vocals is much easier using a computer-based recording system because of the graphical editing environment. There's also the advantage that the editing is non-destructive and, in most cases, undoable, which is not the case with tape, analogue or digital recordings.

Hardware

Although frivolous experimentation is a waste of time and money, it's well worth setting aside a little time to try out different mics and compressors as the vocalist warms up in order to determine which give the best result. There are certain esoteric models known for their good vocal sound, but, as is so often found to be the case, what works magically for one singer may be quite unsuitable for another.

It's common practice to apply a degree of compression to vocals as they are recorded, as this helps to get a good working level onto tape and evens out the worst variations in level. Further compression can be used during the mix, as required. Proper attention should also be paid to giving the singer a workable foldback or monitor mix. Most singers work best with a reasonable amount of monitor reverb to help them pitch their notes. If a singer has problems working with enclosed headphones, try a semi-enclosed type or suggest that they work with one can on and one can off. Spill from the phones into the vocal mic is unlikely to be a problem, except at very high monitoring levels or where a click track is involved.

In recent years, many vocal recordings have been solved by using pitch correction software such as Auto–Tune. In my experience, this requires the audio track to be well isolated from all other sound sources, and it only works effectively if the vocal performance is reasonably good to start with. As a general rule, the pitch-correction rate should be set as low as possible while still giving the required degree of subjective pitch correction, as faster correction times can sound very unnatural. A graphical mode is available for the software version of the Auto-Tune program, which is more able to cope with shorter vocal sections that require more intensive correction. Here, pitch curves can be drawn in, much as with a graphics program.

Drums

If the session requires a lot of real drums, it may be most cost-effective to book some time in a studio that has a good live room and relatively basic 16- or 24-track equipment. Alternatively, you could take your own recorder along. It's important to ensure that the recording media is compatible with whatever other studios may be used for other parts of the project, unless you use the same recorder and take it from studio to studio.

Most pop music tends to make use of sequenced drum parts, often augmented by manual percussion, manual hi-hat and cymbal parts and the odd tom fill. This is an easy way of working because the basic drum rhythm is locked into the sequencer. On the other hand, if the session demands real drums all the way through and some instruments are to be MIDI sequenced, then the drummer usually has to play to a click track generated by the sequencer. Top session drummers can do this effortlessly, but drummers used to setting the tempo rather than following it may take some time to adapt.

Tap Tempo

If a less rigid approach to timing is beneficial, it's possible to record the rhythm section 'live' and then use a tap-tempo facility to create a sequencer tempo map of the actual performance. This usually involves tapping a button in time with the original performance, and it helps to have at least two bars of extra count-in to get the tempo in sync. However, such an approach is rare in pop music, and even very proficient drummers tend to make use of some sequenced rhythm parts, both for convenience and in order to produce a very exact tempo.

Sequencing the snare and bass drum parts avoids the problems of snares rattling or toms booming whenever the bass drum is hit, yet if the player's own drums are sampled and then triggered by a sequencer, the end result can still be very authentic. As a rule, hi-hat and cymbal parts should be played live where a human feel is sought, although for dance music, which is more mechanical, totally sequenced drum parts (or, more often, sample loops) invariably work better.

What follows is a brief introductory overview of instrument recording techniques, a process covered in much greater depth later in the book.

Drum Miking

Recording drums probably involves more decision making than any other aspect of the session, but other than a suitable room, all you need is a good basic desk and a selection of suitable drum mics. Rock drum sounds tend to be recorded with the emphasis on the close mics, with the overhead or ambient mics used to fill in the cymbals. The exception is where a very big, ambient drum sound is required, in which case a studio with a large live room is needed, with additional ambience mics placed at a distance from the kit.

Jazz drums tend to be recorded the other way around, with the stereo mic pair providing the main contribution and close mics used to fill out the sound and fine-tune the balance.

Guitars

Guitar parts may be DI'd (Direct Injected) using one of the many available studio pre-amps or speaker simulators available, although for heavy rock the miked sound is still the preferred option. Ultimately, there is no best way; it's all down to personal choice. In many instances, chordal and rhythm parts can be DI'd very satisfactorily while lead solos might benefit from the interaction between the amplifier and the guitar, especially if feedback is used to prolong sustained notes. Once again, one can mic up either a large stack or a small combo. Both produce their own distinctive sound, although a large set-up needs a large studio to produce the best results. A small valve combo such as a Fender Champ or low-wattage Mesa Boogie can produce excellent results in a small project studio.

Different results can be achieved by varying mic position and by choosing either dynamic or capacitor microphones. If two guitar parts need to be separated in some way, recording one with a dynamic mic and the other with a capacitor mic can help. Further differences can be created by using humbucking or single-coil pick-ups or by the subtle application of effects such as chorus. Additionally, EQ can be used on both the amplifier and the mixing console to emphasise different parts of the sound spectrum and, of course, the two parts can then be panned to different sides of the stereo image. If the resulting sound is still confused, the guitar parts themselves should be examined to see if they're too similar or too busy. Sometimes playing a chordal part in a more restrained and simple way or applying a little string damping solves the problem.

Acoustic Guitars

Acoustic guitars invariably sound better when miked up, regardless of how good the internal bug or pick-up system may be. Important acoustic parts can be recorded in stereo, but where the guitar forms part of a complex arrangement, a mono recording may well give more stability. Because of the problems of sound leakage when working with acoustic instruments, acoustic guitars are invariably overdubbed individually, using closed headphones to prevent spill from the backing track.

If a song needs to start with several bars of solo acoustic guitar but that guitar part must be recorded as an overdub, it's important that the correct number of count-in bars is provided, with a suitable click track or guide hi-hat part. If you ever have to pick up a project where this hasn't been done, it's possible to turn the tape over, so that it plays backwards, and then record extra beats at the introduction of the song in order to extend the count-in to a suitable length. A short, dry sound is best for this, otherwise the timing may appear to shift slightly when the sound is heard in reverse, once the tape is played back normally.

Psychology

Recording can be a very stressful experience, and it is part of the producer's job to be aware of mood problems and to tackle them as they arise. Open discussion should be encouraged, as long as it's not allowed to run on too long, and any individual who is clearly in a less than ideal mood can often be diverted by being given something useful to do, such as looking after a fader level or supervising punch-in points (in a studio where these things are not automated, of course).

The good producer will also recognise the point at which an artist has worked too long to be giving of their best and will change the order of work to give that person a break, if at all possible. Perhaps the worst time is when someone is repeatedly incapable of getting their part right. Insisting on a break at this point can often be far more productive than allowing the person to struggle on stubbornly. Positive encouragement is the key here, because as soon as you start to criticise a musician, his or her confidence

is likely to suffer and the final performance will be worse for it.

If you can spare enough tracks to keep a previous take while allowing the performer to do another, the feeling of security that this gives may enable the player to give a more relaxed performance. Again, digital systems make this easy because most can record far more tracks than they can play back, so that alternative takes may be saved for later 'comping' into a single good take. Also, the use of drugs and the excessive use of alcohol should be discouraged, not least because of their detrimental effect on a performer's musical ability.

Corrective Editing

In extreme cases of inability to perform, it may still be possible to comp together several attempts to provide one good version, and of course it's very common for a one-off good vocal chorus to be copied throughout the song. (Auto-Tune may also save the day, if used within its limitations.) Similarly, several less than pristine guitar solos can often be edited to produce one good one and minor tuning errors or inaccurate bends can be fixed, again with Auto-Tune (provided that the part is monophonic at the part that needs fixing). Session players can sometimes be used to perform critical sections with greater precision than the original musicians, but if these sections are to be edited in with the original parts, great care has to be taken to match the sounds. Even if the same guitar and amplifier is used to play part of a solo, the sound can be quite different simply because of the players' individual techniques. Once all of the necessary parts are safely recorded (and backed up), then it's time for the mix. However, unless time really is tight, this should be done on a different day so that it can be heard with fresh ears.

Once again, this is just a simplified overview of some aspects of a recording session, and in real life each one presents different challenges. The rest of this book is dedicated to examining the various stages in the engineering and production process, but how you put them all together is ultimately your choice, and indeed that's why your style of production will never be exactly the same as anyone else's.

4 ARRANGING

A song may be no more than a set of lyrics and a melody – certainly that's all that's needed to establish copyright – but in most cases a somewhat more sophisticated musical arrangement will be required in order to create a saleable record. Where the song has already been performed live by a band, there will already be an arrangement, possibly arrived at through jamming and other evolutionary processes, although what works well live doesn't necessarily work on record.

When presented with a song to arrange, the producer has to consider not only the musical construction of the piece but also the way in which the various sounds fit together. Thus arrangement can be divided into three distinct areas:

- The order in which the various musical sections are presented (ie intro, verse, chorus, bridge, middle-eight and so on);

- The musical lines and rhythms that make up each part;

- The sounds chosen to play these lines and rhythms.

The order in which a song is arranged is very important – commercial material tends to work to a fairly rigid formula, in that a distinct intro is followed by between three and five minutes of music. The traditional, melodic pop song tends to have...

- an easily recognisable verse/chorus structure, usually with a middle-eight (which, despite its name, doesn't need to be exactly eight bars long);

- one or two 'bridge sections';

- an instrumental solo, although this is not invariably included.

The chorus will be repeated frequently, the song often fading out over a repeated chorus line. Although musical fashions change very quickly, this traditional song structure has proved to be one of life's survivors.

Because of the fickle nature of the commercial music market, a song has to attract the interest of the listener very quickly, and once the intro is over, it usually pays to get to the chorus pretty quickly. This may be achieved by such devices as:

- shortening the first verse;

- using a modified version of the chorus as an intro;

- coming straight in with the chorus after the intro.

Another useful device is to use only part of the chorus when it first occurs, which creates a sense of anticipation, helping to keep the listener interested. Indeed, the ability to create an atmosphere of anticipation is the hallmark of a good songwriter, and often the ends of verses or link sections will contain musical hooks that make the listener want to reach the chorus. What makes a good hook is less easy to quantify, however – it could be anything from a brass riff or a drum fill to a vocal phrase or synthesiser line. The important thing is that it's catchy and easily identifiable. The verse must also contain a hook of some sort, but again this can be created by the clever use of melody, by repetition or simply by the distinctive vocal character of the singer. If you're trying to create a track for the pop market, don't be above using something that sounds childish or musically immature – the majority of singles buyers aren't noted for their appreciation of the finer points of musical construction, and if something sticks in their minds, they're more likely to want to buy it.

Dance tracks tend to have a less formal structure, and there may be little differentiation between the verse and chorus, if any. Even so, most successful dance records combine a driving rhythm with a series of musical hooks to make the result more compelling and to help it stand out from the competition. These could be as simple as using non-standard hi-hat figures or a catchy bass line or a selection of alternative percussion sounds added over the usual bass/snare/hi-hat backbeat. The musical tempo of most such records is quite predictable and lies within fairly rigidly defined limits for each style, but on top of the straight four-to-the-bar rhythm, it's possible bring in other rhythmic patterns to make the whole more interesting.

It comes as no surprise to discover that some of the best dance tracks are mixed by DJs who have worked in dance clubs and have developed an instinctive feeling for what audiences will respond to. The dynamics of the track are also extremely important, as is the placement of any breaks, but knowing where and when to implement these is more of an art than a science. In this respect, there is no substitute for analysing existing tracks to find out what makes them work. Typical pop songs are fairly easy to analyse as there's usually not too much going on at any one time and the vocals tend to be the most dominant feature, underpinned by the rhythm section. I've often felt that American pop arrangements tend to be musically busier than their British equivalents, but it's interesting to note that many of the instruments in US mixes are kept very low in the mix, especially distorted guitars, with the vocal line mixed well up front.

Currently, a significant proportion of British pop music draws elements from dance music, including the use of sampled drum loops and percussive synthesiser motifs, so never be afraid to borrow from one genre to create another. Even if you don't plan to use a drum-loop sample, library loops can provide excellent arranging aids, as they allow you to get a groove going fairly quickly, and once you have a groove, the whole arrangement often comes together that much faster. You can always replace the drum loop later, either with something you've created yourself or with a sample-library format that allows you to change elements of the loop, such as REX files and Groove Control.

Also, don't overlook existing successful records. While you shouldn't aim to copy other tracks, there's no substitute for analysing existing music to absorb song construction and arrangement tricks of the trade. It's also very common for composers to 'borrow' chord sequences from within existing songs and then write a new melody to fit those chords. In most cases, this doesn't infringe copyright, as it's generally perceived to be the melody that defines a song.

Managing The Music

It's tempting for the inexperienced record producer or musical arranger to have too many parts playing at the same time, which can easily make for a cluttered, confused mix. The best way of avoiding this is by identifying the key elements of the music and put these together first. Then you can see what else is needed and what you can either leave out or use at a lower level than originally anticipated.

At the foundation of nearly every pop song is the rhythm section, which might take the form of traditional drums and bass or may be entirely synthesised, using drum machines, drum loops, samples and synthesisers. The source of the sounds is less important than getting the bass instrument and the underlying drum rhythm to work together to establish the rhythm and feel of the piece. The way in which this is approached depends on the type of music with which you're working – definite styles and rules exists for specific musical forms such as funk, reggae, dance and so on, which are quite evident after listening to a few records in the genre. Even though the approach of all these styles may be quite different, the bass and drums work together as a unit and not as independent entities. Even in dance music or hip-hop, the same basic rules apply, even though the sounds themselves may be wildly different, sometimes including distorted drum loops or other lo-fi sounds.

Guitars and vocals tend to occupy the mid ground of the musical-frequency spectrum, as do pad keyboard parts, so it's important to arrange these so that they don't conflict. This can be accomplished partly by the choice of individual guitar and keyboard sounds and partly by the musical lines they play. Where several instruments are playing together and there is a danger of the sound becoming muddled, they can be separated to some degree by changing the basic sounds to make them thinner (removing some low mid using EQ) or by emphasising different parts of the upper mid using subtle EQ boost and panning. However, don't rely on panning to solve all of your problems, as a mix still needs to sound good in mono. If the problem persists, re-examine the musical arrangement and question the role of each sound or musical line you've chosen. Every musical part should exist for a reason, and if you discover a part that has no reason to be there, you're probably better off leaving it out.

At the top of the spectrum are the bright synth sounds, such as cymbals, high percussion and so on, and these add detail and interest to a mix that might otherwise be bass and mid heavy. Bright sounds needn't be loud in order to provide the necessary musical punctuation, and if high synth lines or high percussion parts are planned, it may be prudent to examine any cymbal or hi-hat parts in order to avoid overcrowding. Splashy ride cymbals can have a clouding effect on mixes, so consider using a close hi-hat motif instead if this becomes a problem. Mixing real drums with a sampled drum loop can also produce very useful and satisfying results.

Pad keyboard parts can either be placed low in the mix or they may be filtered so that they occupy a narrower part of the audio spectrum. Removing excess low end and low mid from pads can stop them conflicting with male vocals while limiting the high end prevents the upper harmonics from obscuring high-frequency detail. Listen carefully to commercial records that use pad sounds and you'll often find that they sound fairly restricted both in frequency content and in level. A woodwork teacher once told me that the strength of a joint is down to the amount of glue you squeeze out, not the amount you leave in, and I guess the same is often true of pad parts!

Synthesised sounds can be corrected at source, while organ sounds might be set up using the draw bars and then filtered by means of EQ. For example, it might be useful to roll off all frequencies below, say, 150Hz in order to thin out the sound, which will help avoid potential muddiness in the vulnerable lower-mid part of the spectrum. In computer-based systems, low- and high-cut filters are often provided as plug-ins, and as a rule, the sharper the response, the more surgical you can be. Ordinarily, a filter curve of at least 12dB per octave is necessary, although curves of 18dB per octave and even 24dB per octave are not uncommon.

Riffs played by brass instruments don't usually present a problem, as they tend to be placed in strategic positions rather than allowed to play through, whereas guitar riffs are often allowed to continue below verses or choruses. Clean guitar sounds tend to be easier to integrate into a mix than heavily distorted sounds, hence the popularity of bright guitar riffs for underpinning soul music, and a bright chordal sound cuts through well in any mix without killing other sounds that occur at the same time. Using fader automation or ducking to reduce the level of prominent riffs by a decibel or two during vocal parts can sometimes create the necessary space. In most cases, the difference between a good balance and a bad one is only a matter of very few decibels.

Drum Sounds

While dance music uses very bass-heavy sounds, which are often synthesised, to create a relentless and powerful four-to-the-bar rhythm, pop music can vary enormously, from dance-style sounds to very acoustic-sounding drums. At one time, pop snare drums were usually deep and crisp, but today anything that works goes. Some pop songs demand a brighter, more jazzy snare sound, while for others, more of a techno sound is appropriate, and the electronic sounds defined by the Roland TR range of drum machines are still proving immensely popular.

Dance snares tend to be light, bright and electronic sounding and take back seat to the bass drum, which provides the driving rhythm. These snare parts often play simple rhythmic figures rather than simply beat out two to the bar, and again serious dance-music composers often either sample drum sounds from other records or take loops from sample CDs, which are then further treated with effects or layered with other drum sounds. For those working without a sampler, it's possible to trigger a bass-drum sound from a drum machine at the same time as a low-pitched burst of sound from a synthesiser to create a similar effect, but now that samplers are also available as software plug-ins, and given the high quality of contemporary sample libraries, this type of compromise is less likely to be necessary. In any event, classic analogue electronic drums sounds such as the Simmons electronic kit and Roland TR808/909 machines are often emulated on modern drum machines and rhythm composers, making these ideal for putting together a dance rhythm track. EQ can also be used to change existing sounds to a surprising degree, and the well-known engineer's trick of radically boosting the bass control while applying low-mid cut at around 220Hz adds a lot of weight to the sound. The upper mid can be tuned to between 4kHz and 6kHz and boosted to produce a harder, better defined sound.

Pop hi-hats tend to be fairly natural and bright where a natural drum sound is sought, although many songs make use of the older analogue machine hi-hat sounds that are currently popular for dance music. Additionally, short, resonant synth sounds (sometimes called 'blips and thwips') may be used to augment the rhythm track in place of a conventional hi-hat. As a rule, TR909 kick-drum sounds tend to be the most fashionable (because of their depth and power), augmented by the lighter TR808 snares and hi-hats. Sounds taken from the old Roland TR606 are also usable, and for those who enjoy constructing their own rhythm patterns, rather than relying on loops, numerous sample CDs are available that feature these classic synthetic drum sounds as single hits.

Rock Drums

For rock music, kick drums tend to be recorded with plenty of slap and a little after-ring, while the snares are quite deep and with a well-defined snare sound. Like the bass drums, the toms tend to sound quite solid, with a little ring and a nice, sharp attack. The floor toms tend to be tuned fairly deep, and there may be several higher pitched toms, including smaller concert toms. Rock-cymbal sounds tend to be quite natural, with a fair selection of clangy cymbal 'bell' sounds or earth-ride sounds. The hi-hats often have a fair amount of rattle, but this fits in with the overall sound.

Heavy rock rarely makes use of electronic drum sounds, and most drum machines contain a selection of suitable sampled 'real' sounds. The most important thing is to listen to how a real rock drummer plays and to program the part accordingly – while it's acceptable to use unnatural drum parts for dance music, rock requires a sense of authenticity.

Guitars On Record

Guitar treatments are covered in some depth later in this book, but problems do arise when working with guitar bands because both guitar players often want to play all the time and they both want to play loud! If this is the case, return to the basic song and find out what it needs, not what the players' egos think they would like to give it. A problem often found with bands who play live on a regular basis but have little studio experience is over-busy guitar parts. The band will use a wall of sound to fill up their live sound, but in the studio the result is invariably far too cluttered.

Guitars with single-coil pick-ups take up less space in a mix yet still cut through well, and that holds true for both clean and overdriven sounds. For this reason, Strats and their clones are very popular. If two guitars – both using overdrive – need to play together, examine the musical lines to make sure that they aren't both playing the same thing for no good reason. Space can be created by making rhythm parts more rhythmic rather than merely letting one chord sustain into the next, and it's often possible to reduce the amount of overdrive while recording, which will increase the amount of tonal light and shade present in the sound, even if it is compressed later. Indeed, overdrive is often used as a device to create sustain, and it may be that a far more appropriate sound can be achieved by using much less overdrive combined with a generous helping of compression. The compressor attack time can also be increased to give more bite to individual notes, which can help if the guitar is playing a repetitive part.

It has already been mentioned that miking the two guitars differently can help make them sound distinct, and that choosing one model with single-coil pick-ups and another with humbuckers also helps. Further to these methods, it's possible to use the desk EQ to emphasise the 'bite' of the sound differently for each of the guitars. Typically, the presence or edge of a guitar can be anywhere between 2kHz and 6kHz, and by choosing a different frequency for each guitar, then boosting this by a few decibels, the resulting sounds can be brought even further apart. Additionally, if one guitar part is clearly the lead, with the other playing more of a supporting role, a compressor or gate used in Ducking mode can be used to punch the second guitar down by just 2–3dB while the lead guitar is playing. This small change in level will make a dramatic difference to the clarity of the mix, and the fact that the second guitar swells back in when the lead guitar stops will help to maintain the illusion of power and energy.

Effects can also be useful in making sounds stand out from the mix. A very slow flange effect really lifts a sound without making it appear too processed, while a slap-back echo using a single delay set at 50ms or so also creates a punchy, immediate sound.

Listening to some of the early Rolling Stones albums gives some insight into how a clear, exciting mix can be created with two or more guitars playing most of the time. This is all the more impressive when you consider that the recording equipment available at the time was much less sophisticated than many of us have at home today. Most recording at that time was done on either four- or eight-track machines, and the only effects available were tape delays, plate reverbs and fuzz boxes. Part of the band's characteristic sound was due to the use of alternate guitar tunings, notably the five-string G tuning used by Keith Richards on many of their records. Open-chord tunings aren't always appropriate, but they can be useful in giving an otherwise conventional song a new feel.

Guitar Reverb In The Mix

Excessive reverb can be a problem when used with guitars, especially with dirty sounds, as it tends to make the sound sustain even longer, and this fills up all of the spaces that are so vital in allowing the mix to breathe. Short, bright reverbs work better in busy rock mixes, with longer settings being better suited to slow, melodic solos. Once again, the ducker can be brought into play to hold down the level of reverb in the mix until there is a break in the guitar playing, at which point it will swell back in to create the desired effect.

Assembling Mixes In Sections

Although mix automation makes difficult mixes much easier to handle, some engineers prefer to mix a song in sections and then edit these sections together. This can be done using the *snapshot automation* facilities available on some systems, or it may be easier to assemble the parts in a hard-disk editing system. Provided that the rhythm section and vocal sections retain the same level and character from one section to another, this can be an effective way of working, although you should take particular care not to cut off any reverb or delay that belongs to a part immediately preceding an edit.

5 EFFECTS AND MIXING

Artificial effects, both hardware and virtual, have become an integral part of modern music recording, but it's wrong to think of an effect as something that's added at the last minute to provide a kind of superficial gloss. It's also wrong to assume that using an effect will cover up a mistake or a piece of poor playing, because in most instances it will simply draw attention to it. Nevertheless, one effect can be considered essential, and that is reverberation. Reverb needs to be added to most recordings to simulate a natural acoustic environment, and as an effect it occupies the unique position of being a fundamental part of the natural perception of sound. Virtually all other effects are employed for artistic reasons, and in the case of hardware, it helps to be aware early on in a session of the types of effect that are likely to be needed and, if possible, to work on some presets first so that you don't find yourself in the position of having to built a complex effect from scratch. Most engineers have favourite effects boxes for which they build up a library of useful programs, ideally in a form that can be quickly and easily modified during a session.

Some effects form an integral part of the sounds used in a composition – for example, certain delay-based effects may help to determine the rhythm of a piece of music. In a professional studio, the producer has to decide which effects, if any, need to be added during the recording stage and which can be left until the mix, and the project-studio operator faces the same choices, although some decisions may be determined by the number of recording tracks and effects units available. The world of virtual effects (such as VST plug-ins) has made working with computers a lot more convenient, and in most cases they have user interfaces that are as good as or even better than those of their hardware counterparts. However, if you're recording and mixing in a hardware environment, you'll need to use separate effects units or, in the case of digital mixers, you can also use those effects that are integral to the mixer.

Recording With Effects

Although leaving all effects until the mix gives more room for manoeuvre, it's not always the best way to work, even if the facilities exist to make this practical. Sometimes it helps to record an effect with the original instrument, and indeed in the case of some keyboard sounds where the effect is part of the patch, there's little option. A good engineer or producer will know instinctively when an effect should be added during recording and when it should be left until the end. Indeed, the very open-endedness of leaving everything to the mix can have a detrimental effect on music production; several producers I've spoken to believe that it's a good idea to commit yourself to something fairly rigid at an early stage, as failure to do so can lead to a huge amount of time wasted in exploring different possibilities when all that was needed was a clear sense of direction at the outset. Brian Eno is often quoted as preferring to record in a way that doesn't allow going back and remixing or changing sounds, and although this seems a bit like burning your bridges, at least you know that the only way is forwards.

With systems based on MIDI sequencers synchronised to tape or hard-disk recorders, mix automation and hard-disk digital editing, the opportunities for procrastination and reworking are almost overwhelming. All of these technologies, while wonderful and extremely useful in themselves, can divert much time and effort from the task in hand. Ask anyone who has used an automated mixing system and they'll invariably tell you that the mix takes at least twice as long as it did on a manual desk!

Artistic Considerations

When it comes to adding effects, it's important to consider both the artistic and logistic effects of either recording them to tape or saving them until the mix. The factors in favour of recording the effect to tape with the original instrument are that...

- The player may feel more comfortable and put in a better performance if able to hear the effects while playing;

- Committing effects to tape/disk saves time at the mixing stage...

- ...and frees up the effects device in question for a different task later in the session – for example, a multi-effects unit could provide an echo or delay during recording and then be used to furnish reverb during mixdown.

Conversely, if effects are changed or left out at the recording stage, the original musical performance may no longer work. This is very often the case when delay effects are used, as the musician 'plays' to the effect, but it can apply equally to the chorus-type treatments often used on guitar parts.

There are negative aspects to recording the effects to tape, too, especially if the number of tracks is limited. For example:

- Recording an instrument in mono takes only one track, but if you want to add a stereo effect you need two tape tracks in order to keep the effect in stereo. You could stick with one track, but that would confine the effect to mono.

- Committing effects to tape deprives you of the opportunity to later fine-tune the effect, to change its pan position relative to the dry (non-effected) track and to change its level in the mix.

In truth, there are occasions when one or the other approach is most appropriate, and it's unwise to develop too rigid a method of working that might deprive you of flexibility when you most need it. If time is limited, recording as many effects as possible while tracking certainly saves time when you come to mix. Detailed discussion and applications of individual effects will be left until later in the book, but a few examples are provided here of how effects can be used in a production environment to achieve specific results.

Guitar Effects

Guitar parts tend to be recorded with their basic effects, such as overdrive, spring reverb and expressive pedal effects such as wah-wah. Some analogue effects pedals produce a more musical sound than their better specified rack-mounted counterparts, especially chorus and flange units, while stereo reverb treatments can safely be left to the final mix. Don't be tempted to dismiss an effects pedal purely because of its technical spec; if it sounds good, use it. However, if it produces too much noise, distorts or causes some other problem, discuss it with the player using the pedal and see if you can simulate the sound with your own equipment. Even if you decide to add the effect at the final mixing stage, you should be able to arrange things so that the player can hear his part with the required effect while playing via the headphone monitoring system. This can usually be achieved by feeding the effect to the monitor mix but without recording it to tape.

If it really is necessary to leave a guitar treatment open-ended, it may help to record the sound that the player wants on one tape track and a straight, clean, DI'd output from the guitar (via a DI box) on a spare track. In this way, it's possible to feed the dry guitar track back through an amplifier or recording pre-amp/plug-in with the desired effects and overdrive settings in order to get the desired result when mixing. In a traditional multitrack tape studio, it's not uncommon to play back the guitar track through a guitar amplifier and then mic it up in order to change the sound, and if you can arrange an interesting live acoustic space in which to place the amp and mic, it's often possible to achieve results that would be difficult or even impossible using artificial effects on their own.

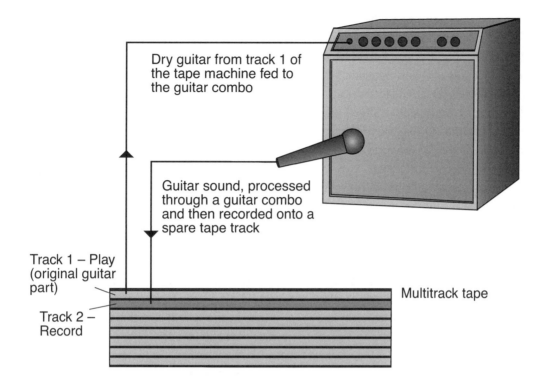

Dry guitar from track 1 of the tape machine fed to the guitar combo

Guitar sound, processed through a guitar combo and then recorded onto a spare tape track

Track 1 – Play (original guitar part)

Track 2 – Record

Multitrack tape

Figure 5.1: Re-recording a guitar track via a combo amplifier

Figure 5.1 illustrates how this is done using tape, but the technique is equally applicable to other multitrack recording systems.

Today, digital-modelling guitar pre-amplifiers are so good that you may not even feel the need to mic an amplifier. A typical modelling pre-amp combines amp modelling, speaker modelling and effects all in one unit, and many purport to emulate a range of classic European and American amplifiers. As you hear exactly the sound you're recording over the monitors while you're playing, you know just how the end result will turn out. However, it's worth pointing out that some of the more unlikely combinations of amplifier models and speaker cabinet models can produce unexpectedly interesting results, so don't just rely on the factory settings.

Some guitarists comment that the sound they hear coming back over the studio monitors isn't the same as what they hear when standing in front of their amp at a gig – which is hardly surprising, since studios seldom monitor at that kind of level. The real question is whether the sound you hear over the monitors is comparable with the guitar sound heard on similar records. If the answer is yes, then this method of recording has a lot of advantages, not least being that you can store all of the settings as a program, enabling you to recreate the sound exactly at a later date, if necessary. (Guitar recording is discussed in much more depth in Chapters 8 and 9, 'Acoustic Guitars' and 'Electric Guitars'.)

Logistics

In some circumstances, it's necessary to record effects with the performance purely because there won't be enough effects units or console sends to go around during the mix. Similarly, if tracks have to be bounced together to conserve space on tape, the necessary effects must be added during the bounce. If track restrictions mean that the bounced signal ends up on a single track, any added effects will also be mono. This is particularly common in home studios, and the usual outcome is that many of the effects that should have been in stereo end up being in mono.

Unfortunately, there's no easy way around this, but it is possible to give some semblance of stereo spread to a mono track by processing it at the final mixing stage with an additional stereo reverb treatment. If the track needs little in the way of added reverb, a short, bright plate setting or an early-reflections program will create a sense of depth and width without making the sound seem as though extra reverb has been added at all.

If the main restriction is in the number of console sends, you should consider using the channel-insert points or direct outputs as sends when adding individual effects to individual tracks. If you have sufficient spare input channels on the mixer, use these as effects returns to enable you to make use of the EQ and pan controls. Be sure that the effects sends are turned down on any channels used as returns, however, or unwanted feedback may result.

Lateral Thinking

Some effects can be created in unusual ways, such as this following application of a pitch shifter. Part of what makes a good engineer is the ability to adapt existing techniques rather than slavishly to follow existing methods. It is well known that pitch shifters can be used to thicken a vocal or instrumental track by providing a slightly detuned version of the original, but with a little thought the pitch shifter may be used in a much more convincing way. This technique requires a spare track, although the type of recorder doesn't matter and it doesn't even need a Varispeed option.

The basic idea is to double the original vocal part by singing along to the original and then playing both back together. Now, there's nothing new in this – in fact it's the classic method of double-tracking a line to make it sound fatter or fuller. The difference is that, this time, the signal feeding the singer's headphone monitor system is processed through the pitch shifter so that it is between five and ten cents sharp or flat. The singer then pitches his or her performance to the shifted sound, with the result that the new take is exactly the right amount out of pitch with the first to create a natural chorus effect.

If the pitch shifter has a delay function, a few tens of milliseconds of delay can be added to shift the second take slightly in time as well as pitch. The advantage of this – apart from having a real second take, as opposed to a synthesised one – is that the quality of the delay or pitch shifter is totally irrelevant, as the shifted sound isn't used in the recording, only for monitoring.

With instruments, you can simply retune the instrument slightly sharp or flat and then record the overdub, although for instruments where retuning isn't possible – the pitch-shifter dodge still works fine. Alternatively, if the recorder does have a Varispeed option, simple change the tape speed slightly and then record a second take without retuning the instrument. Once the tape is replayed at the normal speed, the two slightly out-of-tune takes will produce a chorus effect far more natural than that from any chorus pedal.

The reason why this technique produces better results than regular pitch shifting is because the audio itself isn't processed via the pitch shifter at all. The 'shifted' performance is produced by the singer singing slightly sharp or flat in response to the pitch-shifted monitor mix.

Another favourite method I have for creating double-tracking effects is to use AnTares' Auto-Tune (hardware or software versions, depending on your recording set-up), again in a slightly unorthodox way. This time, record a copy of the original vocal part through Auto-Tune, set up so that the shifted sound is as natural as possible. Even a well-pitched track will be corrected slightly, and the result of adding the natural and the corrected track together produces a good impression of true double-tracking. Adding a few milliseconds of delay to one of the tracks can also help to reinforce the illusion.

VST Effects

Most traditional studio effects are now available as software plug-ins for major sequencers, and these are powered either by the host computer or by plug-in DSP cards. US company Digidesign were the first to open up a third-party effects platform to support their Pro Tools system, but for the project-studio owner Steinberg's VST (Virtual Studio Technology) system was a major step forward, as these are powered solely by the host computer.

Steinberg opened up VST to third-party developers and to manufacturers of other sequencers and audio programs, and it's now one of the most well-supported plug-in formats around – although there are alternatives, such as the Mark Of The Unicorn's MAS plug-in system, for use with Digital Performer, and the generic Direct X format used in certain PC audio programs. Steinberg (Cubase, Cubasis and Wavelab), Emagic (Logic Audio) and TCWorks (Spark and Spark XL) support VST plug-ins directly, as does Opcode's StudiVision, Berkely Systems' Bias Peak stereo editor and the E-mu/Ensoniq Paris system. Additionally, there are other programs available – such as TCWorks' Spark audio editor – that can 'wrap' a VST plug-in to make it work in a different plug-in environment, in this case MAS. Similarly, Cakewalk Pro Audio 9 and Sonar – which have their own plug-in formats – can make use of VST plug-ins via the use of adaptor software. Virtually all music software runs either on Macintosh or PC computers. Be aware, however, that different versions of plug-ins are required depending on whether the host software runs on a Macintosh or PC, and not all products are available for both platforms. Also, a new plug-in format is required to use Mac OSX.

The current VST format, and other advanced plug-in formats, can read MIDI information from the host sequencer, making it easy to automate the plug-in's controls via MIDI. This makes it extremely easy to program effects where one or more parameters change in real time during a mix.

Host-based plug-ins like VST are said to be 'native' because they rely entirely on the host computer's processor and memory for their operation. The greater the number of plug-ins you run at the same time, the more computer power is needed, and there will always be a limit to how many native effects you can run at any one time.

Native plug-ins are used in different ways depending on how the host sequencer or audio editor is designed, but for mixing purposes conventional insert points and aux send/returns are used, just as in a hardware mixer. Stereo-editing packages may use a simpler system where plug-ins are inserted in line with the audio signal path.

Plug-in Advantages

Plug-in effects offer several advantages over their hardware counterparts – they remember their settings when you reload the song to continue work, there are no patchbays to wire up and you can use the same plug-in at several locations at once, as long as you have the computer power to support it. And, of course, they don't wear out!

Almost any effect or processor that can exist in hardware form can be implemented in software, from digitally modelled classic analogue tube equipment to more familiar compressors, equalisers, gates, reverbs and modulation devices. Additionally, there are plug-ins that have no direct hardware counterpart, such as multiband de-noising, de-clicking and de-humming programs.

More creative effects, such as vocoders and ring modulators, are also available, and it's often possible for these to give you far more control flexibility than you'd ever be able to get from analogue hardware. And perversely, there's a strong demand for plug-ins that add deliberate noise and crackle to simulate vinyl recordings or to add various types of analogue and digital distortion to a signal. Add to that synth-style filters, multiband fuzz boxes, vocal-pitch correctors, rotary-speaker cabinets and counterparts to just about every guitar pedal ever conceived and you can see why plug-ins are so attractive to anyone who makes music using a computer. Computers can also provide any kind of graphical interface, often showing compressor slopes, EQ curves and so on as well as the controls. In contrast, most hardware effects boxes are still programmed via a small LCD window and menu buttons.

Plug-ins For Editing

Stereo editors used for mastering are somewhat different to sequencers and are designed to work with two audio tracks rather than dozens. They are used for the cut-and-paste assembling of individual songs and for putting together mixes in the running order for an album. Plug-in support is important, as mastering usually involves processes such as equalisation, peak limiting and compression, where the compression is often multiband.

Summary

Effects, whether real or virtual, are tools, so you not only have to know how to use them but why you are using them. For example, why add double-tracking to a perfectly good vocal part unless you feel there's an artistic need? It's good experience to listen to records or music radio in a critical way to see if you can identify any special effects treatments that make the records stand out, such as the high-cut/low-cut-filtered Britney Spears telephone vocal sound or the obviously artificial double-tracking sound that John Lennon used on some of his trippier songs. Once you've identified the effect, try to think of the different ways you might go about creating it.

6 VOCALS

Even those used to working in an all-MIDI environment will need to work with microphones when it comes to getting vocals onto tape or into a hard-disk recording system. Recording vocals is essentially very simple, but the number of people who really struggle to get an acceptable vocal sound still surprises me. In reality, the first necessity is a vocalist who can actually perform well, but taking that for granted the rest is down to choosing the right type of microphone, putting it in the right position and using the correct degree of compression to control it without choking the life out of it. Room acoustics also have an effect on the sound, even when close-miked, but it should be possible to get acceptable vocal results in almost any room with the aid of a little improvised acoustic treatment.

Pop shields should be used as a matter of course, and it helps to have an effective de-essing system available when the singer's vocal characteristics demand one. A suitable reverb or ambience treatment is invariably needed to add realism to vocals recorded in a dead studio, and both the engineer and producer should work to put the singer at his or her ease in order to stimulate the best performance possible.

It's the producer's responsibility to check that the vocal is of sufficient quality throughout and that any lines containing errors in either lyrical delivery, timing or pitch are replaced, ideally during the same session in order to maintain a continuity of sound. Where sufficient spare audio tracks are available, it's a good plan to keep several takes so that the best sections of each can be compiled into one perfect vocal track. The producer will also need to supervise any harmony parts or double-tracking.

Composite Vocal Takes

It helps to have photocopies of the lyric sheet on hand before the session gets under way so that the producer can add comments and underline any phrases or words that need patching up as they arise. Some producers are happy to get one reasonable take down on tape and then patch this up by replacing sections, while others prefer to capture several complete takes and then use the best sections from each. In studios with a limited number of audio tracks, the first method is less wasteful and the final mix is easier to handle, although many digital recording systems now have virtual tracks that may be used to store alternate takes, disk space permitting.

If the singer isn't comfortable with singing isolated sections of the song, try running the tape all the way through and simply punching in and out of Record on the lines that you want to replace. This will allow the singer to concentrate on creating a whole performance, even though what you finally use will be the result of several different takes. Even with this method, though, you'll often find that one specific line causes trouble, so you may have to tackle this in isolation until it's right. As long as the singer gets a couple of lines of vocals to run into it, everyone should be happy.

The second method of producing a composite take – recording several complete takes and then using the best sections from each – is best suited to larger tape-based systems or digital systems with graphical editing capabilities; in a traditional tape environment, a mixer with mute automation makes it much easier to switch between vocal takes than attempting to do it manually. The composite vocal track will often be bounced to a spare track and the original tracks freed up for re-use.

'Comping' in this way can be time consuming, but it's one thing less to worry about when you come to mix. Also, if you do the job while the recording is still fresh in your mind, you're more likely to remember which are the good and bad sections. If you try to do it several days or weeks later, you may have to listen to and evaluate every take afresh, unless your note-keeping is meticulous.

Ultimately, it doesn't matter which method you use, as long as you end up with a vocal take you're happy with, and if that means putting the best vocal chorus into a large-memory sampler and then firing it back into the mix at the appropriate points using MIDI triggering, or copying and pasting on a digital workstation, then that's fine, too. After all, this is only the 21st-century equivalent of 'spinning in', a practice where vocal sections were transferred to a two-track, open-reel machine, which was then cued up and started manually to do the same job. If you have a spare tape recorder, give this a try, if only to see how much easier it is now! If marker-pencil cue marks are put on the back of the tape and lined up with some integral feature on the machine, the results can be quite repeatable, although some trial and error is involved in getting the start time right.

Vocal Monitoring

Most vocal monitoring is done over headphones, and two types are commonly used. Fully-enclosed headphones are less prone to spillage problems, but some vocalists find that they have trouble singing in tune because the boxed-in feeling distracts them. This is why you often see videos of recording sessions in which the singer has one can on and the other off. In situations where one phone isn't used, it is important to mute it so that it doesn't spill into the mic. Where stereo monitoring is available, this can be done using the Pan control.

Semi-enclosed phones are more comfortable to work with, but they leak more sound, so you could end up with a little of the backing track on the vocal track. This may not seem to be serious – until you suddenly decide to use part of the take unaccompanied! The leakage problem is more serious if any sort of click track is being used – basic pulse-tone metronomes or drum-machine guide tracks tend to spill quite audibly.

The quality of monitoring can have a profound effect on the quality of a vocal performance, so take the time needed to set up a good foldback mix for the singer and add sufficient reverb to the headphone mix to make him or her feel comfortable. The room temperature can also affect a singer's ability to pitch, so don't automatically blame the singer if something isn't going quite right. A song is only as good as its vocal part, so make every possible effort to keep the singer relaxed and in a creative frame of mind.

The Right Mic

Generally, live vocal mics are dynamic models and incorporate a deliberate treble boost of a few decibels at around the 5kHz mark in order to render the vocal more intelligible. While undoubtedly useful in preserving clarity of diction, such a 'presence peak' isn't necessarily a good thing in the studio, where the general aim is to capture as natural a performance as possible.

Most professional studios will use a capacitor mic for vocal use, because these have a high sensitivity and a wide frequency response, extending up to 20kHz or so. Dynamic microphones, on the other hand, tend to perform poorly above 16kHz or thereabouts and are less sensitive than capacitors, and this could lead to problems with electronic noise if the vocalist has a quiet voice. However, some rock vocalists prefer to use dynamic mics in the studio because it gives them a fatter sound, and they use the mic so close to their mouths that low sensitivity isn't a problem.

The wide frequency response of capacitor microphones can emphasise sibilance (a whistling sound accompanying S and T sounds) in a performer's voice, and this problem is further aggravated by large amounts of compression or bright reverb treatments. The usual cure for sibilance is to use a de-esser to attenuate the sibilant sounds, but in some cases a more pragmatic approach might be to use a less bright capacitor model or even a suitable dynamic microphone, as the limited frequency response of the mic will tend to minimise the problem. This need to match microphone characteristics to vocalists is the main reason why a well-equipped studio has so many different vocal mics.

Of course, no single microphone is ideal for all vocalists. If a singer has a bright voice, then a mic with a presence peak may tend to make the overall sound appear excessively harsh, whereas the same mic used on a singer with an indistinct or soft voice could yield a significant improvement. Attempting to achieve the same effect by means of EQ seldom succeeds as well, and for this reason I would recommend recording vocals with little or no EQ. If the sound isn't right, try a different mic or change the position of the one you're using slightly before resorting to EQ. If you must work with just one vocal mic, try to use one that doesn't have too much character, as this will mean that it's more likely to give good results over a wide range of vocal styles, and also fine-tuning the sound later using EQ is more likely to be successful.

Microphone Patterns For Vocals

Unidirectional- or cardioid-pattern mics are the preferred choice for live performance because of their ability to reject off-axis sounds, thus minimising both the spill from other performers and acoustic feedback. In the studio, however, vocals tend to be recorded as separate overdubs, with the singer monitoring the backing mix via headphones, and in this case the need to use a cardioid-pattern mic isn't so great. However, unless the studio is acoustically quite dead, it may be a good idea to use a directional mic anyway in order to minimise the effect of the room acoustic on the recorded sound – unless the room acoustic just happens to provide the sound you want. Figure 6.1 shows the directional characteristics available from different types of microphone.

In circumstances where the room does make a positive contribution to the sound – as it may when recording choral music in a church, for example – the

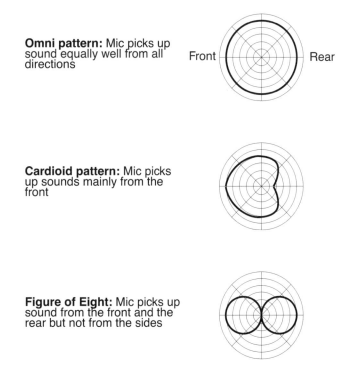

Omni pattern: Mic picks up sound equally well from all directions

Front ———— Rear

Cardioid pattern: Mic picks up sounds mainly from the front

Figure of Eight: Mic picks up sound from the front and the rear but not from the sides

Figure 6.1: Common microphone polar patterns

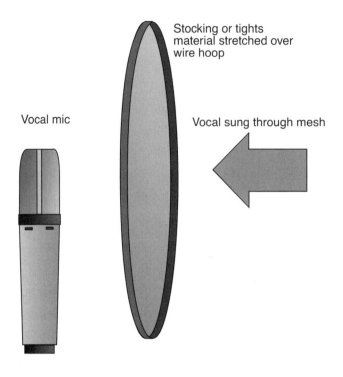

Stocking or tights
material stretched over
wire hoop

Vocal mic

Vocal sung through mesh

Figure 6.2: Improvised pop shield

result will invariably sound more natural recorded via an omni (omni-directional) microphone. As a general rule, omni-pattern mics produce a more accurate overall picture than cardioids because they have the same nominal response in all directions, with the result that both direct and indirect sound is accurately captured. By contrast, the off-axis response of a cardioid mic tends to be very bass-heavy/top-light once you get past 90º from the main axis.

A mic should be mounted on a solid boom stand and a shock-mount cradle should be employed, if available. However, some singers can't perform without a hand-held mic, in which case you should give them one, set up another mic on a stand a couple of feet in front of them and tell them that you need a mix of the sound from both mics. You can then record just the output from the stand-mounted mic!

Pop Shields

Most engineers experience problems with microphones popping, and my experience has shown that simple foam wind shields are virtually useless. The popping is caused by blasts of air from the performer's mouth slamming into the microphone diaphragm and giving rise to a high-level, low-frequency output signal, which comes over as a loud, bassy thump.

Commercial pop filters use fine plastic or metal gauze stretched over a circular frame somewhere between four and six inches in a diameter and positioned between the performer and the microphone. Normal sound, which consists of vibrations within the air, is not affected, but blasts of moving air are intercepted and their energy is dissipated harmlessly as turbulence. Commercial pop shields are very expensive, so here's how to make your own. For the grille, a piece of fine nylon stocking works perfectly. This may be stretched over a wire frame (many engineers use wire coat-hangers) and is then positioned between the microphone and the singer's mouth, as shown in Figure 6.2.

A tidier alternative is to use a wooden embroidery hoop to hold the stocking material in place. Another ready-made option is a frying-pan splash guard. These comprise a fine metal mesh fixed to a wire hoop and are fitted with a handle, making it easy to tape the filter to a mic stand.

Microphone Positioning

Working too close to a microphone will cause significant changes in both level and tone as the singer moves his or her head. A working distance of between six inches and two feet from the mic is most appropriate to studio work, depending on the style of singing and the effect of the room acoustic. Most studio vocal recordings are done in a relatively dead environment so that reverb can be added artificially during the mix, in which case a mic distance of 9–12 inches is typical. In a professional studio, there's likely to be a dedicated vocal booth, but excellent home recordings can be made simply by keeping the microphone well away from the walls of the room and improvising sound absorbers by draping blankets and bedding over mic stands. With a cardioid mic, most of the absorption should be placed behind and to each side of the singer's position. In general, though, the deader the environment the better, and if the acoustic is still less than ideal, work closer to the mic to improve the ratio of direct to reflected sound.

Vocal Groups

If several vocalists are to be recorded at one time, the distance between mics should be at least three times – and ideally five times – the distance between the microphone and the vocalist in order to avoid the phase-cancellation effects caused by spillage. If you can improvise some form of acoustic screening, so much the better.

For larger groups of singers, such as choirs or ensembles, it may be desirable to record them in stereo using a pair of coincident cardioids or an M&S (Middle and Side)pair. For larger choral recordings, more control is available if you use one stereo pair for each section of the chorus, with the microphone pairs mounted above and in front of the performers.

To create the illusion of space when multitracking backing vocals or groups of backing vocalists, try setting up a stereo pair of mics in the room and then moving the performers for each new recording. For example, you could record three tracks with the singers positioned left, then centre and then right of the mics. On playback, this will create the illusion of the three groups of people existing at the same time in a real stereo soundspace. The singers can be made to sound slightly different by using established tricks such as varispeeding the tape slightly for each overdub. (These techniques are described later in this chapter, during the section on 'Double Tracking'.)

Singer/Guitarists

Singers who play acoustic guitar can be difficult to record because of the amount of guitar spill that arrives at the vocal mic and vice versa. One solution is to use figure-of-eight mics rather than cardioids or omnis as these provide almost total rejection for sounds arriving 90º off axis. By aiming the 'deaf' axis of the vocal mic at the guitar and the deaf spot of the guitar mic at the mouth, a few decibels of useful extra separation can be gained. However, because figure-of-eight mics also pick up equally from the rear, this technique isn't ideal where there are other performers playing in the room at the same time. As a rule, placing some sound-absorbing material behind the mics will help produce a cleaner sound, as it will minimise the effect of the room acoustic. (Note that, as with cardioid mics, figure-of-eight mics also exhibit a proximity effect, so it's best not to work too closely and to try to keep a fixed distance from the mic.)

Compression

Compression is invariably needed in pop-music production to keep the vocal level nice and even. A degree of compression applied during the recording stage will help to keep the level going onto tape/disk sensibly high and at the same time guard against loud peaks that might otherwise cause overload and subsequent distortion (this is particularly important in digital systems). Soft-knee compressors are least obtrusive in this application and should be set to give a gain reduction of no more than 6–10dB or so during the louder sections. A singer with a very wide dynamic range, on the other hand, may need a 'hard ratio' compressor set to a ratio of 4:1 or even higher in order to really keep the peaks under control. This is where an experienced engineer is a great asset, as he'll know from the first run-through just how much compression will be required. As a rule, choose a fast or programme-dependent attack time and a release time of around a quarter to half a second.

It is always safer to apply less compression than you need during recording, because you can always add more compression when you come to mix, so in some ways it pays to use the compressor more like a safety limiter than in order to produce a finished vocal sound. The effect of too much compression added at the recording stage may ruin an otherwise perfect take and will be impossible to correct later. The majority of engineers will use additional compression when mixing, but again you have to take care not to use more than is necessary because compression also brings out any noise and sibilance present in a recording. Using an exciter or high-end EQ boost to brighten a vocal track can also bring up the sibilance to an unacceptable level, in which case you might have to resort to using a de-esser.

A gate or expander is useful for cleaning up the spaces between words and phrases, but as the setting up of these devices is quite critical, they should generally be used only on the mix, not while recording, as this will allow you to take as many passes as necessary in order to get the threshold settings and attack/release times right.

Vocal EQ

Vocals will often need some equalisation applied to them in order to make them sit well with the backing track, and over-sibilant vocals may also require the application of dynamic EQ processing via a de-esser. No two singers have exactly the same voice characteristics, of course, so any EQ treatment is likely to be different depending on the singer. However, modifications in certain general areas of the audio spectrum can be considered appropriate for the vast majority of voices, although final EQ settings will have to be tuned by ear with regard to the specific singer being recorded. Be aware that equalisers can sound very different to each other, and the EQ sections found in most small desks are suitable only for making very small, general corrections. For anything more, a good-quality parametric equaliser is essential. For those working with an audio-software package, good plug-in equalisers should be available, but as with their hardware equivalents, the sound quality of these differs according to the design.

Any top boost should be applied quite high, at 6–12kHz or above, but watch out for sibilance creeping in. However, don't settle for a dull vocal sound simply because using the right EQ brings up the sibilance; if you have to use a de-esser to save the day, use it. The most effective de-essers are those that attenuate only the sibilant band of frequencies rather than the whole signal. The simpler, full-band type can make the vocals sound very 'lispy' when processing is taking place. Using so-called 'air EQ' (a wide but gentle boost centred at 12–15kHz) can be effective in adding sparkle and clarity without exacerbating sibilance too seriously, as the boost is applied mainly above those frequencies that give sibilance problems.

Boosting in the 1–2kHz range gives a rather honky, cheap sound to the vocals and so is not recommended, except as a special effect. I try to keep vocals as flat as possible and tend to use the shelving high control or 'air' band to add just a hint of top rather than anything more drastic.

Presence can be added with just a little boost at 3–4kHz, but use this in moderation or the sound quality will suffer, and this is the area where sibilance will be emphasised. Vocals are the most natural sound in the world and our ears soon register the fact that they've been tampered with.

If you're mixing several backing vocals, rolling off a touch of bass might help the vocal to sit better in the mix without sounding muddy. On its own, the equalised backing vocal might sound terribly thin, but once it's in the track the chances are that it'll sound perfectly normal and yet won't fill up the vulnerable lower-mid area of the audio spectrum with unwanted energy.

Double Tracking

Double tracking is a popular trick used to add depth to a voice. It may be used to compensate for a weak voice or to add impact to choruses and so on. Traditionally, the singer performs the same part twice (or more) onto two tracks and then the two tracks are played back together in order to give the effect of two singers in unison. Alternative technological tricks may be used to fake the effect (as described in Chapter 5, 'Effects And Mixing'), but if a singer is capable of duplicating a performance pretty accurately in pitch and timing, the real way always sounds better.

A common problem with double-tracked parts is that words may start together but often sound ragged because the word endings aren't in sync, and nowhere is this more evident than in the case of words ending with T or S sounds. A simple dodge is to perform the second take in a deliberately sloppy manner, by missing off or fading the ends of tricky words. When the two tracks are played together, the result will sound much tighter. The same trick applies to backing-harmony vocal parts.

To create a little difference between the two vocal lines, you could change the speed of the multitrack up or down by a semitone or so before recording the second part, which will give the voice a different character when the tape is returned to normal speed. This is a trick used often by radio-jingle writers to create the effect of a large vocal group when overdubbing just one or two singers.

Another useful trick is to use a delay line to delay the headphone mix by 50ms or so when recording the second track. This has the effect of making the singer perform the second part 50ms later than the first part, giving a short delay effect when the tape is replayed normally. This creates a nice rich effect without compromising the sound quality, because what goes to tape hasn't actually been passed through the delay unit. This means that any old delay box will do the trick, even an old tape-echo or guitar foot-pedal unit.

Faking Double Tracking

Inevitably, some singers can never perform a song the same way twice, in which case any attempt at real double-tracking will sound messy and unacceptable. This is where ADT (Automatic Double Tracking) comes to the rescue. Originally, this effect was created by using an open-reel machine running at high speed to function as a very short delay unit, or by using the short delay setting on a tape-echo unit. But by fine-tuning the delay so that the original sound and its repeat just start to separate, you get the effect of two voices singing slightly out of time with each other. The effect isn't entirely convincing, because the pitching of the delayed part is just too perfect, but later

electronic attempts to simulate the effect using chorus or pitch-shift circuitry can sound rather more realistic.

- A short delay of between 30ms and 100ms is added to the sound but the delay is either subtly chorused or processed via a pitch shifter to give a detuning effect of between five and ten cents (with one cent being one hundredth of a semitone).

- Further depth can be added by panning the original and delayed signals to opposite sides of the stereo mix.

If you only have a basic DDL, you can use this to simultaneously delay the sound and vary the pitch, using it as a kind of delayed chorus setting. After getting the delay time right by ear, adjust the modulation depth and speed so that the pitch wavering effect is just audible – a modulation rate of 2–3Hz combined with a very shallow modulation depth should do the trick nicely. The longer the delay time, the less modulation depth you'll need to create the required degree of pitch shifting.

A more natural effect is achieved if delay is combined with the Auto-Tune trick described in Chapter 5, 'Effects And Mixing'. Here, the untreated vocals are used as the main parts with the delayed, Auto-Tuned parts used to simulate the doubling track.

Reverb And Ambience

Even before digital reverb units came along, some way of adding life to vocals had to be found, because the studio recording environment made them sound quite lifeless without further treatment. Reverb is part of our everyday lives – we exist in reflective environments, so any sound we hear that is totally devoid of any reverb or ambience sounds unnaturally limp. In the early days, live echo rooms, spring reverb units and echo plates were all used to add reverberation to recordings, the most successful probably being the plate, comprising a large steel plate suspended in a rigid frame and driven to vibrate by a voice coil similar to that found on a loudspeaker. The resulting vibrations were picked up by two or more surface-mounted contact mics and amplified

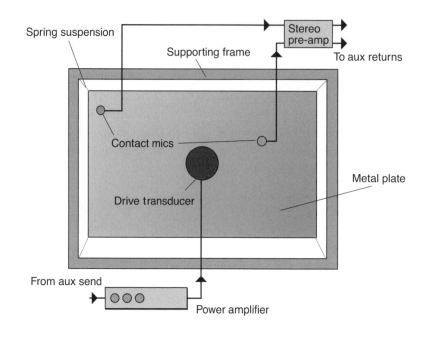

Figure 6.3: Reverb plate diagram

before being fed back into the mix. The final effect was brighter than natural reverb, but it was a musically pleasant sound, which is why most modern digital units have plate-simulation modes as well as settings to imitate rooms, halls and chambers. Figure 6.3 shows how a plate reverb unit works.

Today, few studios have access to plates – nearly all reverb is digital – but the quality of digital reverb units is improving all the time and even the cheaper models offer convincing plate emulations as well as a choice of room and hall settings. Picking the right reverb setting is where the producer's artistic input is vital, because there are many ways of approaching any musical project, with no particular way being more right than others. Even so, there are a few guidelines to follow, based largely on common sense:

- Bright reverb settings give the vocal an attractive sizzle, as long as they aren't so bright that they bring up the level of sibilance to an unacceptable degree.

- If the song is a ballad, a longer, softer reverb might create a better atmosphere.

- Short ambience settings that are rich in early reflections can be used to add life to a vocal while adding no perceptible reverb at all, and trick settings such as reverse reverb also have their place, if used in moderation.

Advanced Vocal Effects

If you have a preset reverb box with few adjustable parameters, you can create a useful effect by setting a DDL to give a single repeat between 50ms and 100ms long and feed this into a reverb unit to provide *pre-delay*. This creates a deeper sense of space and also slightly separates the reverb from the basic sound, which can enhance the clarity. Most programmable multi-effects units and dedicated reverb processors have a pre-delay setting included in their reverb parameters, but this little dodge is still useful for those occasions when your main reverb unit is tied up on another job and you have to create an effect using something more basic.

Another production trick can be achieved by putting a delay unit after the reverb in the signal chain but on only one of the stereo outputs. This splits the reverb so that it starts in one speaker and then moves over

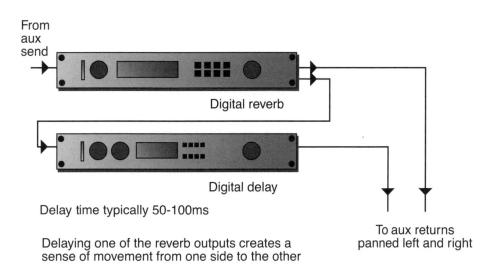

Delay time typically 50-100ms

Delaying one of the reverb outputs creates a
sense of movement from one side to the other

Figure 6.4: Delaying one reverb output

to the other speaker. Again, this treatment adds a sense of movement but without becoming too obvious or gimmicky. Figure 6.4 illustrates how this method might be arranged.

Reverb Panning

Reverb panning isn't limited only to instrumental parts; it can also be used to create movement and interest in vocal tracks without sounding too gimmicky, and if your multi-effects unit includes a panner, shifting the output of the reverb unit from left to right – ideally at a rate that fits in with the tempo of the song – can be very effective. In a software environment, this is very easy, as most plug-ins that provide panning can also be sync'd to the tempo of a song. If you don't have a panner and you're working in a more traditional hardware environment, however, you can create the same effect by using a gate that has side-chain or key inputs.

To pan reverb in this way, using two sounds programmed into a drum machine (which must have at least two assignable outputs), the two sides of the gate can be triggered alternately via the key inputs. Ideally, the drum machine would be synchronised to the master tape using a MIDI sequencer. The stereo reverb is then fed into the main gate inputs and the attack and release times set to give a smooth pan effect. This only takes a little trial and error and is remarkably effective.

If you have two reverb units, try a reverse setting on one and a conventional reverb setting on the other. Pan one reverb unit left and the other right and you'll find that, as the normal reverb decays on one side, the reverse effect will build up on the other, giving a different kind of moving pan effect.

Auto-Tune

No discussion on vocal recording would be complete without looking at the impact that software such as Auto-Tune has made on pop-music recording. Available in both hardware and software plug-in formats, Auto-Tune is designed to pitch correct monophonic vocal (and instrumental) lines by gently nudging wayward notes towards the nearest correct notes in a scale specified by the user. It's possible to leave Auto-Tune set to a chromatic scale, but then it's likely that the pitch of a poorly sung note could go to the wrong note because that's the one it happened to be nearest to. It's a much better idea to input only those notes in the tonality of the piece of music, then the worst that can happen is that a horrendously pitched note will be corrected to the wrong note in the right key! In order to correct the pitch of a note, a system such as Auto-Tune needs to be able to read the pitch of the incoming signal, which is why it can only work with monophonic sources. In some applications, the desired notes may also be 'played in' via MIDI. However, as attractive as all this seems, you must be aware that Auto-Tune and similar products will only sound natural if you use them carefully and if the original performance is reasonably good to begin with; trying to correct a badly sung part will just sound ludicrous. That said, there are some interesting techniques to try by using Auto-Tune in unexpected ways.

Forcing incoming notes to the right pitch is only part of the story, because if that is done too rigidly, you end up with a very flat, pitch-quantised vocal performance that sounds almost vocoder-like. Of course, it didn't take long after this effect was discovered for it to be used creatively, not only on Cher's Number One record 'Believe' but also on many more for the next couple of years afterwards.

The rate at which correction takes place is determined by a control on the device, and by adjusting this carefully, natural bends and vibrato are allowed through unaltered, but as soon as the input settles on a specific note for any length of time, it's pulled into perfect pitch. This is the gentlest way of correcting vocals, but you can also create some interesting effects with instruments such as theremins and fretless basses where their natural slides are retained and yet the pitching is tightened up noticeably. If the tracking is set too fast, the instrument produces discrete, stepped pitches, just like those produced by a keyboard, which can sometimes be used creatively. My favourite trick of this kind – which, I admit, is a digression from vocals – is to use Auto-Tune on lead guitar. If you adjust the tracking speed so that pitch bends are quantised into fast scalic slurs, the whole sound takes on an almost Arabic quality.

Auto-Tune doesn't use any kind of formant correction, so any sound pulled far from its original pitch starts to sound unnatural in the same way as any conventionally pitch-shifted signal. In normal use, the degree of pitch correction is less than half a semitone, so you don't notice the timbral change, but the effect can be abused in creative ways by setting deliberately large intervals. For example, you could set up a target scale containing only octaves and fifths. Then, no matter what you sang, you'd end up with the notes sliding to only one of two possible pitches, often

accompanied by interesting timbral changes. The vocal timbre is transformed in a way that is proportional to the pitch difference between what you're singing and what the nearest scale note is set to. For example, you could sing a steadily rising tone and there would be no pitch change until you got within range of the next note in the target scale, yet the timbre of the fixed note would change as the pitch shifter worked harder and harder to correct it. In this example, the pitch shifter will attempt to push down the pitch of the note to compensate for the higher vocal, so the timbre will take on a darker, larger quality. Then, when the vocal gets within range of the next note in the scale, the timbre will flip as the pitch shifter tries to push the pitch upwards.

Auto-Tune also has the ability to add delay vibrato to whatever sound is being processed, so in theory you could strip out the vibrato from the original performance and replace it with something far more mechanical and precise. The human voice processed with synth-style vibrato can actually be very interesting, purely because it's so unnatural.

There's also Auto-Tune ability to shift pitch according to a MIDI input – ie you can input a MIDI melody and whatever audio input you have will be forced to fit that melody. As I mentioned earlier, moving the pitch too far or too fast sounds unnatural, but unnatural can be good – from a production standpoint, at least. For example, try using MIDI arpeggios to make the voice sing impossibly fast, robotic scales.

A Matter Of Taste

Almost any effect, no matter how bizarre, can be justified in context – it's all a matter of artistic judgment, which is where a good producer comes into his or her own. I've even heard vocals chopped into short, gated sections and then panned between the speakers, giving an effect like a synchronised, intermittent mic-cable fault, but because it was used sparingly and in the right place, it worked. Similarly, a good vocal line can be completely ruined by the gratuitous application of effects. In most cases, clarity of diction is important, in which case the longer the reverb decay time, the lower its level should be in the mix or the sound will become muddled.

One much-used technique is 'telephone vocal' EQ, where the low end is cut very harshly below around 200Hz and where the high end is cut above 5kHz. If this is combined with gentle distortion and/or heavy compression, it can be very effective – although, as with most such effects, it works best when used only for short sections or phrases, not for whole songs.

Art Before Technology

By all means combine two or more different reverb units to create a composite effect that enhances the vocal sound, but always keep your artistic aims at the front of your mind and don't let the technology dictate your actions. The technology is there to serve you, not the other way around. Most pop songs rely on strong, distinctive vocal parts, and it's up to the producer to achieve this by whatever means possible. What's more, although many project-studio owners worry about getting exactly the right type of mic, pre-amp and compressor, often spending a lot of money on tube versions, 99 per cent of a good vocal comes from a good vocalist and good recording techniques. If you can't get a good sound by using one of the budget, large-diaphragm capacitor mics recorded via a decent desk and an affordable compressor, try looking at the sound source and the recording method before blaming the equipment.

Finally, artists tend to ask for effects that they've heard before, and many of these are over-used clichés such as adding repeat echo to the last word in a vocal line or the last word in a song, the Cher 'Believe' effect (mainly Auto-Tune set to the fastest pitch-correction rate) or the Britney telephone vocal. Occasionally, one of these clichés may still be OK to use, but it's much better to do the unexpected than to kill your record with predictability. If you must use a cliché, try to use it in an unexpected way or in an unusual place – for example, adding a gross repeat echo to the very first word in a song might have more impact than using it right at the end.

7 DRUMS

Currently, it seems that more pop records are being made using electronically sequenced drum sounds rather than the real thing, but fashions have a habit of changing, so a good engineer should be prepared for all eventualities. The ability to record a real drum kit is a vital skill that no engineer should be without, for even if the majority of work is done with electronic percussion, it is still common practice to overdub real cymbals and/or percussion to add a spark of humanity to the end result.

The Drum Kit

Provided that the kit to be recorded is well looked after and fitted with decent heads, it should be possible to get a good sound out of it within half an hour or so. Old heads stretch unevenly and the surface becomes wrinkled, causing a loss of tone that no amount of tuning and damping will fix. Contrary to popular belief, drum tuning doesn't have to be radically changed for recording situations; a little careful damping is often all that's needed. Furthermore, most drum recording is close-miked using relatively inexpensive dynamic mics, making it possible to mic the entire kit for around the same price as a couple of good studio vocal mics.

The easiest kit to record is the one that uses single-headed toms. If the toms are double-headed, the bottom heads can normally be removed without problems, although you may find that the nut boxes rattle. If so, a little inventive work with a pack of Blu-Tack will usually cure this. If you prefer the sound of the toms double-headed, they do require more critical tuning, and the bottom head often needs a little careful damping to prevent it from ringing.

Tuning And Damping

Snare drums usually have metal or wooden shells (although some make use of synthetic materials) and they vary in depth enormously: metal shells give a brighter tone with quite a lot of ring while wooden snares tend to produce a warmer sound. Whatever the type you use, it's important to ensure that the snares are in good order and properly adjusted in order to minimise rattling.

The snare head is usually tensioned slightly looser than the batter head, although individual drummers will have their own ideas on tuning. As a starting point, all drum heads should be tensioned as evenly as possible – tapping the head around the edges should give the same pitch all the way around the head. Every drum has a natural range of tuning, and it will be evident if the tuning is too far out as the tone will be either too hard or very lifeless.

Inevitably, the snares will vibrate in sympathy whenever another drum is struck, and although this may be minimised by careful tuning of the snare drum relative to the rest of the kit, it can seldom be eliminated completely. One approach is to gate the snare mic, but this does nothing to remove the buzz picked up by the overhead mics. Some engineers resort to taping coins onto the snare head to pull the head down onto the snares themselves, but in my experience this compromises the tone of the drum.

An undamped drum has a surprisingly long decay time and, worse, it will ring in sympathy whenever other drums are hit. Overdamping, on the other hand, can leave a kit sounding lifeless, yet many inexperienced engineers choke the life out of a kit because they are worried by minor rings and rattles that would probably be inaudible in the context of a complete mix. A little experience will soon give you an idea of the right amount of damping to use. Internal dampers are rarely used in the studio, as they put pressure on the head, and it's far better to use a pad of tissue or cloth held in place with a strip of studio tape.

One trick often used to give a more dynamic tom sound is to tune the head evenly at first but then to slacken off one tuning lug by just a touch. This produces a slight drop in pitch after the drum is struck, rather like the sound produced by an electronic drum, with the effect related to how hard the drum is hit.

Most contemporary drummers will have a hole cut in the front head of their kick drum, which makes miking very easy, although the hole should be as large

as is practical in order to prevent the remaining material from ringing excessively. Don't be tempted to remove the front head completely, however, as this can put uneven stress on the drum shell and may cause it to distort. A wooden bass-drum beater gives a better defined sound than cork or felt beaters, and a patch of moleskin or hard plastic taped to the head where the beater impacts will add a click to the sound. There are specialist drum products for this application, but an old credit card works perfectly well.

Damping the bass drum is best achieved by placing a folded woollen blanket inside the drum so that it rests on the bottom of the shell and touches the lower part of the rear head. Further damping is unlikely to be necessary, although noise gates are often used to sharpen up the decay of the sound.

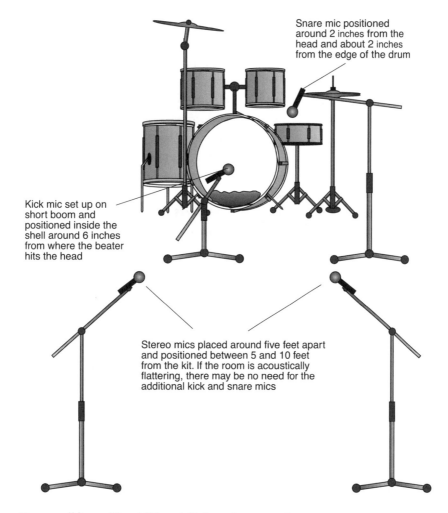

Snare mic positioned around 2 inches from the head and about 2 inches from the edge of the drum

Kick mic set up on short boom and positioned inside the shell around 6 inches from where the beater hits the head

Stereo mics placed around five feet apart and positioned between 5 and 10 feet from the kit. If the room is acoustically flattering, there may be no need for the additional kick and snare mics

Figure 7.1: Stereo miking with additional kick and snare mics

Kit Miking Options

Perhaps the most accurate way of miking a drum kit is with a stereo microphone pair (either coincident or spaced) placed between five and ten feet in front of the kit. This arrangement can capture the live sound of the kit very faithfully, but even so the degree of artistic success is dependent on the actual sound and balance of the drum kit and on the suitability of the room acoustics. If the snare and kick drum need to be made more assertive, additional close mics can be used on these and added to the mix, usually panned to the centre. The mic positions will be similar to those used when a separate mic is used on each drum. This set-up is illustrated in Figure 7.1 and is often used for recording jazz music.

This method of miking is unsuitable for situations in which spill from other instruments might cause a problem. Furthermore, for pop-music work, the natural sound of the kit is often the last thing the producer wants to hear, though it has applications in some fields of pop music, as well as jazz. More often, the kit is recorded with closely positioned mics on the individual drums with an additional stereo pair located above the kit to capture the ambience.

Close Miking
Snare And Toms

Snare drums produce the brightest sound in the kit, other than the cymbals, so a dynamic mic with a respectable top end or a capacitor mic is desirable. Most engineers use cardioid-pattern mics for all of the drums in an attempt to give the greatest immunity against spill, but in reality omni mics don't fare much worse than cardioid in this respect and have the benefit of being able to pick up off-axis sounds more accurately. In other words, they may pick up a touch more spill from the other drums, but at least they'll pick it up accurately. A further benefit is that omni mics don't suffer from the proximity effect and so are less susceptible to unpredictable tonal changes when used close to an instrument, as is the case when miking drums. That doesn't mean you should rush out and buy a set of omni mics, but if you have access to some already, you might want to try them to see if you get very different results. The usual mic position for the

snare and toms is a couple of inches above the drum head, a couple of inches in from the edge and angled towards the centre of the head. The mics should also be angled away from other nearby drums or cymbals in order to minimise spill (where cardioid mics are used). Any damping should be positioned so as not to be between the mic and the drum.

Kick Drum

Kick-drum mics are invariably mounted on boom stands so that the mic can be positioned inside the drum shell. A good starting position is with the mic pointing directly at the point on the head at which the beater impacts and at a distance of six inches or so. By changing the distance slightly or by moving the mic to one side, a significant tonal change can be achieved, giving the engineer a means of controlling the sound at source rather than by using EQ. Because of the low frequencies involved, a mic with a good bass response is essential, and it must be able to stand the high sound levels that occur inside a kick drum. Dynamic cardioid or figure-of-eight microphones tend to be used in this role, and most manufacturers include a dedicated kick-drum mic in their range. On paper, some kick-drum mics look to have very odd frequency-response curves that are far from flat, but if the subjective end result is what you were looking for, that's all that matters.

Cymbals

Capacitor mics should be used as overhead/ambience mics to preserve the cymbals' transient detail. Depending on the kit set-up, you may also find a separate hi-hat mic useful, especially if the close drum mics are to be gated. Positioning the hi-hat mic a few inches from the edge of the cymbals and angling it from above or beneath will avoid the mic picking up the sound of air being expelled when the cymbals are closed. The angle of the mic should also be chosen carefully in order to minimise spill from the snare drum. Figure 7.2 shows a fully miked kit.

Percussion

General percussion, such as congas, may be miked from overhead in either mono or stereo, and unless separation is a problem the mic distance may be

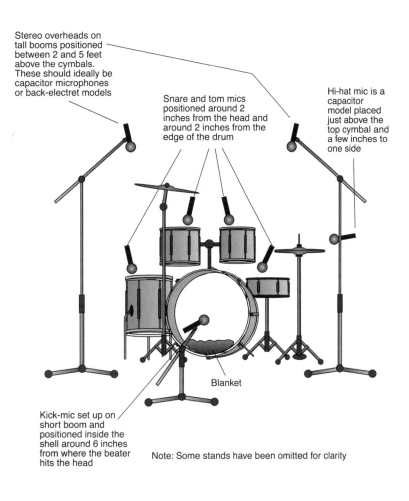

Stereo overheads on tall booms positioned between 2 and 5 feet above the cymbals. These should ideally be capacitor microphones or back-electret models

Snare and tom mics positioned around 2 inches from the head and around 2 inches from the edge of the drum

Hi-hat mic is a capacitor model placed just above the top cymbal and a few inches to one side

Blanket

Kick-mic set up on short boom and positioned inside the shell around 6 inches from where the beater hits the head

Note: Some stands have been omitted for clarity

Figure 7.2:: A fully miked drum kit

increased to anywhere between one and three feet from the drum. In situations where the mics are placed at a distance, the room will have more of an influence on the sound, whereas close miking will capture little of the room ambience, giving a drier sound that may then be processed further during mixing. Capacitor mics render a better sense of detail and will also interpret the high end of bell-like percussion more accurately.

Tracking Drums

The number of tracks allocated to the drum kit depends on the total number of tracks at your disposal and on the requirements of the rest of the instrumentation. If you're working with a computer-based system or with a digital all-in-one workstation, there will be a limit to

the number of physical sources that you can record at one time. Ideally, six tracks should be considered a minimum for drums, divided up as kick, snare, stereo toms and stereo overheads, and be sure to check that the overheads are panned the same way as the tom mics! If spare tracks are abundant, however, a separate track for each tom might be useful, although in the smaller studio there may be only four tracks reserved for drums, or even fewer. In this case, it may be advantageous to mix the bass drum and snare drum together on one track and all the toms on another, keeping just the overheads in stereo. Provided that a significant amount of the stereo overhead signal is used in the mix, some degree of stereo imaging will be restored. If the snare is gated to reduce the effect of spill, a separate hi-hat mic will help to prevent the level of the hi-hat changing as the gate opens and closes.

Machines And Samples

Drum machines provide an easy way of obtaining high-quality drum sounds, although they need to be programmed by someone with a good feel for percussion if the end result is to be acceptable. Many sequencer users prefer to use their drum machines or samplers merely to provide the sounds, with the actual programming being done by playing the drum part in real time, either on a MIDI keyboard or on some form of MIDI drum-pad system. Usually, the part is built up in layers rather than all in one go, and it helps to hold the timing together if a straight guide rhythm is recorded first. This may then be quantised, if necessary, before the rest of the drum part is added and then deleted once the recording is complete.

Even the best drum machines sound less than convincing when playing fast tom fills because each beat produces exactly the same sound, unlike a real kit, which has subtle variations in tone. For this reason, some producers prefer to program the kick-drum and

snare-drum parts but play the hi-hats, cymbals and toms on acoustic drums miked conventionally. This eliminates such problems as sympathetic resonances in the bass drum or snare rattles and improves separation, allowing for a cleaner result. The slight timing errors of a real player also make the whole thing sound more human, but the overall sound is cleaner and the essential rhythm elements – the kick and snare – can be made as tight as is desired. Another alternative is to use specialist drum-sample sets where multiple versions of each drum are mapped to different keys on the keyboard, enabling more realistic rolls to be programmed.

Drum Sound Replacement

Drum samples can also be used to replace sounds on tape that have been properly played and yet the sound is inadequate in some way. This technique relies on the drums being recorded on separate tracks, but on most sessions at least the kick and snare drums will have their own tracks.

If tape tracks are limited, gate the sounds while recording to isolate them from any spill. (For this

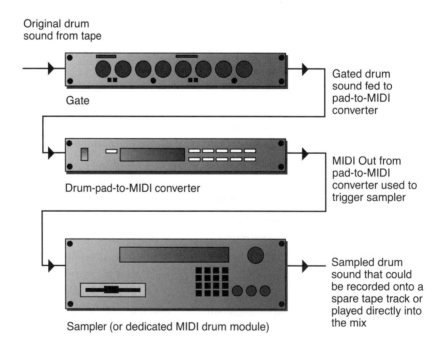

Original drum
sound from tape

Gate

Gated drum
sound fed to
pad-to-MIDI
converter

Drum-pad-to-MIDI converter

MIDI Out from
pad-to-MIDI
converter used to
trigger sampler

Sampler (or dedicated MIDI drum module)

Sampled drum
sound that could
be recorded onto a
spare tape track or
played directly into
the mix

Figure 7.3: Replacing drum sounds with samples

application, gates with key filters cope much better than straightforward gates.) If there are plenty of tape tracks available, record the drums onto individual tracks and then gate afterwards. This allows more than one take if the gate settings aren't properly optimised.

The output from the gate should then be fed into a pad-to-MIDI converter, although some drum modules have these built in. However, it is essential that the trigger system allows the user to set a *retrigger inhibit time*, preventing a sample from being triggered twice in quick succession due to spill breakthrough or a careless stick bounce. Most trigger systems can be made responsive to the loudness of the triggering signal, but in the majority of pop work, the levels of the bass and snare drums need to be kept even, so it may be advantageous to turn off this facility or to make sure that the input is always high enough to ensure that the sample is played at or near its maximum velocity. Figure 7.3 shows a typical set-up.

Drum Pads

Drum pads provide a convenient means of triggering sampled drum sounds or sounds generated from a drum machine or sound module, which are less problematic to record than real drums, especially in the home studio. Pads played with sticks allow a more natural feel to be imparted to the playing than that obtained by drum parts played from a keyboard, and they allow drummers to become involved in sequencer programming rather than leaving it all to the keyboard player. Inexpensive transducers are also available that can be attached to acoustic drums, allowing them to be used in place of pads. Most are based around simple piezo-electric transducer discs, and it's possible to make your own by attaching piezo-electric sounders (normally used as computer bleepers) to a drum head with double-sided sticky foam pads. These sounders may be obtained from a variety of electrical component suppliers at very low cost. Figure 7.4 shows how this is done.

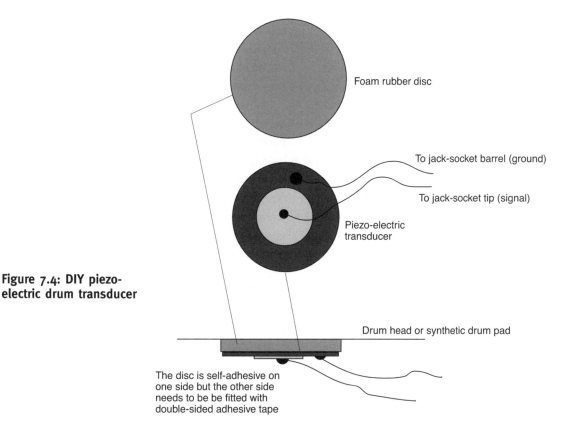

Foam rubber disc

To jack-socket barrel (ground)

To jack-socket tip (signal)

Piezo-electric transducer

Figure 7.4: DIY piezo-electric drum transducer

Drum head or synthetic drum pad

The disc is self-adhesive on one side but the other side needs to be be fitted with double-sided adhesive tape

Note: It's advisable to protect the soldered joints with small blobs of silicone rubber in order to prevent damage through vibration

DIY Piezo Drum Transducers

While it's commonplace to quantise bass-drum and most snare-drum parts, leaving drum fills unquantised helps to maintain a natural feel. When working with a sequencer, it's usually easiest to program drum parts in layers rather than try to record the whole kit at once (unless you have a set of pads that includes kick-drum and hi-hat pedals). Each pass can be recorded on a different track and then merged when all of the parts are complete. As ever, it helps to get the straight rhythmic parts – such as the kick and snare – down first and then overdub the hi-hats, cymbals and fills. If this isn't practical, program a simple guide rhythm and then erase this later.

In order to preserve the feel of the unquantised parts, the quantised parts should be recorded onto one sequencer track and the unquantised parts onto another – if you put them all on the same track, the same quantisation will apply to everything. My earlier comments regarding mixing programmed and miked drum sounds apply equally when using pads. Natural hi-hats can often help tremendously in making a programmed part sound convincing.

Drum pads are also ideal for playing tuned percussion such as vibes and marimbas, where only a small selection of notes is required. When triggering drum samples, it's also possible to create convincing 'talking drum' effects by creating a looped sequencer track containing nothing but pitch-bend information on the same MIDI channel as the drum samples. Then, when the drum part is played from either the pads or the sequencer, the pitch-bend information is merged with the note data and produces the talking-drum effect. Creating the bend information requires a little trial and error but is best done while a typical drum part is playing so that the effect can be heard. Subtle pitch bends work best, and if the loop is made to be an odd length, the pitch-bend pattern will appear to be constantly changing. I have used this technique very successfully to make sampled congas sound more like tablas.

Drum Loop Samples

Drum samples are available as single hits or as loops, the latter of which sound more natural, as they are often recordings of real performances, although they may not be at the required tempo. You could apply time stretching to change the tempo of a loop without changing its pitch, but this may introduce unacceptable processing artefacts (although many early dance tracks used this as an effect in itself). A better way is to use sample loops that have been prepared in either REX or Groove Control format as these can be manipulated to an extensive degree before they start to sound unnatural.

Groove Control is a system developed by Spectrasonics where the loops are in fact sliced into individual beat-sized chunks, which are then triggered by short MIDI sequences (which usually look like chromatic ramps of MIDI notes), provided as MIDI data. In concept, this isn't too different from Propellerhead's REX format, which uses their own ReCycle software to slice existing drum parts into the REX format. With ReCycle, you can do the slicing work yourself, whereas creating Groove Control material isn't an end-user process. On the other hand, the REX file format has to be supported by the application in which you wish to use REX material while Groove Control can be used within any software or hardware sequencer. The key benefit of the slicing approach offered by these two techniques is that the sound quality remains constant over a wide range, regardless of fluctuations in tempo.

As supplied, the Groove Control MIDI data determines the feel of the drum groove, as it provides the timing pulse that drives the groove along. However, it's easy to change the feel of the pattern by using the quantising and swing features of the sequencer. Alternatively, you can use the Groove Control MIDI pattern to create a custom quantise template for syncing up other elements within the song.

Groove Control patches can also be used as playable drum- or percussion-sample kits, as each 'slice' is allocated to a different MIDI note. Some slices will be single drum sounds while others may be two or more drums playing on the same beat – it all depends on how the original loop started out. By treating the slices as samples, you can create your own loops, and interesting effects can also be achieved by changing the timing of the Groove Control loops – by layering two parts and offsetting them in time, for example, or by quantising the two layers to different values.

With ordinary loops, the balance is fixed, but

because Groove Control is driven by a MIDI file, you can use normal sequencer editing techniques to change the levels of individual beats or slices. It's also possible to achieve a deliberately chopped sound by changing the MIDI gate time of the Groove Control sequences. You can also change or even modulate the pitch of the samples using a pitch-bend wheel, because the tempo will always stay the same.

8 ACOUSTIC GUITARS

Steel-strung acoustic guitars are wonderfully expressive instruments and their sound encompasses almost the entire audio spectrum, with the exception of the lowest couple of octaves. The instrument also has a very wide dynamic range, and while an enthusiastically strummed rhythm part might be relatively loud, a melodic section played with the fingers or with a pick might sound very much quieter. Because acoustic guitars possess such a broad range, both in terms of frequency and dynamics, you should use the very best mic you can get your hands on when recording a critical acoustic-guitar part. Some of the better dynamic microphones are sensitive enough for all but the quietest playing, but the higher sensitivity of a capacitor model is a distinct advantage. Similarly, the extended frequency range of a capacitor microphone is better able to capture the subtle high-frequency detail of the instrument.

Of course, not everyone can afford a top-quality capacitor microphone, but there are now so many inexpensive imported capacitor models that still produce great results that there's little reason not to buy at least one. Where phantom power is unavailable, a battery-powered back-electret model can produce similar sound quality, although in my experience mics designed to run on battery power tend to be less sensitive than true capacitor microphones because of the limited voltage – and hence headroom – available.

Mic Positions

If getting enough level while recording an acoustic guitar is proving a problem, it's tempting to put the mic very close to the soundhole. This produces the largest signal, but unfortunately the tone is likely to be heavily coloured by body resonances and tends to

be both dull and boomy. These body resonances are part of the natural timbre of the instrument and are what give the guitar sound its depth, but the essential detail that completes the picture comes from elsewhere. No amount of equalisation can make a good guitar sound out of a bad one, and the key to a good sound is to use the right mic in the right position.

As with all instruments, the various parts of the guitar vibrate in different ways, and different parts of the instrument generate different sounds. The strings, the neck, the air within the body and the wood of the body itself all contribute to the overall sound. Add to this the effect of room acoustics and it's easy to see why a single microphone positioned close to one point on the instrument's surface isn't going to do it justice. This is why contact mics or piezo-electric bridge pick-ups rarely give a more accurate sound.

It could be argued that the only place you're going to get a good guitar sound is where the audience would normally be, several feet from the guitar. Fortunately, you can get good results far closer than this – after all, the person actually playing the guitar usually hears a passable sound, and he's very close to the instrument! On top of that, the required recorded sound isn't necessarily the exact sound that the audience would hear at a live performance, especially in the context of pop music.

Tone

A steel-strung acoustic rhythm guitar may need to be both brightened and have some bass rolled off to make it sit better in a mix without taking up too much space. Conversely, a solo acoustic guitar is normally miked to sound fairly natural, but even then the performer may want to vary the sound slightly, by the choice and positioning of microphones, by the use of equalisation or by some form of electronic enhancement. My own preference is to use as little EQ as possible but, where it does prove necessary, to use 'air EQ' (a wide boost at around 14kHz), to open out the top end, combined with a shelving low-cut control if I need to thin out the sound. In any event, avoid making harsh boosts, as these will invariably make the guitar sound unnatural or honky, although you can be more relaxed about cutting problem frequencies, as the human ear is much less likely to detect dips in frequency than peaks.

The Right Microphone

The most important thing to do when recording an acoustic guitar is to choose the right mic. If the chosen model is insufficiently sensitive or has a restricted frequency response, this will reduce the number of positioning options available. Most dynamic microphones are insufficiently sensitive to do justice to the acoustic guitar, and their lack of top-end response leads to a somewhat lifeless sound. However, if a dynamic mic is all you have, you can still get passable results by taking a little extra care. For instance, don't point it directly at the soundhole in an attempt to get enough level, and by the same token don't place it too close to the guitar. A position between 12 and 18 inches from the guitar is quite close enough, and if you're using only a single dynamic mic you could try aiming it at the point where the neck joins the body. You may pick up a little noise, but better that than a dreadful sound. Figure 8.1 shows this approach in practice. Adding air EQ will help to open up the top end, but for EQ to work, the frequencies have to be present in the first place. Admittedly a harmonic enhancer such as an Aphex Aural Exciter can be used to synthesise the missing high octave, but it probably still won't sound as pleasant as choosing the right type of microphone in the first place.

Ideally, a capacitor or sensitive back-electret mic should be used for any serious work and any type of polar pattern may be used, depending on the situation. Unless the room acoustics are particularly flattering, I'd be inclined to stick to a cardioid model, unless two guitars are being recorded together, in which case it may be better to use omnis rather than cardioids. This will result in a little more spill between the mics, but because omnis tend to have a better

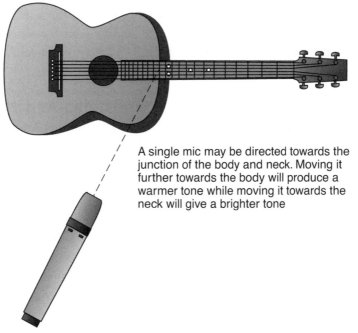

A single mic may be directed towards the junction of the body and neck. Moving it further towards the body will produce a warmer tone while moving it towards the neck will give a brighter tone

Figure 8.1: Using a single close microphone

off-axis response than cardioids, the spill will at least be sonically accurate.

When using multiple microphones, try to keep in mind the 'three to one' rule for mic positioning. For example, if the mics are placed two feet from the guitars, make sure that they're at least six feet apart. If they're too close to each other relative to their distance from the instruments, the resulting spill will produce significant phase-cancelling effects that will colour the sound, usually to its detriment. Getting the desired tone by choosing a suitable mic and mic position always sounds better than using EQ, and if you need a brighter tone then choosing a mic with a presence peak and siting it in the right position will invariably give a more natural result than applying EQ. As a rule, moving the mic away from the guitar body and closer to the neck will produce a brighter, lighter tone.

In some situations, a figure-of-eight mic can be useful in rejecting spill due to the null area that exists exactly 90º off axis, resulting in sound approaching from this direction being completely cancelled out. This 'deaf zone' is very narrow, so it may be best to adjust the mic position while monitoring through headphones, and don't expect total cancellation of off-axis sounds because room reflections will bounce back sound at different angles. Beside this, of course, most sound sources aren't narrow lines or points. Even so, you can expect to add a few decibels to your best efforts by using cardioid mics, especially if you place sound absorbers behind the mics as well as behind the performer.

Before The Session

Unlike electronic keyboards, you can't just assume that a guitar is going to play properly and in tune as soon as it comes out of the box, so intonation problems and buzzes should be fixed before the session starts. With steel-strung instruments, using a relatively new set of strings is a good idea, particularly if you're after a bright sound.

Ideally, the performer should play seated in order to avoid unnecessary movement of the guitar relative to the microphones. Ensure that the chair doesn't creak and try to exclude other sources of noise such as spill from headphones, especially if you intend to work with a click track. A degree of finger squeak is inevitable, but if it becomes excessive it can ruin an otherwise excellent performance. There's no complete cure for this, but a dusting of talcum powder on the player's hands might improve matters, and there are also commercial string lubricants available that may help. Other unwelcome sources of noise include rustling clothing, crackling lyric sheets and excessive breath noise, and it also pays to keep an ear open for ticking watches. It can be argued that breath noises are normal, but if you have several overdubs to do, the result can sound like a chorus of heavy-breathing dirty phone callers!

Click-Track Spill

When working with click tracks, choose a sound for your click that isn't too strident, as some spill is likely, even from enclosed phones. You could route the click signal through a compressor set up in Duck mode so that the click track gets louder when the guitar is played louder and quietens down during quiet sections or pauses. This will ensure that the click is audible to the performer at all times, but it will be quietest when there is little else going on to hide it. Alternatively, the engineer can ride the level of the click track manually, dropping the level during pauses or very quiet sections in the music. There are also some processing tricks that can help to minimise recorded squeaks and breathing, which will be discussed later in this chapter.

Rooms And Mic Positions

Before getting down to the finer points of microphone placement, it's helpful to look at the surroundings in which the recording is to be made. Most instruments are designed to sound best when played in a room with a certain degree of reverberation, and acoustic guitars are no exception. However, most small studios tend to be on the acoustically dead side, so it may pay dividends to look for another room in the building that has hard surfaces and is a more live environment. In the absence of a suitable live room, an artificial live environment can be created by covering the floor with hardboard, shiny side up.

Of course, if you're in a situation where spill may

be a problem, a live environment may work against you, in which case opt for a deader environment in order to preserve separation. Don't worry too much if the sound still isn't as live as you'd like it to be, as some electronic reverberation can be added at the mixing stage. Ambience patterns that are rich in early reflections are good for creating a sense of space and life without making the reverb too obvious.

I really can't over-emphasise the importance of microphone positioning when recording acoustic instruments. That's not to say that there's only one right way to do the job, though; there are many different miking methods that produce excellent results. Placing a single mic between one and two feet from the instrument, pointing toward the spot where the neck joins the body, is always a good starting point, as shown back in Figure 8.1. If the sound is too heavy, the mic can be positioned further away from the soundhole or moved upwards so that it's 'looking down' on the instrument. To add more weight to the sound, the mic can be brought closer to the soundhole, but make sure that the sound doesn't become boomy as well as full.

This is by no means the only viable mic position in this kind of situation – I've had quite a lot of success when pointing the mic over the player's right shoulder, looking down on the guitar body from a distance of between 18 inches and two feet. The theory here is that, if the guitar sounds OK to the player, it should sound OK to a mic located close to the player's ear, and Figure 8.2 illustrates this set-up. Equally, you might find that pointing the mic at the floor to pick up mainly reflected sound gives a well balanced result.

A good engineer will move around the playing position as the performer warms up, listening out for any 'sweet spots' that may crop up. This careful listening invariably yields some improvement, and when you've identified these sweet spots, try moving the mic to hear what difference it makes. One effective way of finding sweet spots is by monitoring the output from the mic over good-quality closed headphones plugged into the mixer, then manually moving the mic as the guitarist runs through the number. By using this method, any coloration of the sound by the microphone or mixing console or other part of the recording chain is taken into account.

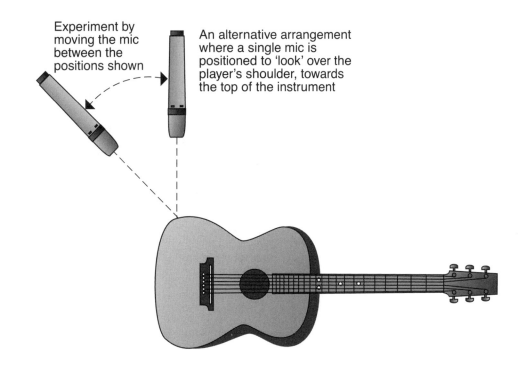

Experiment by moving the mic between the positions shown

An alternative arrangement where a single mic is positioned to 'look' over the player's shoulder, towards the top of the instrument

Figure 8.2: Miking over the shoulder

Mono Or Stereo?

If an acoustic-guitar line is simply part of a full pop mix, a mono recording is generally adequate and may even be beneficial, as it produces a more stable, solid sound. However, in small acoustic bands, or in the case of solo performances, stereo miking greatly enhances the sense of depth and reality of the sound. The easiest way to make a stereo recording is to place a stereo pair of microphones a couple of feet in front of the instrument, although in practice you can use any of the existing stereo-miking methods, including M&S (Middle and Side) pairs, spaced microphones or spaced boundary mics.

I'll often pick two mic positions that don't necessarily produce an accurate stereo picture as such but yet do provide me with the sound I want, plus a sense of depth. One arrangement that I find works particularly well is to position one mic in the usual end-of-neck or 'looking down' position, thus capturing the main part of the sound, and then position another a foot or so away from the neck, pointing towards the headstock or halfway up the neck. This produces a bright, detailed sound that works particularly well with picked or folk-style playing. I'd normally use cardioid mics, but you can use omnis if they're available, or even one of each. One advantage of this method is that, as one mic picks up a very full sound and the other a relatively bass-light sound, it's possible to change the tonal quality after recording simply by balancing the levels from the two mics (provided that you've recorded them on separate tracks, of course). It really doesn't matter how you get a result as long as you get it! Figure 8.3 shows how the microphones are arranged in this kind of set-up.

Using two boundary or pressure zone mics (sometimes called PZMs), you can obtain a very natural sound by placing these on a tabletop a couple of feet in front of the performer, with the mics three feet or so apart. Alternatively, these could be set up as a conventional stereo pair, as outlined in Chapter 10, 'Miscellaneous Miking Techniques'. Even inexpensive PZMs can sound surprisingly good when placed on a low table in front of the performer. Alternatively, if a guitar is fitted with a bridge transducer, this may be used in conjunction with either one or more microphones to create a stereo effect, although personally I've never really liked the sound of transducers when compared directly to good mics.

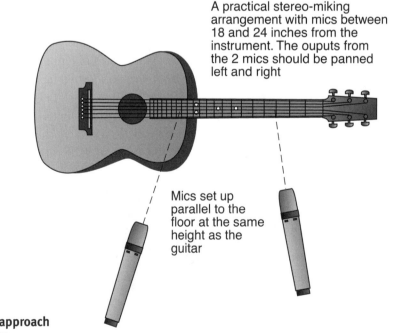

A practical stereo-miking arrangement with mics between 18 and 24 inches from the instrument. The ouputs from the 2 mics should be panned left and right

Mics set up parallel to the floor at the same height as the guitar

Figure 8.3: An approach to stereo miking

Acoustic Guitar EQ

In an ideal world, equalisation wouldn't be necessary, but in the studio, where reality isn't always the main objective, some EQ may be required. There's no reason to be afraid of using a lot of equalisation, as long as you know what you are trying to achieve, but if you're in any doubt, or if you're after a more natural sound, you should use as little as you can get away with. If the mic positions were correct and the instrument sounded good in the studio when the material was recorded, you shouldn't need to do much to get a good sound, but you may often have to contend with a less than perfect recording, in which case a little electronic repair work will be necessary.

One of the most persistent problems with acoustic guitar recordings is boominess. This centres around a certain fixed frequency, and you can find out just what this frequency is by doing the following:

- Turn up the boost on your lower-mid equaliser and then sweep through the frequency range until the boominess really jumps out at you.

- Having found this frequency, which will probably lie between 80Hz and 220Hz, you can bring the boost control back into its cut position, applying just enough cut to tame the resonance. Adjust the width of the EQ (if you're using a fully parametric equaliser) to see how narrow you can make the cut without losing effectiveness. This is the optimum setting for removing the problem frequencies without adversely affecting other parts of the audio spectrum too seriously.

Top End

- General brightening can be achieved by using the high equaliser on the mixer to add the required degree of top boost. In circumstances where this is insufficient, don't just go on cranking up the top, as all you'll do is bring up the noise and make everything sound harsh. Instead, either re-record the track or use an exciter/enhancer to add a little artificial top end.

- Sparkle can be added to the sound by boosting between 5kHz and 10kHz, although I prefer the 'air EQ' trick of adding a broadband parametric boost at around 14kHz, as this produces clarity without incurring harshness.

- Harshness or honkiness in the upper-mid range can usually be reduced by cutting frequencies between 1kHz and 3kHz.

- The exact frequency that you need to work on is best identified by setting the relevant equaliser section to full boost and then sweeping through the frequency range. When you hit the area you need to boost, it should be obvious. Then all you need to do is back off the boost until the sound is as you want it. (During this process, keep checking the sound against the EQ bypass position because the ear soon gets acclimatised to radical EQ changes and you may not realise that you've gone too far.)

- In some mixes, you may feel the need to take out all of the bottom end to produce a bright, thin rhythm sound. This is common practice and really helps to keep a mix sounding clear. The low EQ control may be sufficient to achieve the desired result, but if more cut is needed you should try tuning the lower-mid control to somewhere between 80Hz and 150Hz and applying more cut with this. Alternatively, if you have a computer-based system, try using a shelving filter plug-in with a slope of 12dB per octave or steeper. In situations where you have few facilities, at least use the low-cut switch on the microphone and/or on the desk when you need to lighten the sound; it's invariably more musical to use EQ cut rather than boost, and it also reduces the danger of causing clipping, with the possible consequence of distortion. More importantly, as stated earlier, the human ear really is more forgiving of EQ cuts than it is of boost.

Unwanted Noises

Earlier, I mentioned the problems caused by string squeaks and over-loud breathing. This can be reduced by the careful use of a parametric or variable-frequency shelving equaliser, but accepting that some users don't have these, I've discovered a way of using the side-chain filters in my gates to achieve the same result. In the Drawmer DS201 gate – as with other models working on a similar principle – the side-chain filters are variable-frequency, 12dB-per-octave devices that can be inserted into the audio path simply by selecting the key or side-chain Listen mode. This bypasses the gate section and leaves just the filters in series with the input signal, acting as a kind of super equaliser.

The great thing about these filters is that they have a fairly sharp response, which means that you can take out a high-frequency sound without seriously affecting the frequencies directly below. I've had surprising success in filtering both acoustic and electric guitars using these devices, and setting them up is quite simple. Alternatively, in a computer system where you have plug-in filters available, try a high-cut filter of 12dB per octave or steeper and again adjust the cut-off frequency so that you reduce the squeaks without killing the high end of the guitar sound. Start off with the high filter in its maximum position and then bring it down slowly, while listening to the effect on the recorded sound. You should find that you can take the edge off the breath and string squeaks without affecting the tone of the guitar too seriously. (Of course, if you turn the filter setting down too far, you'll hear the top go from the guitar as well.) For a sharper response, you can put both channels of the gate in series, which will produce a filter response of 24dB per octave if you set the filters to the same frequencies.

The final resort, if you need to tame those squeaks, is to use a de-esser, ideally the type that filters out only those frequencies in the 4–8kHz range, where sibilance tends to occur.

Further Processing

Recording the basic guitar sound and then applying a little EQ may be all you need to get exactly the right acoustic guitar sound, but on the other hand it might be just the beginning. There are some engineers who wouldn't dream of recording an acoustic guitar without compressing it at some stage, and it's certainly true that compression does even up the sound a lot. In the case of a strummed rhythm part, compression can smooth out the sound, making it less ragged, fuller sounding and more cohesive. By increasing the compressor's attack time to 10ms or so, the attack transients of the guitar remain intact, whereas a short attack time tames the natural attack of the instrument, giving an altogether more consistent sound.

The release-time setting of the compressor is also important, because setting it too short can cause the sound to 'pump', especially when a lot of compression has been used. Conversely, setting it too long means that gain reduction may still be applied well after the sound that caused it has fallen back below the threshold, resulting in uneven level control. The ideal setting depends on the speed of the performance and on how much pumping can be tolerated, but as a rule between 250ms and 500ms usually does the trick.

Very generally, compressors that sound good on vocals also sound good on acoustic guitars. Soft-knee compressors are usually easier to set up and give consistently decent results, although if you want to juggle the compressor-attack time to enhance the attack of the instrument, a hard-knee or strict ratio compressor might give you more positive control. By compressing the sound to give a gain reduction of between 6dB and 12dB on the loudest sections, it should be possible to even up the sound without inviting too much noise during pauses or quiet sections. If more compression is considered necessary, you should consider using a compressor with a built-in expander gate or you should gate the signal before compressing it. Some of the newer compressors also have a built-in enhancer feature that restores any brightness lost during heavy compression. Those that I've tried work well on acoustic guitar and help maintain an edge to the sound, even when a lot of compression is being applied.

When combining EQ and compression, my preference is to equalise after applying compression, as working the other way around sometimes means that the compressor is trying to undo what you've just done with the EQ. For example, if you've added some high-end boost, the compressor will react more strongly to that and pull down the signal level. In some situations, this is musically appropriate, so by all means try both ways of connecting your compressor and equaliser to see how great the difference is. You should also make the final adjustments to the EQ after setting up the compressor, as your choice of compressor setting will have some effect on the final tonality.

Reverb For Acoustic Guitar

To achieve a natural guitar sound, it shouldn't be necessary to do much more than add a hint of compression and a suitable amount of reverb to the recorded part, and in the case of mono recordings a stereo reverb can be used to give the sound a sense of space and width that it wouldn't otherwise possess. If the basic sound is sufficiently live but is lacking in width, you could appropriately add a short room reverb or early-reflections pattern, which will create a sense of space and identity without making the sound muddy. You might also find that a bright reverb setting will add life to the sound in a way that EQ can't.

If a longer reverb is required, don't just solo the guitar and then pick a flattering setting because you'll find that everything sounds different once the rest of the mix is up and running. It's far better to set up a rough mix first and then add the reverb. Rolling some bass off the reverb returns can help to keep the sound clear when a lot of reverb is added, but take care when doing this that the remaining reverb doesn't sound too edgy and thin. There is a tendency to add too much reverb to instruments in a mix, and professional engineers have come to understand that less is often more. Music relies on contrasts in level, and although reverb does create a sense of space, it also fills the valuable spaces between the notes. On an interesting psychoacoustic note, reverb also creates the illusion of distance, so if you're after an up-front, in-your-face acoustic-guitar sound, don't pick a long reverb time. Instead pick a short room, plate or early-reflections setting and be sparing in how much you add to the dry signal.

Other Effects

In the context of pop music, a gentle chorus effect works well on the acoustic guitar, giving it an enhanced sense of presence and depth but without making it sound too unnatural or processed, while a shallow, mild flange achieves a similar effect. However, it isn't always necessary to resort to electronic effects. Take the example of chorus. The effect is designed to create the illusion of two or more instruments playing together, but by using a multitrack recorder, you can do this for real by playing the same part twice on two different tracks. If you can't afford the space to leave them on separate tracks, you can always bounce them down onto one afterwards. For a more subtle effect, place these modulation effects before the reverb so that the dry sound is unaffected. The randomising effect of the reverb turns the normally heavy cyclic effect of a chorus or flanger into a textural shimmer.

To achieve a more 'detuned' chorus effect, you could detune the guitar slightly when you do the second take, but a far easier approach is to make use of your recorder's Varispeed control, if it has one. Instead of recording one part at the normal speed and one at a slightly altered speed, try recording both parts with the Varispeed on, recording one take with the recorder running slightly fast and the other with it running slightly slow. A pitch change of around 5–10 cents is all that's needed. Then, when the recording is replayed at the normal speed, this will place the average pitch somewhere between the two, which is more likely to sound in tune with the rest of the track. On the other hand, if you record one part at the normal pitch and then add a second part that is a few cents sharp, the average of the two will still appear slightly sharp.

A shift of less than one per cent in each direction should be sufficient, but do a few trial takes to determine which settings give the most appropriate chorus depth. (It's worth noting down these settings for future use.) The two tracks can then be panned to the two sides of the mix, unless you've had to bounce them, in which case a subtle stereo reverb will help recreate the lost sense of space.

It's possible to further exaggerate the chorus effect by delaying one of the guitar parts by a few tens of milliseconds, and this technique is particularly effective if the two tracks can be kept separate for left/right panning. Rather than use a delay unit to create the effect while mixing, try using a delay unit to delay the headphone feed slightly when recording the second part. In other words, the guitarist is being forced to play late because he's hearing the backing track after

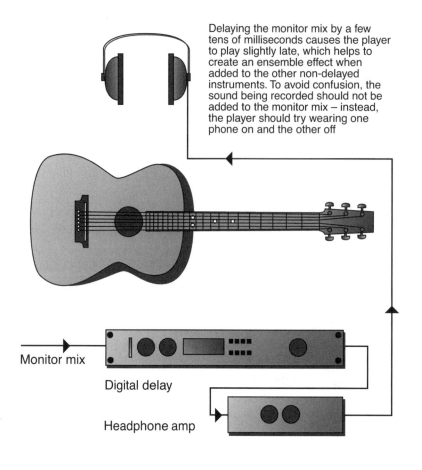

Delaying the monitor mix by a few tens of milliseconds causes the player to play slightly late, which helps to create an ensemble effect when added to the other non-delayed instruments. To avoid confusion, the sound being recorded should not be added to the monitor mix – instead, the player should try wearing one phone on and the other off

Monitor mix

Digital delay

Headphone amp

Figure 8.4: Delaying monitoring for a natural ensemble effect

it's been delayed. Figure 8.4 shows this method of delayed monitoring.

If you think about it, this approach is bound to produce better results than using a DDL (Digital Delay Line) in the mix because the recorded sound hasn't been processed at all, which means that the quality of the delay line is quite unimportant; even a budget delay pedal can be used and it won't affect the recording.

When recording into a sequencer, you can duplicate this effect extremely easily, either by using the Track Delay facility or by physically dragging the track to a slightly later start time. Similarly, where mild pitch detuning is needed, this can often be achieved with best results by using offline processing (via plug-ins or the sequencer's built-in audio capabilities) rather than by using real-time pitch-shifting systems.

9 ELECTRIC GUITARS

Even though synthesisers and samplers are now far more widely used in mainstream music production than they once were, the electric guitar remains one of the most popular contemporary instruments, not least because of its diversity of sound and its expressive capabilities. The electric-guitar sound is the result of a unique symbiosis as, unlike other instruments, it relies on its amplification/loudspeaker system to enhance the sound in a creative way rather than simply to make it louder. Because there are so many different types of guitar and guitar amplifier and so many playing styles, the range of sounds that can be coaxed from this instrument is vast and varied. The method of recording the instrument adds a further variable, and this potential for creating radically different individual sounds undoubtedly accounts for the continuing popularity of the electric guitar in all forms of contemporary popular music. As the sound is produced via a loudspeaker rather than directly from the instrument, it's useful to examine the guitar amplifier further.

Guitar Amplifiers

Guitar amps are usually fitted with 10" or 12" speakers, often in multiples, mounted in cabinets, which may be sealed or open-backed. The distinctive overdrive sound is caused by harmonic distortion added in the amplifier, but if fed through a full-range monitor speaker system the result is invariably buzzy and unpleasant. Guitar speakers are built with a deliberately poor frequency response, and this has the effect of filtering out the less musical harmonics, resulting in a sound that still has plenty of edge but doesn't sound buzzy or nasty. Furthermore, many guitar speakers are specifically designed to add distortion at high sound levels.

Open-backed cabinets tend to have a fatter sound than closed ones and are often referred to as having a *bass thump*. This is because the speaker doesn't have a cushion of air to damp it, so low-frequency sounds caused by the player's hands hitting the strings cause the speaker cone to move a considerable distance, producing an audible thump. This characteristic also affects the more musical sounds of the instrument to quite a large extent, especially on the lower notes. Different players will argue on whether the open- or closed-back cabinet sounds best, but both are quite easy to record.

Most rock guitar players still express a preference for valve amplifiers, as these have a sound quality that is difficult to emulate using solid-state circuitry. Valve circuits, with their transformer output stages, can reproduce transient peaks well in excess of their average rated power-handling capacity, while their distortion characteristics when overdriven are considered more 'musical' than those of solid-state designs. The vast majority of guitar amplifiers would be considered technically disastrous, from a hi-fi point of view, but the high orders of even harmonic distortion that they produce have become synonymous with rock guitar sounds worldwide.

The Guitar

The basic design of the electric guitar has changed little since it was invented – indeed, one of the most popular guitars today is the Fender Stratocaster (or one of its many copies), which was one of the first ever production electric guitars. The electrical principle of the guitar pick-up is fairly straightforward and isn't too far removed from that of the magnetic microphone, except that the guitar string takes the place of the diaphragm. The string vibrates within a magnetic field generated by a permanent magnet, causing a signal voltage to be induced in a coil of wire wound around the magnets. It works very well, but as the pick-up coil behaves exactly like the coil of a transformer, it also picks up stray magnetic fields from transformers and mains wiring, resulting in a background hum.

Humbuckers

It's possible to cancel out most of the hum by using a pick-up with not one but two coils, one wound in the opposite direction to the other. This is the humbucking principle, which was originally devised to cancel the hum generated in loudspeakers in the days when their magnets were energised from the mains current. A well-designed humbucker has almost perfect immunity from picking up hum, but because of the different coil impedances and the spaced magnetic pole-pieces, they invariably have a significantly different tonal characteristic than the simple single-coil pick-up.

Unfortunately, the guitars that are currently popular tend to feature single-coil pick-ups, and these can be a nightmare in the studio because nearly every piece of equipment radiates mains hum to some degree. It is possible to rotate the instrument to find a position of least hum, but this imposes restrictions on the player and rarely leads to perfect cancellation. Furthermore, now that computer monitors are commonplace in studios, the problem is worsened, as these radiate a high level of buzz, which will interfere with the operation of a single-coil pick-up at distances of ten feet or more.

One solution is to use one of the newer mini-humbuckers that are fitted on some instruments and are available as replacements for standard instruments. These locate the two sets of magnets very close together, in an attempt to combine the noise-rejection capabilities of a humbucking pick-up with the tonal qualities of a single-coil model. Different manufacturers meet this challenge with differing degrees of success, although few side-by-side humbuckers get close to the sound of the original single-coil pick-up that they're designed to replace.

To retain the original tone of a guitar such as a Stratocaster, a better option is to fit one of the new generation of 'stacked' humbuckers, the best of which use elaborate coil-winding and screening techniques to retain the tonal characteristics of the original pick-up while being very effective at reducing noise. Because the two humbucking coils are located one above the other, the appearance of the original pick-up can also be maintained. Currently, the most accurate-sounding replacement pick-ups of this type are available from the Australian company Kinman, although alternatives are also available from a number of major American pick-up manufacturers, including Fender.

Active Pick-ups

Another approach is the so-called *active pick-up*, which usually comprises a low-impedance pick-up followed by a battery-powered electronic buffer. These still suffer from interference, although of a lesser extent than a standard pick-up, and they offer the advantage that they can be DI'd without the need for a DI matching box if a clean sound is sought. Some active models do, however, produce a noticeable degree of background noise, due to the amplifier circuitry, and when boosted by the extra gain of an overdriven amplifier or effects pedal, the noise level can become obtrusive.

Setting Up

Obviously, it's up to the musician to ensure that their instrument is properly maintained, but the reality is that many guitar players turn up at the studio with an instrument that is inadequately set up and frequently unrecordable. Professionals are unlikely to fall into this trap, but amateur players coming into the studio for the first time can easily be let down by their instrument. In this situation there are a few things that you can do to help ensure a good result.

• Old, worn strings can turn an expensive guitar into an unresponsive, dull and thoroughly uninspiring instrument, so if you know that you have a session coming up where the players are inexperienced, ask them to check that their strings are OK and, if not, to replace them a day or two before the recording so as to give them time to settle in. Changing strings directly before a session frequently results in tuning problems.

- Problems concerning action and intonation can defeat the most talented player, and here a little first aid can be administered by an engineer with a little guitar experience. Although this is, again, not the engineer's responsibility, he is inevitably the one who gets the blame when a session goes badly, whatever the true cause. Furthermore, if he can demonstrate an ability to sort out minor problems with guitars and drum kits, he's more likely to win the respect of the artists, which will help the session go more smoothly and possibly win repeat business.

- Ideally, the guitar's strings should be as low as possible without buzzing, and the correct neck shape to allow this is not dead straight but slightly concave. If you hold down a guitar string on the first and last frets simultaneously, you should be able to see a small space between the middle of the string and the frets over which it passes. If it touches all the way down the neck, it's either too straight or, worse still, a touch convex. Slackening the truss rod an eighth of a turn at a time should correct this problem, but be sure to give the neck a few minutes to settle before making any further adjustment. A twisted or warped neck will also cause problems with the action of the guitar, but this is beyond the scope of first aid and requires the attention of an experienced guitar technician.

- Poor intonation is probably the easiest fault to fix and is mainly caused by incorrectly positioned bridge saddles. Using an electronic tuner, compare the pitch of the string fretted at the twelfth fret and the harmonic struck at the same position. If the fretted note is sharper than the harmonic, the bridge saddle needs to be moved to lengthen the string slightly until the two pitches are the same. Conversely, if the fretted note is flatter than the harmonic, move the bridge saddle slightly towards the neck and try again.

- Another less well-known source of intonation error is insufficiently deep nut slots. Aside from making the guitar harder to play, this forces fretted notes to be slightly sharp, as the string is stretched by a small amount when fretted. Owners of such guitars frequently distrust electronic tuners because, whenever they tune their open strings, the fretted notes are sharp! Unfortunately, most production guitars suffer from this fault to a greater or lesser extent. A junior hacksaw blade is normally fine enough for deepening nut slots, but be sure to take off only a little material at a time, then refit the string into the slot and check the action.

- One final tip that can help keep tuning stable is to keep a roll of plumbers' PTFE tape in your spares kit and slide a piece beneath the strings where they cross the nut. The tape will be stretched down into the slots, where it will act as a very efficient lubricant to prevent the strings from sticking when notes are bent or a tremolo unit used. The tape is thin enough not to affect the action or sustain, but it does help to ensure that a bent note returns to its previous pitch when released. This is, obviously, unnecessary when using a locking nut system or a replacement low-friction nut.

  If you have a house guitar fitted with a tremolo system via a low-friction nut, low-friction bridge saddles and fitting locking tuners can make a huge improvement to tuning stability.

Guitar Noise

Noise is a particular problem with guitars, not just because of the propensity of the pick-ups to act as aerials for interference but also because guitar amplifiers tend to be noisy. This isn't down to bad circuit design but is more a function of the tonal voicing of the amplifiers and the high levels of gain needed to produce overdrive sounds. If an attempt is going to be made to remove some of the noise by electronic means, it may be best to leave this until the mixing stage so that an incorrectly set gate or noise filter doesn't ruin a good take.

A dynamic noise filter such as the Symetrix 511A, Drawmer DF320, Rocktron Hush or dbx Silencer can be a powerful ally when cleaning up noisy guitar tracks, and these are generally far less obtrusive in operation than conventional gates. Also known as single-ended noise-reduction units, these devices work by reducing the audio bandwidth as the sound level falls; the filter action is so rapid that attack transients pass through with very little change. As any natural sound decays, the higher harmonics almost invariably decay most rapidly so no significant tonal change is noticed as the filter closes. The filter action is further aided by the fact that electric guitars have a relatively low upper-frequency limit anyway – most of their energy is below 3kHz. Because these filters only tackle high-frequency noise, many models are fitted with an integral expander that shuts down the audio path once the signal level has fallen below a threshold set by the user.

Noise Removal

There is currently digital noise-removal hardware available that works by tackling hum and hiss separately. To deal with hum, they are either set to 50/60Hz, as applicable, or they automatically track the mains frequency and then apply a series of very narrow notch filters to remove both the fundamental and the harmonics that make up the hum/buzz. Because of the precision available with digital filtering, even quite severe buzzes can be removed with little or no subjective effect on the wanted part of the sound.

High-frequency hiss is taken care of by means of a multiband expander, which produces far fewer audible side-effects than using an analogue dynamic filter. Such units are still relatively costly in hardware form, but in a studio specialising in electric-guitar work they might still be a worthwhile investment. Conversely, software noise-removal systems (frequently available as plug-ins for the major sequencers or stereo editors) are relatively inexpensive and the best of these can produce excellent results. If you're recording to a sequencer rather than to a hardware recorder, this is the best option in the majority of cases.

In the absence of a dynamic filter, a gate may be used to clean up the pauses between notes or phrases, but as electric guitars can sustain for a long time, there may be few periods of true silence where the gate can be effective. In any event, the gate release time needs to be set long enough to allow the guitar to decay naturally without being cut short.

Whether you use a gate or a noise filter, it's sensible to use either to process the guitar sound before any delay or reverb is added. This way, the reverb or delay will decay naturally and will help to cover up any slight truncation of the original sound caused by the action of the gate or filter. Any attempt to filter or gate a sound that contains added reverb is almost certain to change the reverb-decay characteristics quite noticeably.

Gate Filters

There is another technique that can be used for cleaning up electric guitar tracks, and this relies on the limited bandwidth of guitar amplifiers. Rolling off some EQ above 3kHz should, in theory, remove high-frequency hiss and noise but allow the guitar sound to pass with little subjective change. In practice, however, the slope characteristics of conventional equalisers restricts their effectiveness in this application because the response is simply not sharp enough. In other words, if the EQ is set to remove the high-end noise, the chances are that it will have a significant effect on the wanted sound, too.

A solution presents itself in the form of the side-chain filters included in many studio gates, including the popular Drawmer DS201. These are variable-frequency filters with a 12dB-per-octave characteristic designed to process the side-chain input with a view to reducing the risk of false triggering. By selecting the Key Listen mode, it's possible to place these filters in the audio path, enabling the unit to be used as a filter rather than as a gate. And in the fight against noise, the sharp filter response is a powerful ally.

By setting the upper cut-off frequency to between 2.5kHz and 3.5kHz, it's possible to improve significantly the signal-to-noise ratio of a typical electric-guitar sound without dulling it noticeably. If an even sharper filter response is required, the two channels of the gate can be wired in series and, with both switched to Key Listen mode, a filter of 24dB per octave can be created simply by setting the upper-frequency controls to similar values.

In this application, the sound is usually treated after being recorded so as to eliminate the risk of irretrievable over-processing – the gates are connected to the console via the appropriate channel insert points as normal, but they're switched to Key Listen mode. As you may have noticed, this technique is very similar to that described in the previous chapter, 'Acoustic Guitars', for removing finger noise and squeaks, but it can also be surprisingly effective in reducing distortion on tape caused by over-recording of clean electric-guitar parts.

Once again, anyone using a sequencer with audio-recording capability is likely to find high- and low-pass filters available as plug-ins, and these may be used in exactly the same way as the gate filters just described. In most applications, a slope of 18dB or 24dB per octave will give the most useful results.

Microphones

When miking up a guitar amp, it's important to realise that the speaker cabinet should be treated as an instrument in its own right. Much of the sound comes direct from the speakers, but there's also a lot of sound emitted from the back and sides of the box, especially in the case of an open-backed cabinet. The sound is different close to the speakers than it is further away in the room, which gives several miking options, including close miking, ambient miking at a distance and a combined approach with two or more mics set at different distances.

Most British recording engineers choose fairly unsophisticated cardioid, dynamic microphones to record electric guitar, as neither sensitivity nor high-frequency extension is a priority, due to the fundamental nature of the electric-guitar sound. In other words, guitar-amplification systems aren't short on volume and produce very little in the way of true high frequencies.

American engineers, on the other hand, often choose a capacitor microphone for the job, which undoubtedly contributes to the sound of American rock guitar, which isn't as fat as the English sound and has more top, to the point at which a British engineer or producer might consider it too buzzy. A mic with a presence peak will help a sound to cut through a mix, but a sound that's already quite abrasive may sound smoother if a fairly flat mic is used. As with vocals, it's down to matching the choice of microphone with the sound you're recording.

Amp And Mic Set-up

To recreate the sound of a live stack, the textbook approach is to set up a full stack in a big studio, play it loud and then mic it from several feet with an additional close mic to enhance the bite. The more distant mic captures the direct sound from the speakers plus room reflections, including any phase cancellation effects caused by multiple drivers. Sound is also reflected from the floor, creating further comb filtering when it arrives at the microphone via different paths.

In other words, the distant mic hears the performance much as an audience would. It's possible to omit the close mic, but in this case things then tend to sound indistinct and distant, even after applying considerable EQ.

Close Miking

A more common approach – especially in smaller studios – is to close-mic a smaller amp, such as a single-speaker, open-backed combo. In this case, the mic is initially positioned very close to the speaker grille and pointed directly at the centre of the speaker cone. If a less bright sound is sought, the mic can be moved slightly to one side, which will give a warmer result. Again, an ambient mic may also be used, positioned several feet away. Figure 9.1 shows an electric- guitar combo being recorded via a single microphone.

An even warmer sound may be achieved by miking the rear of the cabinet; indeed, there's no reason not to mic both the front and the rear simultaneously if this arrangement produces a sound you like. The phase of the rear mic should, strictly speaking, be inverted so that its output is in phase with that of the front mic, but try both phase positions in any case, as what's technically correct doesn't always give the best sound.

If you want to try an ambience mic, place it several feet from the cabinet and add this to the close-miked sound, either summed in mono or with one mic panned left and the other right. The ambient mic may be pointed directly at the guitar amplifier or, alternatively, aimed at a reflective surface within the room. Check the sounds individually and you'll soon notice the weighty power of the distant mic compared with the incisive edge of the close-miked sound. For a brighter ambient sound, use a capacitor mic as the distant mic.

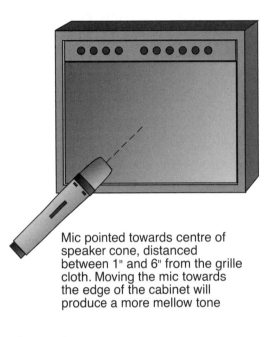

Mic pointed towards centre of speaker cone, distanced between 1" and 6" from the grille cloth. Moving the mic towards the edge of the cabinet will produce a more mellow tone

Figure 9.1: Close-miking a guitar combo

By combining these two mics in different proportions, a wide range of sounds can be achieved.

If the guitar is played in the control room with the amp itself in the studio, a capacitor microphone may be used to pick up the direct sound from the guitar strings. In isolation, the miked strings will sound very thin, but when mixed in they will add definition to the notes, rather like an exciter. Again, though, this is a matter of preference – some engineers and producers use the technique a lot while others would never bother to do it. A similar effect can be achieved by splitting the guitar output and feeding some of it direct to the console via a DI box.

A practical method of miking is to combine the above techniques by using two close mics, one on axis and one off axis, plus one mic at a distance from the cabinet. The maximum flexibility is achieved if the close mics have very different characteristics – for example, a capacitor mic on axis and a dynamic mic off axis. The distant ambience mic should almost certainly be a capacitor model, but don't let that discourage you from trying the alternative. By combining the outputs from these three mics using a mixer and then balancing the contributions of the different mics, a great variety of tonal characteristics can be obtained without having to move or change mics. Switching the phase of individual mics can often yield interesting and musically useful results. It is also possible to delay the ambience mic to increase its distance, in effect, when combining it with the other mics. Each millisecond of delay will make the signal from the mic appear to have travelled approximately 12" further. Where the difference produced by inverting the phase is too great, this can be a useful 'in between' option.

Processing

Most engineers would agree that adding effects at the mixing stage allows greater creative flexibility, but for a guitarist the effect may be so much a part of his sound that he can't play the part properly without it. Obviously the right overdrive effect must be set up prior to recording, but effects like chorus, echo and wah-wah can also be very important to the performance. Ultimately, the performance is what really counts, so many producers believe that, if the player really wants to use his own effects live as he plays, it's best to let him. If delay or reverb effects are being used live during the performance, any gating should be carried out prior to the effects, ideally using a pedal-style gate designed specifically for guitar use.

Having said that, if some of the effects are too noisy for serious recording and they can't be cleaned up – with dynamic noise filters, for example – consider patching them in to allow the player to monitor the desired effects while playing, but record the signal unprocessed. In this way, you can simulate his effects with high-quality studio processors when you come to mix, and this technique has the added benefit that the effects can be in stereo, they can be fine-tuned and their level can be changed.

Guitar DI

As an alternative to miking up guitar amplifiers, there's a variety of DI recording techniques available, some of which are very effective and can save a lot of studio time, as well as allow for greater separation between instruments being recorded simultaneously. It's almost standard practice to DI bass guitars for the majority of pop recording, for example, and even where the amplifier is miked up, some proportion of DI'd sound is often added.

Many players have had bad experiences with DI guitar techniques, to the point that they may even refuse to try them. It's true that a DI's signal seldom sounds exactly the same as a miked-up amplifier, but modern recording pre-amps and speaker simulators can work exceptionally well. Nevertheless, simply plugging a guitar into an overdrive pedal and the output of the pedal into the desk will produce a disgusting sound because there's no speaker or speaker simulator there to filter out the unwanted higher harmonics.

However, there are very genuine problems that stand in the way of achieving a good DI'd electric-guitar sound, not the least being that the output impedance of a passive guitar pick-up is too high for a mixer's mic or line input. This results in an electrical mismatch, causing loading on the pick-ups, which adversely affects the sustain and tone of the instrument.

Any active DI box will solve the impedance-matching problem, but still the tone is unlikely to be right. In a guitar amplifier, the frequency response isn't flat but is 'voiced' to sound good; in addition, the guitar speaker completely changes the characteristic of the sound. A basic rhythm sound can be achieved by using a DI box and then applying some corrective or creative EQ. A dedicated guitar processor will give better results if you actually want the authentic sound of an amplifier, but sometimes the clean, artificial sound of DI, coupled with a little compression, produces a result that works musically.

Recording Processors

Direct-recording guitar pre-amps started with the all-analogue Rockman, invented by Tom Scholtze of Boston fame, which combined compression, delay, chorus, equalisation and overdrive to give a workable clean or dirty guitar sound straight into the mixing desk. The designers appreciated the effect that the speaker has on the overdrive sound and included filtering to simulate this. Although the sound wasn't much like a real miked guitar amp, it was probably the first time that a genuinely usable DI'd guitar sound could be obtained.

Since then, many advances have been made, using a variety of technologies. Some designers have chosen to go back to tubes in order to capture the authentic tube-amp sound, some have built digital circuits to simulate the same effects and others (such as the makers of the successful Sans Amp) have employed solid-state analogue circuitry to do the job. However, the majority of guitar-recording systems now use physical modelling, a process designed to recreate the characteristics of specific guitar amps and speaker cabinets.

Many of these systems are quite sophisticated and offer MIDI-programmable digital multi-effects as well as the more obvious overdrive, EQ and compression. The quality of design has improved over the years and some of the latest units really do come very close to the sound of a miked-up cab. Even so, guitar players always tend to complain that the sound coming back over the studio monitors isn't the same as what they hear when standing in front of a loud stack at a gig – although this is hardly surprising, since studios seldom monitor at that kind of level.

The only fair way to judge such a guitar processor is to hear if it gives the kind of sound over the studio monitors that you'd expect to hear from a conventionally miked guitar amp on a record. At the time of writing, the best-sounding guitar-recording pre-amps either use analogue tube circuitry (and the good ones tend to be expensive) or they use physical modelling, and even some of the cheaper pre-amps that employ this principle can produce very high sound quality as well as be able to emulate many types of amp and speaker. Furthermore, they invariably include effects and are programmable. Analogue units, on the other hand, take very little time to set up and can be processed via any studio effects unit. Their control layout is very similar to that of a regular guitar amplifier, and their speaker emulation is generally preset or switchable, offering a very small number of options.

Speaker Emulators

A more basic approach to DI'd guitar is to use a conventional guitar amplifier and to plug in a speaker simulator instead of the usual speaker. A typical speaker simulator comprises a reactive dummy load, allowing the amplifier to work normally, followed by circuitry that approximates the filtering effect of a guitar loudspeaker. Apart from the dummy load – which is, by necessity, passive – the circuitry may be either passive or active and the output will appear as either a mic- or line-level signal that can be plugged directly into a mixing console. Most models can handle up to 100W of input power, which means that the majority of guitar amps can be run flat-out to get the best overdrive sound. Figure 9.2 shows how a speaker emulator is connected.

Some of these devices include switchable filters, enabling them to simulate open- or closed-backed speaker cabinets, and the difference in sound produced by the different models is surprisingly great. As a rule, valve amplifiers produce a nicer overdrive sound when used with speaker simulators than solid-state amplifiers, but in any event speaker simulators can come very close to the sound of a miked-up amplifier. All that's missing is ambience, which can be applied with a studio reverb processor. Having some electronic reverb is an advantage, however, even if the guitar amp has a built-in spring reverb, because few guitar amplifiers have a stereo output. Adding even a small amount of stereo digital reverb really opens up the sound and creates the impression that it was recorded in a real space.

Some engineers have been known to use a guitar sound on tape to drive a guitar amplifier, which is then miked up and re-recorded onto a spare tape track

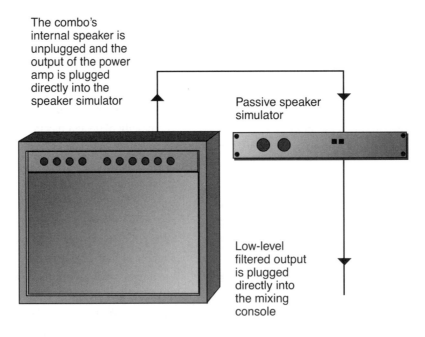

The combo's internal speaker is unplugged and the output of the power amp is plugged directly into the speaker simulator

Passive speaker simulator

Low-level filtered output is plugged directly into the mixing console

Figure 9.2: Using a speaker simulator

prior to mixing. This means that the original sound can be modified by the character of the amplifier, additional overdrive can be added and different EQ settings tried.

It's also possible to mic up the amp in a room with a flattering acoustic, which can contribute to the sound – concrete stairwells, corridors and basements have all been used at one time or another, and the way in which a basic guitar sound can be changed by this method is little short of dramatic.

Guitar EQ

The electric guitar sound is not natural, so there are no hard-and-fast rules concerning how it should sound. Invariably, some EQ will be necessary to fine-tune the sound and it is quite acceptable to add EQ during recording as well as when mixing. However, don't go overboard with EQ while recording, because few console equalisers are good enough to undo a previous EQ treatment, even if you happen to remember the exact settings used.

Final EQ settings should always be decided in the context of the entire mix, as sounds optimised in isolation seldom work properly when everything else is playing. Here are a few guidelines:

- Cut applied at between 100Hz and 250Hz can help sort out a boomy or boxy sound, while boost in the same range can fatten a thin sound.

- Cabinet clunk can be accentuated by boosting at around 75–90Hz, although it can be argued that there's little point in adding EQ boost much below 100Hz on a conventional electric guitar as the fundamental of the lowest note is in the order of 80Hz. All you'll do is bring up the boom of the cabinet or the room resonances, which is generally not what you want.

- Bite can be added to the sound anywhere between 2kHz and 6kHz, depending on the effect you're after. The electric guitar isn't a natural instrument, so the only rule is to get the sound you want. Don't add any really high-end boost unless the guitar is DI'd; nothing much over 4kHz comes out of a guitar

speaker, so boosting higher than this would simply bring up the background noise for no reason.

- Two similar-sounding electric guitars can be separated by adding bite at different frequencies – for example, at 3kHz on one guitar and around 4kHz on the other. It also helps to choose two different types of guitar if the parts are both busy – perhaps one single-coil model and one with humbuckers.

- Single-coil guitars cut through a mix without taking up too much space, so they may be the best choice in a busy mix. Conventional humbucking pick-ups create a thicker sound, which can help when you're aiming for a full sound from a small rock band such as a three-piece lead, bass and drums outfit.

Further Processing

Aside from optimising the EQ, what else can you do to a guitar sound? The answer to that question really depends on whether you merely wish to enhance the sound or make it significantly different. In extreme cases, the guitar can be so heavily treated that it is no longer recognised as a guitar at all.

Multi-effects processors are relatively cheap, and most allow the user to create reverb, delay, chorus, phasing, flanging, vibrato, pitch shifting and so on. More up-market models offer extras such as panning, exciters, complex equalisers, compressors, gates and auto-wah. The list of possible effects is endless but, as in the worlds of art and music composition, it's often what you leave out that makes more difference than what you put in.

Reverb

If you're after a fairly straight rock sound, the basic overdrive sound – however it's achieved – need only be treated with a little EQ and reverb to make it sound right, and the only problem is in choosing the right type of reverb. For a raunchy, live sound, a short reverb with a fairly bright character is ideal, and the shorter the reverb decay, the more of it you can add into your mix without making the mix sound cluttered. If the original amplifier sound had reverb added, you may even find that an early reflection or ambience program works best, as this will add brightness and interest as well as open up the stereo spread, but without changing the essential character of the original sound too much.

More abstract musical forms may demand a longer, more flowing reverb and these can be combined with repeat multi-echo effects to create a sense of vastness. Further interest can be added by feeding the effects signal through a chorus or flange unit before it gets to the reverb unit. There are no hard-and-fast rules, but in general terms the less busy the guitar part, the more reverb you can add before you run into problems. For a more in-depth discussion of the effects of reverb, read Chapter 11, 'Reverb'.

Compression

Compressors are commonly used on guitar tracks of all types to increase sustain and to keep an even level. In this application, compressors with program-dependent attack and release times are very helpful, as they will automatically adapt to the different sounds produced by different playing styles. Even a heavily overdriven guitar can be made to sound more powerful if compressed, as its average energy level is increased.

Of course, manual compressors may also be used, in which case the attack time of the compressor may be increased slightly to give individual notes more attack if desired. Optimum release time depends on playing speed, but around half a second is usually adequate.

Using a faster release time in combination with a high degree of compression can cause audible level pumping, but this may be used creatively to enhance the feeling of power. As a rule, a medium compression ratio of between 3:1 and 5:1 is adequate, with the threshold set to give between 8dB and 15dB of gain reduction on the loudest notes.

It must always be borne in mind that 10dB of compression also means a 10dB deterioration in the signal-to-noise ratio during the quieter sections, where noise is most likely to be obtrusive, so tracks containing guitar solos are best kept closed down until the moment before their entry. This may be done manually, but is more easily handled by an automated mute system, either on a hardware mixer or on a software recording system. Remember that guitar amplifiers produce more noise than almost any other instrument (especially during heavy overdrive), which means that special care must be taken if the end recording is not to be compromised.

10 MISCELLANEOUS MIKING TECHNIQUES

There are well-established microphone techniques for all the more common musical instruments, but the musical world is a large place, and there is an abundance of ethnic instruments for which no standard miking methods exist. Nevertheless, there are a couple of simple rules that can be applied to virtually every instrument conceived to give you a good starting point.

Most instruments produce sound from more than one place. Take the acoustic guitar – some sound comes out of the soundhole due to air vibrating inside the body, the wooden panels making up the body resonate, the strings themselves produce sound and the neck and headstock vibrate. What we identify as a good acoustic-guitar sound is in fact a combination of all of these separate sounds. The same is true of all acoustic instruments, and even in the case of an electric instrument, such as an amplified guitar, it could be argued that the cabinet vibrates and contributes to the sound directly produced by the loudspeaker. Unless we capture all the elements that make up the sound as perceived by a listener at a distance from the instrument, the result is likely to sound less than natural.

Mic Distance

Choosing the right miking distance can be a challenge, because if we bring the microphone too close to the instrument, we start to focus on just one part of it, which means that we are no longer capturing the composite sound of the whole instrument. It is tempting to put the microphone close to the part of the instrument that seems to be making the most sound, such as the bell of a trumpet, the soundhole of a guitar or the head of a drum (especially tempting if you are using insensitive microphones), and though it is occasionally possible to obtain usable results in this way, what we actually get is not really representative of the whole instrument.

On the other hand, placing the microphone too far away could capture the necessary components of the sound but could also pick up other unwanted sounds or room ambience. For this reason, it's always easier to record an instrument if it's played in a sympathetic acoustic environment, and most western instruments need a little reverberation because they were designed to be played indoors. The same is not necessarily true of ethnic instruments, as many are only ever played outdoors and thus need a less reflective environment.

Universal Rule

As acoustic instruments vary enormously in loudness and frequency content, I'd normally choose a capacitor microphone in order to be confident of having a high enough degree of sensitivity and the ability to capture the full audio spectrum. Most instruments sound reasonably accurate to the person playing them, which gives us one fallback position straight away: if all else fails, put a mic close to the player's ears. As I mentioned earlier in the book, I've used this technique to good effect when working with acoustic guitars, where a cardioid mic 'looking' over the player's right shoulder will often produce a natural and well-balanced sound when other positions have failed.

The other method I've developed is based on rules normally applied to the stereo miking of ensembles. When working with stereo, it's common practice to create an approximately equilateral triangle, with the musicians forming one side of the triangle and the stereo-mic array occupying the point opposite. This ensures that all the instruments in the ensemble are roughly the same distance from the mics, yet the mics are close enough to the performers to exclude external sounds to a useful degree. But what happens if we apply this rule to a single microphone?

Single Instruments

A typical drum kit is around five feet in width, so a single mic placed five feet in front of the kit should give a usable result without favouring one drum above the others. Of course, few people would record the drum kit with a single mic these days, but this arrangement serves to illustrate the principle.

This rule may be extrapolated to accommodate single instruments by considering the various parts of each instrument to be a kind of mini-ensemble. It's necessary to estimate only the longest dimension of the instrument and then place a cardioid-pattern mic at that distance from the instrument, pointing towards its centre. For example, a drum kit is normally miked from between four and five feet, while a piano might be miked at between five and eight feet. This is only a rule of thumb, however, and if it's desirable to capture a little more of the room ambience, the mic can be moved a little further away until the desired balance is achieved. Even so, if you check the mic position calculated via this method against the standard mic positions for known instruments, you'll be surprised at how closely they correlate. Virtually all of the wind-instrument mic positions can be worked out in this way. Likewise, the acoustic guitar can be recorded using a single mic at a distance of around three feet. As before, avoid the temptation to point the mic at the loudest part of the instrument and experiment with both the angle of the mic and the distance once you've heard the initial results. Also, monitoring the results on enclosed headphones as you move the mic can speed up the process considerably.

The 5:1 Rule

A further consideration arises when several instruments are being recorded together, as it may be necessary to compromise the individual microphone positions in order to minimise leakage or spill between the instruments. Using cardioid-pattern mics, it's best if the mics are separated by a distance of at least three and, ideally, five times the distance between the microphones and the instruments upon which they're trained, a principle illustrated in Figure 10.1. A slight improvement

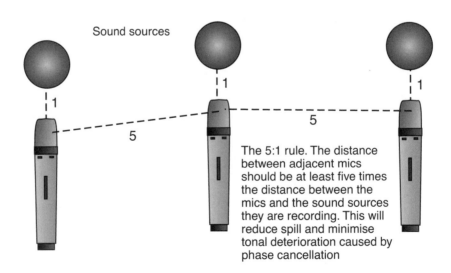

Sound sources

1

1

1

5

5

The 5:1 rule. The distance between adjacent mics should be at least five times the distance between the mics and the sound sources they are recording. This will reduce spill and minimise tonal deterioration caused by phase cancellation

Figure 10.1: The 5:1 rule

in preventing unwanted leakage can be achieved by using a tighter microphone pattern, such as a hypercardioid or supercardioid, but it could also be argued that omnis will produce just as good a result. Omnis may pick up more spill, potentially causing phase problems, but because of their improved off-axis response, this spill will at least be recorded faithfully.

Cardioids, on the other hand, will produce slightly better separation (and consequently fewer phase problems), but because of their inferior off-axis response, what spill is picked up may be tonally inaccurate, leading to a less accurate representation of the performance when the outputs from all the of mics are mixed. Of course, there are cardioids on the market with excellent off-axis responses, but these tend to be rather specialised and very expensive.

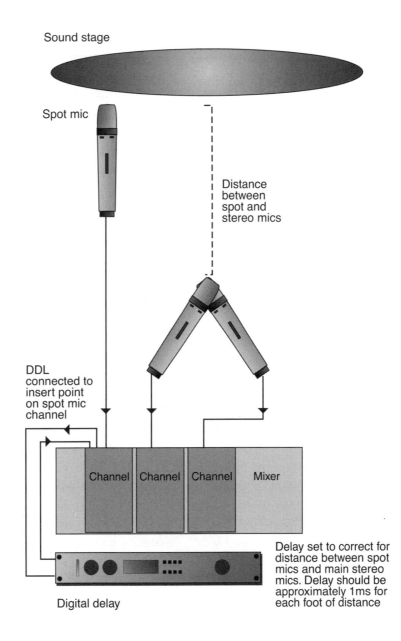

Sound stage

Spot mic

Distance between spot and stereo mics

DDL connected to insert point on spot mic channel

Channel | Channel | Channel | Mixer

Delay set to correct for distance between spot mics and main stereo mics. Delay should be approximately 1ms for each foot of distance

Digital delay

Figure 10.2: Using a delay line to correct timing

Stereo

When attempting stereo recordings of large ensembles, the classic approach is to use a stereo mic pair, usually M&S (Middle and Side) or XY (coincident), mounted in front of the performers. In a venue with suitable acoustics, this can produce excellent results, with the outputs from the mics being recorded directly to DAT, MiniDisc or a stereo hard-disk recording device. Realistically, though, the balance is unlikely to be exactly as you would wish it and, although individual performers can be moved around to compensate to some extent, most engineers resort to using spot microphones to reinforce the weaker sections. When working with a small folk duo or string quartet, this may not be a problem, but in situations such as orchestral recording sessions, where much greater microphone distances are involved, the time delay between the sound reaching the spot mics and the main stereo mics becomes significant.

Delay Correction

The problem of time delay can be corrected by using a high-quality delay line to delay the spot mic outputs by exactly the right amount so that the signals arriving from both sets of mics are brought back into phase with each other. As sound travels at roughly 300m per second, this isn't too difficult to calculate, and the spot mics (suitably panned) can then be added to the main stereo-mic signal before being recorded onto the stereo machine. Alternatively, the performance can be recorded onto a multitrack recorder for subsequent mixing, enabling different delay settings to be tried at the mixing stage. Figure 10.2 shows how a delay line can be connected in this way.

To do this properly, you'll need a separate digital delay for each spot mic, but in all but the most serious classical recording situations, this might be considered a touch extravagant (although most digital mixers provide exactly this facility). It's often sufficient to delay all the spot mics by the same amount, which is easily achieved by creating a stereo subgroup of the spot-mic signals (either while recording or during mixing) and then using a good-quality stereo delay unit to delay the subgrouped signal by the required amount.

It's essential that the spot mics are panned to the correct positions in the stereo soundstage so that they corroborate the image produced by the main stereo-mic array. In an analogue mixer, the delay unit may be connected to the subgroup insert points, and if the business of adding delay can be left until the mixing stage, this gives the added flexibility of being able to fine-tune the delay time by ear to achieve the best subjective result.

Esoterica

There's some disagreement as to whether the sound from spot mics should be delayed until it's exactly in phase or whether subjectively better results are produced if the spot mics are slightly over-delayed. The logic behind this is that, when over-delayed, the sound from the spot mics blends in with the early reflections picked up by the main stereo mics. This has the effect of changing their subjective level without having to make the timing absolutely accurate.

It must be stressed that these are very highbrow considerations and are the subject of debate between engineers at different leading classical record companies. However, it strikes me that, if a compromise must be made and all of the spot mics have to be processed by a single stereo delay line, over-delaying the sound very slightly, rather than under-delaying it, might achieve a better result – bearing in mind that it's impossible to give all of the spot mics exactly the right delay time using a common delay line.

Figure-Of-Eight Mics

Elsewhere in this book I've cited examples of where figure-of-eight mics might be useful in cutting down spill due to their near total rejection of sounds approaching from 90º off axis. By aiming this 'deaf spot' at the source of the spill, you can win a little extra separation, although the results will vary depending on how reflective the room is and on the physical size of the sound source. Because figure-of-eight mics are equally sensitive on both sides, the side not addressing the performer should be aimed at an acoustic absorber in order to minimise spill from room reflections and to reduce the effect of room acoustics.

11 REVERB

Reverberation is undoubtedly the most important studio effect at our disposal, and no book on engineering or production would be complete without a section devoted to this subject. In pop-music production, and indeed in some classical recording situations, reverberation tends to be added using digital-reverberation simulators rather than contributed by the natural acoustics of the studio or performance venue. Digital-reverberation units were originally very costly, due to the complexity of their circuitry and the research that went into their development and production, but as new circuit technology was developed and as the principles of artificial reverberation became better established, inexpensive units became commonplace. Nowadays, a basic digital reverberation unit offering very respectable performance can cost less than £200.

The more expensive professional-studio reverb units usually have a better technical specification in terms of noise, audio bandwidth and distortion than their ancestors, and they also produce a more realistic effect. However, although budget units may be technically inferior, most now employ 24-bit converters and offer surprisingly good reverb simulations that are generally quiet enough (if used with care) to make good master-quality recordings. Some models offer a choice of preset reverberation treatments while others allow every detail of the effect to be programmed. My preference is for something in the middle, where you can access a handful of key parameters very quickly without having to get bogged down in lengthy edit menus. Admittedly, it's useful to be able to control the more important parameters that make up the reverberation effect, but it's arguable whether the very

detailed programming possible on some models is worthwhile. A basic unit offering a choice of over 100 preset reverb treatments (as many now do) will cover most eventualities, and such models make ideal second reverb units.

Vital Statistics

When a sound impulse is fed into a reverb unit, there is a short delay before any reverberant sound is heard. This is known as the reverb *pre-delay* and is often used to increase the impression of room size, although it can also be useful in separating the reverb slightly from the dry sound, especially on vocals, thus increasing vocal clarity.

Directly after the pre-delay come the so-called *early reflections*, which are really closely spaced, discrete echoes representing the first reflections from the room boundaries. These discrete reflections quickly build up into a dense, reverberant pattern that further increases in density as its level decays. In a real room, these early reflections help the listener to localise sounds, and in a digital reverberation simulator they help create the illusion of space around the sound. Figure 11.1 over the page shows how reverberation develops and decays following a percussive sound.

Early Reflections

Herein lies one major difference between real rooms and artificial reverberators: in a real room, every instrument in an ensemble produces a different early reflection pattern because the performers each occupy different positions relative to the room boundaries. As a consequence, the early reflections from the different instruments tend to blend, creating a more dense, more

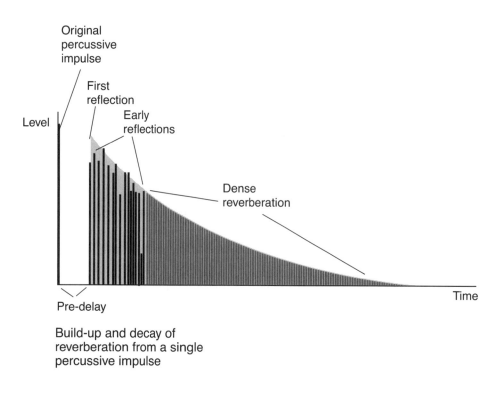

Build-up and decay of
reverberation from a single
percussive impulse

Figure 11.1: Anatomy of reverberation

complex pattern than would be produced if all created the same early reflections pattern.

Most artificial reverb devices produce a fixed pattern of early reflections (one exception is the TC System 6000 processor, which can calculate different reflection patterns for a number for a number of input 'positions'), which has the effect of placing every instrument in our imaginary room in the same position. This isn't always a problem, especially when producing pop music, as artistic considerations come before the need for authenticity. However, in classical or other acoustic work, it helps to turn down the level of early reflections if the reverb unit is programmable or to choose a hall setting with a slow reverb build-up, if the unit offers a choice of presets. Not only does this prevent the everything-in-one-place effect but it also sounds more natural, as most digital reverberation units produce early reflection patterns that are far more obtrusive than those found in real concert halls.

Mono Into Stereo

Reverb units usually take a mono sound source and create a pseudo-stereo output by producing different reverberation patterns for the left and right channels. This is a perfectly viable approach and closely simulates what happens when a single sound source (which can be considered as mono) is heard in a reflective room – different reverberant patterns arrive at the listener's left and right ears, creating the impression of space. Those units which have stereo inputs invariably combine the two channels to mono for processing, leaving only the dry portion of the sound in stereo. The reverberant sound is generated from the summed mono signal and processed to provide stereo (left and right) outputs. A similar strategy can be employed to create a reverb processor that will work in a surround-sound manner, although in most instances using two stereo reverb units – one for the 'front' of the mix and one for the 'rear' – will produce believable results. Adding more pre-delay to the rear reverb and perhaps using a slower build-up and less high end can help create the impression of a larger acoustic space, such as a concert hall.

Real-Life Acoustics

During a real musical performance, all of the instruments normally play in the same room and so are influenced by the same natural acoustic environment. It therefore follows that, in order to simulate this sound using artificial reverberation, all of the instruments in the mix should be treated with the same type of reverberation. In the production of pop music, however, we are under no such constraints, as a natural-sounding result isn't necessarily the most artistically pleasing result. Consequently, it's common practice to use several different reverb settings on the same mix – for example, the vocals might have a medium length, warm-sounding reverb while the snare drum might be treated with a short, bright plate or even a gated setting. Other instruments could be treated with other reverb types or be left completely dry. Furthermore, the relationship in level between reverb and dry sound is likely to be different in each case. The choice of settings for individual instruments or parts is a purely artistic one, but there are some points to take into consideration, which might make this choice more logical.

Psychoacoustics

In nature, reverberation is used by our ears to determine something about our immediate environment. If we hear a sound with a lot of reverberation, we assume that it's quite distant because nearby sounds contain far more of the direct portion of the sound and less reflected sound. This is true both in and out of doors, though outdoor reverb is only evident in places where there are large reflective surfaces such as buildings, cliffs or densely growing trees. Furthermore, bright reverbs suggest hard surfaces, while duller or warmer reverbs characterise softer environments such as concert halls.

It can be deduced from these facts that, if the level of reverberation following a sound is increased, the sound can be made to seem more distant, and this provides a way of creating a front-to-back perspective in a mix, as opposed to the simple left/right positioning offered by pan pots. Also bear in mind that high frequencies are absorbed by the air, so distant sounds tend to be less bright than nearby sounds. This applies to both the direct and the reverberant sound, which means that a sound may be placed in the far distance by using a very high level of reverberant sound with a low level of direct sound and a degree of high-frequency cut. Conversely, the illusion of proximity can be created by placing a relatively bright, dry sound against a backdrop of less bright, more reverberant sounds; this explains why highly reverberant lead vocals need to be mixed at a high level in order to prevent them from receding into the background.

Small Rooms

Small rooms tend to have pronounced early-reflection patterns with a fairly rapid reverb decay, and electronic small-room emulations can be used to create an intimate club atmosphere. Alternatively, using an ambience setting that comprises mainly early reflections with very little ensuing reverberation helps to bring a sound alive without making it seem obviously processed. That's because this simulates the type of acoustic in which we're used to living and working – one that we recognise as normal and take for granted. The better reverb units contain specific ambience or early-reflections programs which provide a very useful alternative to conventional rooms or plates for those occasions when you want to create a sense of space but without obvious reverberation. They are also useful for processing tape tracks that have been recorded with a mono effect and which need to be given a sense of width – for example, a vocal recorded using a mono reverb can be processed using an early-reflections setting to create the illusion of depth and stereo width. This process is extremely useful where tracks are limited.

Further Effects

Reverberation used alone is a very powerful effect, but it can also be combined with delay to make things more interesting.

- If you're using a digital reverb with no programmable facilities, you can add pre-delay

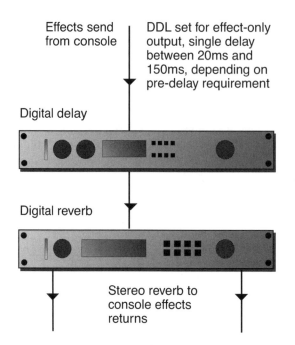

Effects send from console

DDL set for effect-only output, single delay between 20ms and 150ms, depending on pre-delay requirement

Digital delay

Digital reverb

Stereo reverb to console effects returns

Figure 11.2: Adding pre-delay to reverb

simply by patching a DDL into the reverb input, using a single repeat at between 30ms and 300ms, depending on the effect required. Figure 11.2 shows how this is patched up.

- Multitapped delays can be used to create very spacious reverb effects, especially if the delay is patched before the reverb unit.

- Setting longer, multiple echoes gives a very rich echo effect because each individual echo is surrounded by its own individual halo of reverb.

- Modulating the delay very slightly creates a kind of chorus echo, which can work beautifully on guitar or synthesiser.

Multi-effects units don't always allow you to connect the effects in the order that you would prefer. This is significant because the order in which effects are connected makes a profound difference to the end result. However, if you're using software plug-ins, you can usually patch these in series in any order you want.

Autopanned Reverb

- Processing a reverb signal via an autopanner, to sweep it from side to side at a rate of one sweep every couple of seconds or so, creates a nice sense of movement without sounding too obvious or gimmicky.

- A mono-in/stereo-out autopanner must be fed with a mono reverb signal, which can be obtained from the reverb's mono output, if the unit has one, or by combining the two channels using a mixer. Panning this signal from side to side at the rate of half a second or so per sweep creates a distinct side-to-side movement, and if the pan time can be made a multiple of the song tempo the result can be very subtle. This works particularly well when trying to make backing vocals more interesting or for treating instruments in new-age or ambient music productions. When working with plug-ins, it's generally very easy to synchronise panning effect to tempo, and if the song includes tempo changes, the panning rate can be made to follow this.

- Alternatively, a stereo panner can be used to treat both the reverb's left and right outputs, causing the left and right signals to cross over and back again, in effect, as the pan progresses.

It's also worth experimenting with processing the send to the reverb unit as follows:

- Applying a small pitch detune to the reverb send can thicken the sound, especially if the reverb level is high in the mix. This may be used to good effect on parts such as backing vocals or synthesised strings.

- Similarly, applying chorus or mild flange to the reverb input helps add movement and spread to the sound, while the random nature of the reverb breaks up the cyclic nature of the chorus or flange.

Multi-Effects Processors

The hardware required to produce additional studio effects is little different from that used to generate reverb, so other than a few high-end reverb processors, most commercial effects boxes combine reverb with a choice of other effects, sometimes available singly and sometimes as multi-effect combinations. Depending on their cost and sophistication, these units may be preset or programmable and may allow anything between 2 and 20 effects to be used in combination at the same time. There is usually a limitation to which effects can be used simultaneously and in what order they can be used, the permutations often being grouped into so-called *algorithms*. These algorithms are, in effect, pre-assigned configurations of effects where the user can change the parameters of the various effects and store the modified composite effect as a patch for later recall.

Most multi-effects units offer reverb, delay and modulated delay effects such as chorus, phasing, flanging and vibrato as standard. More sophisticated models may provide pitch shifting, exciters, compressors, gates and equalisers, while guitar-specific models often include overdrive and speaker simulation. These days, it's common practice to use guitar multi-effects units to process synthesisers or samplers in

order to produce overdriven synth guitar sounds or distorted organ simulations.

While the same reverb is often used on several instruments or voices in a mix, this is not really true of complex multiple effects patches. These tend to be created with a specific musical part in mind, are often confined to a single vocal or instrumental part and may only ever be used in one song.

It's becoming increasingly popular to include real-time MIDI control over key parameters within an effect. This allows a performer to change reverb decay time or amount of pitch shift, for example, from a MIDI pedal unit. By the same token, these same parameters may be controlled from a MIDI sequencer, which opens up new avenues for automated effects processing. In this application, some units work better than others – for instance, on some models the parameter being changed will shift smoothly, while on others the change will be heard as a series of fine steps. Obviously, the smoother the change, the better.

Automation of effect parameters is one area where plug-ins really do make life a lot easier, but when it comes to reverb I've yet to hear a high-quality reverb plug-in that doesn't take up an extravagant amount of processing power. For this reason, hardware reverbs or reverbs based on DSP cards are often used with computer systems to provide the best results.

Innovative Reverb Effects

While most effects can be generated using either dedicated effects units or digital multi-effects processors, it's possible to create something a little out of the ordinary just by using a little ingenuity. Indeed, most of the recordings still regarded as pop classics were made in the days when very few effects units were available and engineers had to improvise. Fine examples can be heard on records by The Beatles and early Pink Floyd, to name but two.

Some of the most powerful effects are the most simple to create, and one of my favourites is true 'backwards reverb'. This is quite unlike the 'canned' reverse effects that come as standard on most reverb units because it actually comes before the sound that caused it. Obviously, this can't be done in real life, and it can't be done in real time, either, because the reverb unit would have to know what sound was coming next. Nevertheless, it's an easy effect to produce with analogue tape after recording, because of the ease with which tape can be reversed. It's also possible to create the same effect using digital, tapeless recording systems, but sadly it isn't possible with digital tape such as ADAT or DA88. To make the methodology clear, I'll explain the analogue-tape method first.

• Record the original take dry onto the multitrack tape, then turn the tape over so that the track plays backwards, from the end of the song to the start. (Turning the tape over also reverses the track order so that, on an eight-track machine, track 1 becomes track 8 and vice versa, so make sure that you don't record over any wanted stuff while the tape is reversed.)

• With the recording now running backwards, the track to be treated is used to feed a conventional stereo reverb set to a medium-to-long decay setting (two to ten seconds) and the reverb recorded onto an empty track (or pair of tracks, if you can afford the luxury of keeping it in stereo).

• Once the reverb has been recorded, the tape can be switched the right way around and played normally. Now the reverb will start to build up a couple of seconds before the track starts and produce an unnatural pre-echo effect. This works very nicely on vocals, but it can also be used on pitched-instrument sounds or drums.

• Panning the dry sound to one side of the mix and the reverse reverb to the other creates a strong sense of movement, and it's a worthwhile exercise to experiment with combined effects such as adding artificial reverse reverb to the track at the same time and panning this to the opposite extreme.

Recreating this effect in a computer sequencer is even easier. Simply copy the part to be processed to new track, reverse it using the sequencer's Edit functions and then add a suitable reverb using a plug-in. What you'll hear is a backwards track with conventional reverb applied. Set the Reverb Mix

to 100 per cent and then record this to a new track. Finally, reverse the reverb part you've just recorded so that the reverb is now backwards but the musical order is back as it originally was. Line up this reverb track with your original dry track and fine-tune its position so that it sounds properly in sync. What you'll hear is the reverb starting out quietly, then building rapidly to a peak as the dry sound plays. The result is exactly the same as that described for analogue tape and is simple to achieve in most sequencers.

While you can't achieve this effect with digital tape, you may be able to record and reverse the audio in a hardware sampler, add reverb and then sample the result again before reversing it again. By triggering the sample just before the original dry sound, a similar reverse effect can be created.

Ducking

Another useful trick that works well in conjunction with the previous technique is setting up a compressor (or a gate with a ducking facility) as a ducker and triggering it from the vocal track. The backwards-reverb vocal track is then processed via the ducker so that the reverse effect is loudest in the pauses between vocal phrases, a technique shown in Figure 11.3. A normal, short reverb can also be added to the vocal track to make it sound natural. The secret is not to overdo it. The reverse sound doesn't have to be used all the way through a song; it can be brought in and out of the mix as required at the touch of a fader.

Pitched Reverb

Normally, a reverb unit will be fed directly from the track being treated, but there are a couple of tricks that can be used to make the effects more interesting. One technique is to feed the effects send through a pitch shifter before it goes to the reverb unit and drop the pitch by an octave. This means that the original sound will be unchanged but its reverb will be an octave lower than normal. Used on musical sounds, the pitch shift must be either an octave up or an octave down in order to maintain a true musical relationship, but smaller shifts can be used with drums and percussion. Small

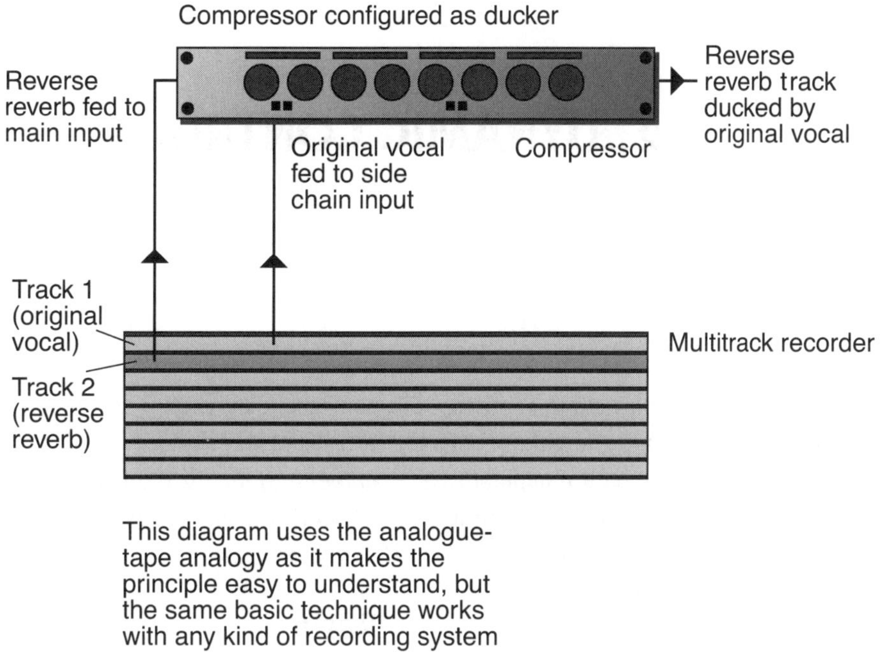

Compressor configured as ducker

Reverse reverb fed to main input

Reverse reverb track ducked by original vocal

Original vocal fed to side chain input

Compressor

Track 1 (original vocal)

Multitrack recorder

Track 2 (reverse reverb)

This diagram uses the analogue-tape analogy as it makes the principle easy to understand, but the same basic technique works with any kind of recording system

Figure 11.3: Ducked reverse reverb

pitch-detuning effects used with pre-reverb can also be effective in creating a richer reverb sound.

Reverb And Flange

Flanging is a very dramatic effect, but by the same token, it can be obvious. However, if a flanger is patched in between the aux send output and the reverb input, the result is far more subtle than that achieved by putting the flanger after the reverb output. In this case, instead of a heavy modulation effect, the flanging is fragmented and randomised by the reverb to create a shifting reverb effect that can add sparkle and interest to vocal or guitar sounds. This also works nicely with synthesised string sounds as the flanger creates a sense of detail and movement in the reverberant sound without changing the dry part of the sound.

12 DYNAMIC CONTROL

The term *dynamic control* is generally held to apply to any automatic process that changes the gain of an audio signal. In the context of outboard equipment, the term refers to compressors and gates, although it could equally cover mixer automation and autopanners. Gates and compressors were originally designed for corrective purposes, but they also have a creative role in the studio and few modern recordings are made without the help of these devices.

Compressors

A compressor is a device designed to reduce the dynamic range of an audio signal – in other words, it reduces the difference between the loudest and quietest parts of a piece of music. Compression is invariably necessary when recording vocals, as singers' voices vary in level a great deal, depending on the notes they're singing and on their phrasing. Certain instruments – such as bass, electric and acoustic guitars – also benefit from the use of a compressor to help produce a smooth, even level. The compressor plays a vital role in pop-music production, where dynamics need to be quite strictly controlled, and it also increases the average signal level of a recording – which, when applied to music, helps produce a full and punchy sound. In non-musical applications, such as in the processing of broadcast speech, compression is used to ensure intelligibility at all times.

All conventional compressors work on some form of threshold system and are arranged so that signals exceeding the threshold are processed while those falling below the threshold pass through unchanged. This threshold may be set by the user, either by varying the threshold level relative to the input signal or,

conversely, by varying the input signal level relative to a fixed threshold. A further stage of gain, called *make-up gain*, is then provided after processing, allowing the user to restore or make up any gain lost during processing.

Ratio

When a signal exceeds the threshold set by the user, its level is automatically reduced, with the amount of reduction depending on the ratio setting. On many compressors, the ratio is variable: the higher the ratio, the more severe the degree of compression. (High ratios produce an effect known as *limiting*, where the input signal is prevented from ever exceeding the threshold.) The best way to understand the effect of a compressor ratio is by giving an example: if a compression ratio of 5:1 is set, an input signal exceeding the threshold by 5dB will cause an increase in level of only 1dB at the output. The concept of threshold and ratio are illustrated in the graph in Figure 12.1.

Soft-Knee Compression

A standard compressor has a well-defined threshold – for instance, if the input signal is just below the threshold, no compression takes place, but if it's just over, the full compression ratio is applied. An alternative approach is the so-called *soft-knee compressor*, which 'blurs' the threshold level over a range of 10dB or so, inasmuch as the ratio gradually increases in the vicinity of the threshold rather than coming in all at once. This type of compressor is less able to exercise really positive gain control than the fixed-ratio or *hard-knee* types, but its real advantage is that it sounds less obtrusive, making it suitable for compressing complete mixes or

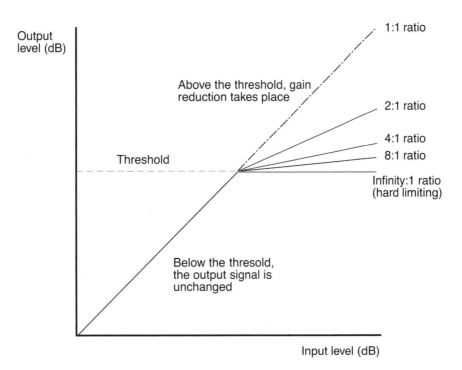

Output level (dB)

Above the threshold, gain reduction takes place

1:1 ratio

2:1 ratio

4:1 ratio

8:1 ratio

Infinity:1 ratio (hard limiting)

Threshold

Below the thresold, the output signal is unchanged

Input level (dB)

Figure 12.1: Compressor threshold and ratios

for treating instrumental or vocal sounds that need to retain a natural quality. Figure 12.2 over the page shows how soft-knee compression appears on the threshold/ratio graph.

Soft-knee compressors give a more progressive kind of level control because the compression ratio is gradually increased up to the value set by the user rather than applied abruptly. Hard-knee compressors are used to better effect where a more firm degree of control is needed or when it comes to making deliberate modifications to the sounds of percussive or picked instruments.

Attack

The term *attack* when used in the context of compressors refers not to the attack of the sound being processed but to the reaction time of the gain-control circuitry within the compressor. The attack-time control determines how long the compressor takes to respond once the input signal exceeds the threshold. If the attack is set to a fast degree, the signal is brought

under control very quickly, whereas a slower attack time might allow the input signal to overshoot the threshold before gain reduction is applied. Allowing deliberate overshoot to occur in this way is a popular way of emphasising the attack characteristics of instruments such as guitars or drums, while the slower the attack of the compressor, the more pronounced the attack of the sound being treated.

Release

The release setting determines the time it takes for the compressor to restore the gain to normal once the input signal has fallen back below the threshold. If the release time is set too short, the gain returns to its normal level too quickly, resulting in an audible surge in volume, often referred to as *gain pumping*. On the other hand, if the release time is set too long, the compressor may still be applying some gain reduction when the next sound comes along, and if this is a quiet sound, it will still be suppressed and the benefit of compression will be lost. Long release times can be

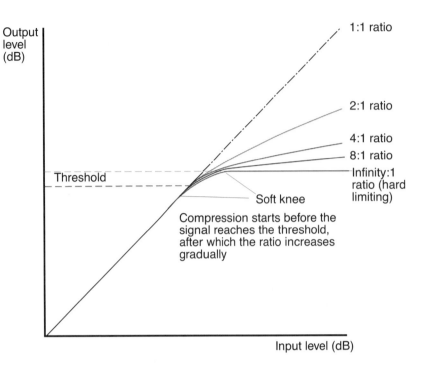

Figure 12.2: Graph showing soft-knee compression

Compression Side-Effects

A common problem that arises from using compression is that a loud kick drum (which produces mainly low frequencies) will trigger the compressor and consequently pull down the gain of everything else that happens to be passing through the compressor at the time, even though those other sounds might not need to be compressed at all. If the compressor is acting on a solo kick-drum track, then clearly this isn't a problem, but if the whole drum kit is being compressed, high-frequency sounds such as hi-hats and cymbals (which carry relatively little acoustic energy) will be compressed along with the kick drum, often causing a subjective dulling of the sound during times of heavy compression. Careful use of the attack and release controls can help to

useful when trying to even out long-term changes in levels, such as the differences in level of different songs on a radio broadcast. However, in music mixing applications, a typical release time is in the order of a quarter to a half a second.

reduce this problem, but where complete mixes need to be compressed transparently, a multiband compressor will invariably do a better job. The latter half of this chapter explains in detail the principle of multiband compression.

Auto Mode

Optimising the attack and release settings of a compressor isn't difficult when the dynamics of the signal being processed are consistent, but if the dynamics are consistently changing – as is the case with most complete mixes, slap-bass parts and some vocal lines – the ideal settings are less obvious. In such situations, it's often better to use a compressor that has an auto attack/release feature. On these devices, when Auto mode is selected, the compressor analyses the dynamics of the incoming signal and changes its attack and release times 'on the fly' in order to maintain maximum control with the minimum number of side-effects. Auto mode is usually most effective for complex mixes or signals with varying or unpredictable dynamics.

Problems With Compressors

Compressors aren't without their negative aspects, of course. For every decibel of compression applied, the background noise is also brought up by 1dB. This might not be obvious at first because, as I've said, a compressor only affects signals exceeding its threshold, and even then it turns the sound level down, not up. However, the reason for the increase in noise is obvious if you think about it. If you use a compressor to reduce the highest signal peaks by, say, 10dB, you're likely to use make-up gain to restore the peak level of the signal to its original value. This means applying 10dB of gain to the whole signal, with the result that any noise present in the signal will also be boosted by 10dB. This will be most apparent when there's no wanted signal to hide the noise, as with low-level signals that don't exceed the threshold.

Excessive noise can be alleviated to some extent by using a gate or expander before the compressor, thus ensuring that breaks and pauses are completely silent, and many compressors now come with a built-in expander for this very reason. However, this is a corrective measure and, as such, is less satisfactory than the preventative measure of ensuring that the original signal is as free of noise as is possible. In practice, an expander used to clean up a well-recorded signal with a low noise content produces very good results.

Where And When?

Most engineers tend to compress their signals while recording and then again during mixing. There are good reasons for this, the main one being that compressing a signal while recording it makes the best use of the tape's dynamic range and, at the same time, helps to prevent unexpected signal peaks from overloading the tape machine. Because any processing applied during recording is irreversible, it's normal practice to use rather less compression than might ultimately be needed so that a little more can be added at the mixing stage, if required. It's at this later stage that the expander or gate is best applied to clean up the pauses. If the gate setting is incorrect, the tape can always be run again, but if a mistake is made during recording, an otherwise perfect take can be ruined.

When recording into an audio sequencer, it's not uncommon to use a voice-channel type of microphone pre-amplifier with a built-in compressor to add compression while recording and then to use a software plug-in compressor to add more compression while mixing.

Compressor Sound

Much of what I've explained so far is common knowledge in recording circles, but what may be less obvious is why different models of compressor can sound so different to each other. Part of the difference can be attributed to the *side-chain detector circuit*, that part of the system that analyses the dynamics of the incoming signal. There are two distinct types of circuit in use: *peak detecting* and *RMS detecting*. A peak-detecting circuit – as its name suggests – will respond to peaks in the input signal regardless of how short they are, while the RMS detector averages the signal level over a short period of time.

The latter approach is more akin to the workings of the human ear and so tends to give a more natural type of dynamic control, but it has a disadvantage in that short signal peaks can get through undetected. Of course, short peaks may also get through any type of compressor unchecked, unless the fastest attack time is set, which is why, in some critical applications, a fast peak limiter is also required. A good example of this is digital recording, where signals larger than the maximum permitted level must be avoided, or serious audible distortion will result. It's possible to patch a separate limiter after the compressor, but in critical applications such as digital mastering or broadcasting it may be desirable to use a compressor with a built-in peak limiter.

The limiter threshold is invariably set higher than the compressor threshold and such limiters are very fast acting, thus preventing any overshoot. In practice, most employ a clipping circuit that physically arrests any signal trying to exceed the limiter threshold until the necessary gain correction has been applied. Although this kind of limiter action is pretty drastic, the sound that it produces can be useful in a creative way, especially when recording in rock music.

Another reason why some compressors produce a

different sound is that many don't have a linear input/output ratio above the threshold. With some designs, soft-knee compression may continue above the threshold, while in others the degree of compression may level out a few decibels above the threshold and then increase again for higher signal levels. Compressors that work on the optical principle, where photo-resistors are illuminated by LEDs or lamps powered from the side-chain circuitry, often have extremely non-linear compression curves, which gives them a very distinctive sound.

Side-Effects

Most of the energy in a typical music signal resides in the lower frequencies, which means that the bass drum, bass guitar and (to a lesser extent) snare drum control most of what the compressor is doing. This shows up one real weakness of compressors, which is that any high-frequency sounds occurring at the same time as a low-frequency sound will be reduced in level as the compressor responds to the input signal level – for example, a quiet hi-hat beat occurring at the same time as a bass-drum beat will be reduced in level, even though it isn't too loud. The usual way around this is to set a longer attack time on the compressor in order to allow the attack of the beat to get through unchecked. Even so, if a lot of compression is applied to a complex mix, the sound can become dull as the high-frequency detail is overruled by the low-frequency peaks.

Some of the early valve compressors seemed to suffer less from this problem than apparently more sophisticated later designs, and here's one of the reasons why: most valve compressors introduce a significant amount of even harmonic distortion, which increases as gain reduction is being applied. This has the effect of brightening the sound, very much like an exciter, which helps to compensate for the over-reduction in level of high frequencies. A little even-order harmonic distortion can actually make a signal sound brighter and cleaner than it really is. As it was, valve compressors were adding this distortion quite unintentionally.

Some early FET-based (Field-Effect Transistor) designs also introduced a similar kind of distortion,

which is why FET compressors can sound very similar to valve models. More recent designs have attempted to recreate this serendipitous combination of effects by building in a degree of harmonic distortion or dynamic equalisation, which provides a subtle treble boost related to the amount of gain reduction taking place. This can work very well in maintaining a detailed and relatively transparent sound, even when heavy compression is taking place.

Ducking

Although compressors are used mainly to smooth out large fluctuations in signal level, they may also be used to allow one signal to control the level of another. This technique is generally referred to as *ducking* and is frequently used by radio DJs to allow the level of background music to be controlled by the level of the voice-over. When ducking is applied, as the DJ starts to speak, the level of the background music drops, but whenever there is a pause in the speech, the background music will return to its normal level at a rate determined by the setting of the compressor's release control.

Such techniques are possible only if the compressor being used has side-chain access. Normally the side chain of a compressor is fed from its own input signal, but if it's fed from an external source instead, the dynamics of that external source will control the gain-reduction process. In the previous DJ example, if music is fed into the main compressor input and the DJ's voice is fed into the side-chain or external input, whenever the DJ's voice exceeds the threshold level, gain reduction will be applied to the music. The amount of gain reduction will depend on the compression ratio that has been set; many engineers prefer to use a gate with a dedicated ducking facility instead of a compressor because this produces more predictable results.

Apart from the obvious application just described, ducking can be very useful when mixing pop or rock music. Loud, relentless rhythm guitar or pad-keyboard parts can be forced down in level to allow the vocals to punch through. The amount of ducking needed to make this work is surprisingly small – a drop in level of just 2–3dB is often sufficient to avoid conflict, and the slight gain-pumping effect caused by the gain change can add a sense of power. It's important not to overdo the effect, however, as once the gain changes start to become noticeable, they cease to be pleasant.

Apart from controlling one instrument level with a voice or other instrument, such as solo guitar, ducking may also be used to control the output level from an effects unit. Reverb or delay are very powerful effects, but if too much is used in a busy mix, the result can be very cluttered. Nevertheless, the same mix might have sudden breaks or stops where a high level of reverb or delay is necessary. The solution to this problem is to use, say, the drum part to feed the external side-chain input of the compressor and feed the reverb or delay outputs through the compressor's main input. Now, whenever the drums stop, the effect level will return to normal, but when the drums are playing, ducking will take place and the level of the effect will be reduced. Figure 12.3 shows how a ducker might be used in the context of using a voice-over to control the level of background music.

Note that, although this is the 'classic' method of setting up ducking, the process is often easier to achieve and more controllable if you use a gate that includes a dedicated ducking facility, as this will allow you to control directly the amount by which the signal is ducked, whereas ducking with a compressor involves a certain amount of trial and error.

Compressor Distortion

I've already touched on valve and FET distortion, which can work to your advantage by brightening heavily compressed sounds, but there are other, less pleasant distortion mechanisms of which you should also be aware. Normally, a compressor's side chain follows the envelope of the signal that's being fed into it, but if the attack and release times are set to their fastest positions, it's possible that the compressor will attempt to respond not to the envelope of the input signal but to individual cycles of the input waveform.

This is particularly significant when the input signal

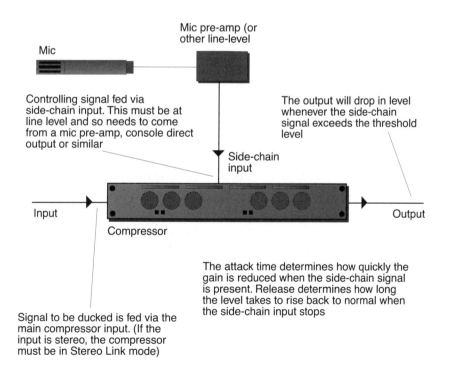

Figure 12.3: Using a compressor as a ducker

is from a bass instrument, as then the individual cycles are relatively long. If tracking of the individual waveform cycles is allowed to occur, very poor distortion is audible as individual cycles of the waveform are compressed 'out of shape'. The best way of getting around this problem is either to increase the release time of the compressor or, if your model allows it, to increase the compressor's hold time. The hold facility is a simple time delay that prevents the compressor from going into its release cycle until a certain time has elapsed after the input signal has fallen below the threshold. If the hold time is set longer than the lowest audio frequency likely to be encountered, the compressor will never be able to release quickly enough to distort individual cycles. A hold time of around 50ms should cover all eventualities, and some manufacturers build a fixed, preset hold time of this value into their compressors in order to make them undistortable, in effect. Such a short hold time is unlikely to restrict the flexibility of the compressor in any way.

Distortion may also be introduced by the gain-control circuitry itself, especially in older, valve-based designs, and in many cases this can sound musically interesting. However, this form of benign distortion shouldn't be confused with waveform-shape distortion (produced by using attack and release times that are too fast, as described earlier), as this kind of distortion generally sounds quite unpleasant.

De-essing

A typical compressor reacts equally to all input signals, whether they're bass sounds or high-pitched instruments. For routine gain-reduction applications, this is exactly what's required, but sometimes it's desirable to have the compressor react more strongly to some frequencies than to others. The prime example is in de-essing, where it's necessary to remove or reduce the sibilant content of a vocal signal. Sibilance is caused by breath passing around the lips and teeth of the singer and manifests itself as a very high-pitched whistle, which can be distracting and is further exacerbated by high-frequency EQ, heavy compression or digital reverberation. This can be ameliorated in the following manner:

- If an equaliser is inserted into the side-chain signal path of a compressor, the equaliser can be used to determine which section of the audio spectrum is compressed the most.

- Sibilance normally occurs in the 5–10kHz region of the audio spectrum, so if the equaliser is tuned to the offending frequency and set to give, say 10dB of boost, compression will occur at this frequency at a level 10dB lower than that applied to the rest of the audio spectrum.

- Both graphic and parametric equalisers can be used in this application, the parametric providing more control. The equaliser can be set up by listening to the equaliser output and then tuning the frequency control until the sibilant part of the input signal is most pronounced.

- By carefully setting the threshold and ratio controls, the sibilant sounds can be pushed down in level quite dramatically without significantly affecting the wanted sounds. However, if the amount of processing is too high, there will be a noticeable drop in gain whenever a sibilant sound occurs, and this can be almost as annoying as the sibilance itself. Figure 12.4 shows how a conventional compressor may be used as a de-esser.

Dedicated De-essers

A better approach is to use one of the more sophisticated, dedicated de-essers. Using a compressor as above results in the gain of the whole signal being reduced whenever a sibilant sound occurs, and when heavy de-essing is being applied to a vocal a very obvious lisping effect can be created. Ideally, only the level of those frequencies that make up sibilance should be reduced. Some of the more refined, dedicated de-essers do just this by using either a *shelf* or *notch filter* to reduce the gain in the 5–10kHz region whenever a sibilant sound is detected. This allows more processing to be applied without any undesirable side-effects becoming noticeable, and as a rule, the narrower the band of frequencies affected, the less noticeable the side-effects. However,

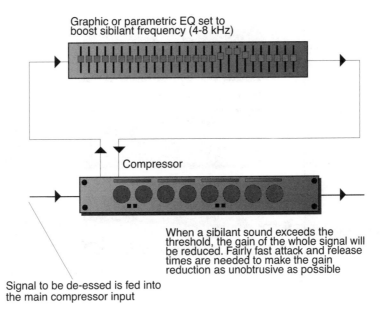

Graphic or parametric EQ set to
boost sibilant frequency (4-8 kHz)

Compressor

When a sibilant sound exceeds the
threshold, the gain of the whole signal will
be reduced. Fairly fast attack and release
times are needed to make the gain
reduction as unobtrusive as possible

Signal to be de-essed is fed into
the main compressor input

Figure 12.4: De-essing with a compressor

prevention is much better than cure, and if possible you should use a different microphone or change the microphone position in order to reduce the sibilance at source.

Multiband Compression

In some situations, the side-effect of full-band compression may be unacceptable, which is why multiband compressors are very often used when it comes to mix compression and mastering. A multiband compressor comprises a set of filters, similar to a PA system's active crossover, that splits the audio signal into two or more (usually three) frequency bands. After having passed through the filters, each band of frequencies is fed into its own compressor, after which the signals are recombined, as shown in Figure 12.5 over the page. By treating the frequency bands separately, a loud event in one band won't trigger gain reduction in the other bands, so when a loud kick-drum beat comes along, only the low-frequency sounds will be compressed, leaving the mid range and high frequencies unaffected. The same is true of a loud peak in any of the other bands – only the relevant band is subjected to gain reduction. Any

change in tonality caused by heavy compression in one or more bands can usually be restored by adjusting the levels of the three compressor bands relative to each other.

Conventional compressors designed for stereo use generally feature two audio channels as well as a *stereo link switch*. The link switch sums the two side-chain signals and then uses this signal to control both compressor channels so that the same amount of gain reduction is always applied to both channels. Without this, there could be audible image shift on signals that were significantly louder on one channel than another. A multiband compressor works in a similar way, except that each band has its own side chain, so a three-band stereo compressor would have three stereo-linked sections to control high frequencies, mid frequencies and low frequencies.

Crossover Frequencies

Multiband compressors generally allow the user to adjust the crossover points, but where is the best place to set them? Setting a crossover point in the middle of the vocal range can compromise the sound, so it's safest to set the low crossover point below the main

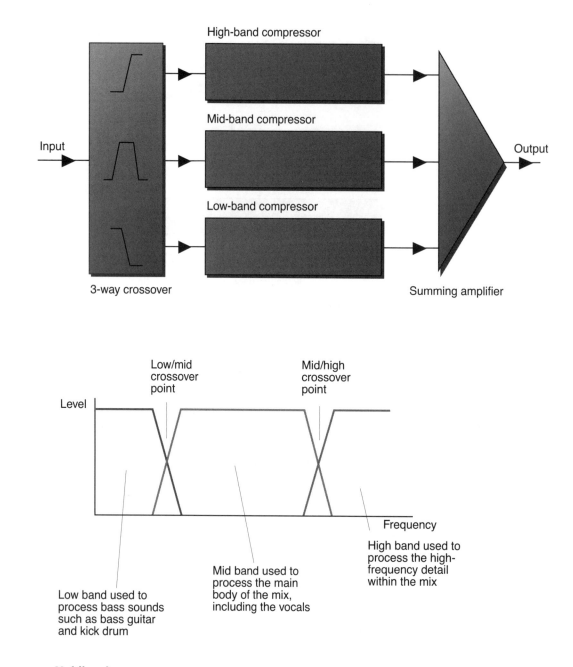

Figure 12.5: Multiband compressor

vocal frequency range and set the high crossover point above it – at 120Hz and 4kHz respectively, say. This puts the low crossover point above most of the bass elements in a typical mix, and by placing the high crossover point at 4kHz you'll retain plenty of control over the high end of the spectrum with impinging too much on the important mid range.

Settings

Very often, compressors are used to control only those signals that are too loud, in which case first the threshold is set, then a compression ratio is applied so that gain reduction is applied to anything exceeding the threshold level. If you need to tame peaks or other occasional excesses, this is the conventional way of using a compressor, whether it's a full-band or multiband model.

Another approach, which I often use when mastering, is to set the threshold fairly low and also to use a low ratio, typically less than 1.2:1, with a threshold of −20dB to −40dB. Then, instead of applying a lot of compression only to peaks, apply a little compression to all but the quietest sound. This adds density and energy to a mix and helps to integrate the different elements, although it won't help much with unexpected peaks. This method of compression is therefore best applied to material that's already mixed and at a reasonably consistent level.

With this technique, you also have the luxury of being able to use different compressor settings in the three bands, so if you're working on a track that seems to be bass-light, using a higher ratio in the low band and then restoring the balance using the band-gain control can work wonders. Similarly, by applying heavier compression to the high band, it's possible to create an effect similar to that produced by an enhancer. As a rule, it's best to process the mid band by the least amount, partly to help create a sense of loudness and partly because the mid range is the most vulnerable part of the audio spectrum and so must be treated gently.

As a starting point for the attack and release settings, try using double the release time on the bass band as you do for the mid band and half as much as the value for the mid band in the high band. As a rule, the mid-band settings should be similar to those that you'd use on a full-band compressor – ie, slow the attack time further if you want to enhance transients and use the shortest release time you can without causing gain pumping.

What applies to complete mixes also applies to subgroups where two or more instruments are mixed, so multiband compression may still offer advantages, especially where high- and low-frequency sounds are mixed together and you need gain control without obvious compression.

Different instruments may require different crossover frequency settings – a bass guitar or bass synth might benefit from a low crossover point set to around 50Hz or 60Hz and an upper crossover point of just a few hundred hertz. Much depends on where the bulk of the sound energy for a particular instrument resides. As there's very little bass-guitar energy above 2kHz, setting a 6kHz upper crossover frequency, for example, would make little sense.

Synthesisers also benefit from multiband compression where the sound is based around a resonant filter sweep. If you apply full-band compression here, the whole sound is reduced in level – sometimes dramatically – regardless of the filter frequency. In contrast, multiband compression keeps the filter's resonant peak under control but without changing the level in the unaffected frequency bands.

13 GATES AND EXPANDERS

As far as I'm aware, gates were first devised to solve a problem in the film industry, where dialogue was often recorded under less-than-ideal conditions due to the need to keep the microphone out of shot. Their purpose is to shut down the signal path when the signal falls below a threshold set by the user. Normally, this threshold will be set just above the ambient noise floor. When the gate is open, both the wanted signal and the unwanted noise pass through, the noise (hopefully) being masked by the signal. During pauses in the wanted signal, the gate closes and, in doing so, shuts off the background noise, which would otherwise be clearly audible in the absence of any signal large enough to mask it.

Gates have undergone a process of refinement since their invention, and modern models can be quite sophisticated. Like the compressor, they have attack and release controls that determine how quickly they respond, enabling them to be used to process most types of sound without undue difficulty. The fastest attack settings are used to allow percussive or highly transient sounds to pass through cleanly, while slower attack settings enable the gate to open more smoothly when processing signals that themselves have longer attack times, such as bowed strings.

The variable release time of a gate is also vital in that it enables the gate to close gradually when sounds with a slow decay are being processed. Examples of such sounds are plucked strings, some synthesised sounds, and sounds that have a long reverberant 'tail'. As with the compressor, problems can arise if the fastest attack and release times are set, as this means that the gate triggers on each individual cycle of the input, producing a badly distorted, gritty sound. The solution is the same as that for the compressor – many gates have a hold feature or a built-in hold time. In the absence of hold time (where the gate is forced to remain open for a short time after the signal falls back below the threshold), it's necessary to extend the release time until the problem disappears. The envelope structure of a typical gate is shown in Figure 13.1.

The hold facility may also be used in a creative way to produce hard 'gated' reverb or ambience sounds. If the reverberant sound is fed into the gate and then triggered externally using a mic located close to the drum, the gate can be used to impose an envelope on the reverberant sound. A fast release time combined with half a second or so of hold time produces the familiar gated drum sound when used to treat percussion.

Today, gates are available as hardware units, software plug-ins and also as part of the processing capability of most digital mixing consoles. As a rule, gates are really effective against noise only when used on individual tracks rather than complete mixes, although their creative uses shouldn't be underestimated.

Side-Chain Filters

A common feature on many gates is *side-chain filtering*. This usually takes the form of a pair of shelving equalisers, one high-pass and one low-pass, connected in series with the side-chain circuitry. By varying the filter settings, it's possible to make the gate respond only to a selected band of frequencies, which helps avoid false triggering in situations where spill from other instruments is present. An example of a situation in which filters can be helpful is when miking a drum kit, where sounds from all of the drums spill into all

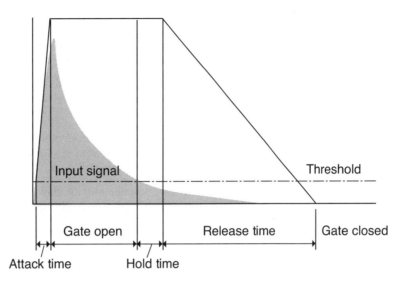

Figure 13.1: A typical gate envelope

of the mics to a greater or lesser degree. By making the gate frequency selective, it's possible to reduce the risk of, say, the hi-hat triggering the snare gate.

By setting the filters to minimise the amount of hi-hat spill fed to the side chain while at the same time maximising the amount of snare signal, a greater degree of separation can be obtained. This can only be achieved by listening to the filter output while adjusting the controls when 'Key Listen' is selected during setting up. It's important to realise that the filters are only connected in series with the side-chain signal path and so don't affect the sound of the main input in any way. The only exception to this rule is when the filters are deliberately used as an equaliser by leaving the gate set to the Key Listen mode.

Gating While Mixing

Gates are very important in multitrack recording, even when the recordings appear to be relatively free of noise. In a multitrack situation, the noise from all of the tracks is cumulative, so if a track can be gated into silence when nothing is playing, the finished mix can be made considerably cleaner. For example, the vocalist won't be singing during instrumental breaks and solos, so it makes sense to gate the vocal track in order to mute any tape noise from that track, as well as breath noise and any spill from the headphones that might otherwise be audible during pauses in the singing.

It's also desirable to gate electric guitars, as they have a relatively poor noise performance, especially when used for overdriven or heavily distorted lead-guitar sounds. Using a gate will remove the hum, hiss and buzz generated by a guitar amplifier and can significantly improve the clarity of the final recording.

Gating is best carried out after the signal has been recorded rather than during recording, for the obvious reason that an incorrectly set gate at the recording stage can ruin a take beyond any hope of salvage. Nevertheless, sometimes it's necessary to gate while recording – for example, in situations where several signals have to be mixed onto one tape track and only one of these is to be gated. In this instance, it's wise to set the gate attenuation control to give only as much attenuation as is really necessary and to err on the side of caution when setting the threshold. It's better to put up with a little unwanted spill than to have a signal with vital sections cut out of it by an over-zealous gate!

Gate plug-ins are useful for cleaning up audio tracks recorded into a sequencer or other multitrack software program, as no permanent change needs to be made to the audio file. Once the gate settings have been optimised, the processed track may be bounced to a new track in order to make the changes permanent, but still without discarding the original version, enabling you to go back to it later if required. Where gate plug-ins have a side-chain access facility to permit chopping or ducking effects to be created, these are normally fed from a designated audio track rather than from a live input.

Alternative Filter Applications

The side-chain filters used in gates necessarily have a very sharp response curve – usually 12dB per octave. This makes them far more selective than most conventional equalisers, and in some circumstances the filters in a spare gate can be used to supplement the basic desk EQ. To do this, it's necessary only to leave the gate switched to Side-Chain Listen; the gate will be bypassed and the filters placed in line with the signal path.

The low-pass filter can work wonders in removing high-frequency noise from an electric-guitar track without significantly changing the character of the basic guitar sound, while the high-pass filter can be used to remove low-frequency hums and rumbles as well as to 'thin out' rhythm-guitar or backing-vocal parts. In very desperate circumstances, the low-pass filter can even be used to reduce the effects of overload distortion on recordings of rhythm guitar and other dynamic sounds, where a little too much enthusiasm on the part of the player can drive the tape machine or mixing console into clipping. When working with plug-ins in a software environment, a shelving-filter plug-in can be used for this purpose.

External Control

Gates can be triggered externally via their side-chain access points, allowing the level of one signal to be controlled by another. An 'External' switch is usually provided to enable the side-chain input, although some models may simply be fitted with a side-chain-access jack wired in the same way as a console insert point. Used normally, this facility enables the signal routed through the gate to be turned on and off by the signal fed into the side chain. This is commonly known as

chopping because, if fast attack and release times are set, extremely abrupt, rhythmic effects can be created. Where the triggering source is very short (as it would be if a beat from a drum machine was used), the 'on' duration of the gate must be set using the Hold Time control. Here are some practical examples:

- A sustained sound fed through the gate could be turned on and off by a drum beat fed into the side-chain input. The rate at which it turns on and off depends on the attack and release settings, but it does provide a novel way of synchronising a sustained sound with a percussive one. Figure 13.2 shows how this might be set up. This technique is often used to beef up kick-drum sounds by adding a gated, low-frequency synthetic sound and works well in the context of dance music. In this instance, the gate would need a fast attack but a slightly longer release time to create the impression of a decaying drum sound.

- Synthesiser chords can be gated from a rhythm pattern to create a synchronised arpeggio effect.

- Bass-synth or bass-guitar sounds can be gated so that they're audible only when a kick drum is present. A popular trick is to use the kick-drum track to trigger the gate while passing the bass-guitar track through the gate. The Attenuation Range control may then be set to reduce or even remove any bass-guitar notes not falling directly on top of kick-drum beats, which can help to tighten up an otherwise sloppy track. The gate Release Time control is set to allow the bass-guitar notes to decay at an appropriate rate.

Gate Ducking

If the gate has a Duck facility, it can be used as a ducker in a similar way to a compressor. The Attenuation control of the gate can be used to determine exactly how much the signal level drops once the side-chain input signal (a voice, for example) exceeds the threshold, and as this control is calibrated directly in decibels, it's much easier to set up a precise ducking effect using one of these gates than it is using a

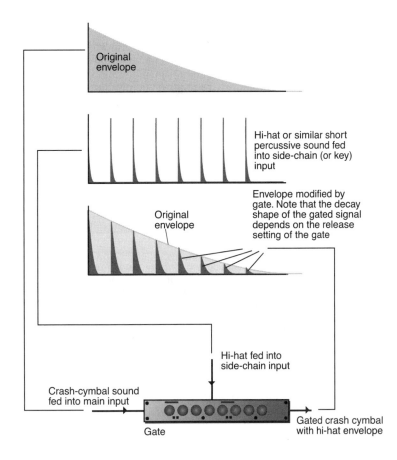

Figure 13.2: Gating a slowly decaying sound with a percussive sound

compressor. Again, the gate's attack and release times determine how fast the ducked signal will fade out and in again in response to the side-chain input.

Gate Panning

The side-chain access facility of a gate also means it can be used to produce a limited range of panning effects, which can be useful in a hardware recording environment as relatively few sophisticated panners are available. In a software environment, dedicated panners are usually available with Tempo Sync facilities, so it may not be necessary to use a gate to achieve the effect, but it's still worth knowing how to do it.

• If the signal to be panned is fed into both channels of a two-channel gate, the side-chain inputs could

alternately be fed with percussive sounds from a drum machine (synchronised to the track) to act as timing triggers.

• By setting the attack and release times of the gate to fairly long values and panning the two outputs hard left and right in the mix, the signal will appear to move back and forth between the speakers as first one channel is triggered and then the other. Figure 13.3 over the page shows how this is done.

• If the gate has a ducking function, the process is simplified further: one channel is set to gate, the other to duck, and the two channels are linked for stereo operation. Feeding a single pulse or drum sound into one side-chain input will cause the signal to pan and then return.

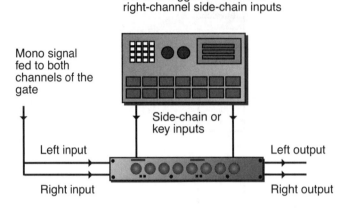

Drum machine feeding alternate beats to trigger the left- and right-channel side-chain inputs

Mono signal fed to both channels of the gate

Side-chain or key inputs

Left input

Left output

Right input

Right output

By setting a long attack and long release time, the signal can be made to pan from one gate output to the other. The exact settings will need to be adjusted to suit the tempo of the trigger inputs. Note: on a gate with a dedicated ducking facility, panning may be achieved simply by setting one channel of the gate to duck and the other to normal gate operation. In this case, the gate should be set for stereo operation and only a single trigger input will be required

Figure 13.3: Panning with a gate

- If the tempo of the drum machine is synchronised to that of the music by means of a tape time code track or something similar, the pan timing will remain accurately synchronised to the tempo of the music. Furthermore, the pan triggers don't have to be evenly spaced but can follow a suitable rhythm, allowing more complex effects to be created. Given the extent to which this technique is used in dance-music production, it's surprising that more time-clocked rhythmic effects haven't been produced.

- This basic triggered-pan set-up can be further modified to produce a rough approximation of a rotary-speaker simulation simply by feeding the two gate outputs into two equalisers, each set to give a noticeably different sound, as shown in Figure 13.4.

Expanders

Although they perform a similar task to gates, expanders are easier to understand if you think of them as compressors in reverse. Compressors reduce the gain of a signal once it exceeds a predetermined threshold whereas expanders apply gain reduction to signals that fall below the threshold. Whereas a gate will close completely when the signal falls below its threshold, the expander reduces the gain of signals that fall below the threshold by a user-definable ratio, in just the same manner as the compressor. For example, if the expansion ratio is set to 1:2, for every 1dB the signal falls below the threshold, the output will fall by 2dB. This produces a more progressive and more subtle muting effect than can be achieved by using gates but, because the action of a gate is smoothed considerably by its Attack and Release controls, both gates and expanders behave in a very similar way, subjectively, when used to clean up sounds. The smaller the expansion ratio, the more subtle the gain-reduction effect, while a high expansion ratio will make the expander behave in exactly the same way as a gate. Expanders are often incorporated into compressor designs because they are less critical to set up than gates and yet still provide a worthwhile reduction in noise during pauses in the signal.

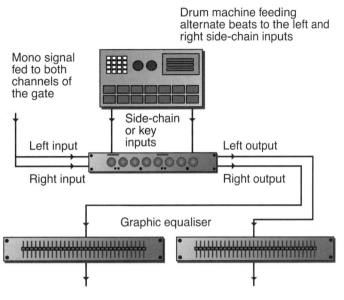

Drum machine feeding
alternate beats to the left and
right side-chain inputs

Mono signal
fed to both
channels of
the gate

Side-chain
or key
inputs

Left input

Right input

Left output

Right output

Graphic equaliser

Use different EQ settings on each side
to create a Leslie speaker type of effect

Figure 13.4: Rotary-speaker simulation using panned EQ

Summary

Gates in all their forms are useful to keep pauses silent in individual tracks but are of little use on mixed material as in this case there are unlikely to be many true pauses for the gate to work on. With modern 24-bit recording systems, noise in the recording chain is no longer a problem, but source noise is a different matter, especially with instruments like electric guitars, which have pretty poor signal-to-noise performance when used with overdrive.

The creative use of gates to modulate the envelope of one signal under the control of another is an area of control that's well worth exploring and, with a little ingenuity, it's possible to set up some very sophisticated-sounding rhythms using very simple source material.

14 MINIMUM SIGNAL PATHS AND DIRECT INJECTION

In the studio, we rely on the mixing desk and patchbay to such a extent that we often forget about alternative methods of routing signals to the recorder. In this era of high quality digital or analogue/Dolby S recording, engineers are becoming more quality conscious and in some circumstances passing an electrical signal through an entire mixing console just to get it onto a recorder track isn't the best way to do the job. No matter how well the mixer is designed, some signal degradation must take place, and the more circuitry the signal has to pass through, the worse the degradation will be. Take the example of a single microphone signal that needs to be amplified and then routed to a single track on the recorder: sending it through the console might be the easiest method, but think about all the circuitry, switches and controls in a typical mixer channel and then add that to the routing switches and the group-output electronics. It's hardly surprising that the signal suffers.

Mic Pre-amps

A more purist approach to recording vocals is to use a separate, high quality microphone pre-amplifier plugged directly into the recorder. This is known as the *minimum-signal-path approach*, and the more discerning engineer may choose to record important parts such as lead vocals in exactly this way. If the vocal needs compressing on the way to the recorder, a compressor may be patched between the mic amp and the recorder or a compressor with a built-in mic amp (sometimes called a *voice channel*) may be used instead. Aside from avoiding unnecessary circuitry in the mixer itself, it's possible to bypass the patchbay, too, by plugging directly into the back of the recording machine. Although

patchbays contain no active circuitry, contact corrosion and dirt can add considerably to the noise and distortion present in a signal passing through the patchbay. Figure 14.1 shows a practical approach to recording vocals without going via the mixing console.

Where the recording system is based around a computer sequencer with audio capability, voice channels provide an ideal means of getting signals into the system and, in situations where tracks are recorded one or two at a time, this is also a cost-effective strategy. Where a high quality digital output option is available for the pre-amp, this will prevent the audio quality from being compromised by a less well-specified audio interface or soundcard. When used in this way, the sequencer must be set to External Digital Sync so that the pre-amp becomes the clock master. The only exceptions to this rule are when using a recording system that features sample-rate conversion at the input or where all of the equipment in the studio is clocked from a single digital clock source (Word Clock). Most audio-recording software is capable of mixing and adding effects, so a mixer may not be necessary at all unless there is a need to add the output from the computer's audio interface to the outputs of external MIDI synthesisers and samplers.

DI Boxes

Line-level signals can also be recorded directly preferably via a DI box, which will match the impedance of the source to that of the recorder input and may also offer some form of level control, allowing the recording level to be optimised. Line-level signals include the outputs from guitar pre-amps and speaker simulators as well as active guitars, basses and some

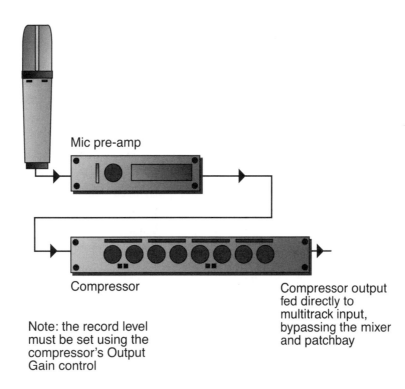

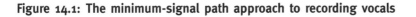

Mic pre-amp

Compressor

Compressor output fed directly to multitrack input, bypassing the mixer and patchbay

Note: the record level must be set using the compressor's Output Gain control

Figure 14.1: The minimum-signal path approach to recording vocals

electronic instruments. Passive guitars have high-impedance pick-ups, which in theory means that an active DI box will give the best matching. Even so, a good passive (transformer) DI box can give surprisingly good results and may produce a more natural sound than an active model. The lower input impedance may also reduce the effect of interference on the signal, giving a cleaner result.

Guitar-speaker simulators and pre-amps designed specifically for direct recording have now reached a high level of sophistication. Whereas a few years ago few people would have dreamt of using anything other than a mic to record a guitar, the direct approach is currently very popular, even on serious guitar-album projects. The advantages of this way of working are immediately obvious – the sound heard by the performer over the monitors is the same sound that's going into the recorder and, perhaps more importantly, there is complete isolation between the guitar and any other instrument being recorded at the same time. Problems of acoustic spill are therefore completely

eliminated, making the guitar as easy to record as the keyboard synth.

Rhythm Guitar

Clean rhythm sounds can be recorded directly using a simple DI box, although some EQ is usually necessary to simulate the way in which guitar amplifiers are voiced, and compression will help to even out the sound. However, be aware of the following:

• A significant amount of upper-mid boost is often needed to emulate the voicing of a guitar amplifier and, if this may be achieved by using something like an upper-mid sweep equaliser tuned to between 3kHz and 6kHz, the necessary brightness can be produced with a smaller noise penalty than would be the case if high-shelving EQ was used.

• It can be advantageous to over-boost the upper mid and then back off the high-frequency shelving control a little to compensate. This will result in a reduction in high-frequency noise without dulling the guitar sound unduly.

- A popular approach to recording rhythm guitar is to feed the guitar into a suitable compressor, via a DI box, and then directly into the recorder. A suitable compressor is really any model that sounds good, although valve compressors or those using photo-electric gain elements (ie optical compressors) are often chosen for the warm, smooth sound that they produce. In general, if a compressor sounds good on vocals, it should work well with guitars.

While the above DI methods will produce a usable clean sound, they won't simulate the on-the-edge distortion that you get from a good tube amplifier, so if you need more of an amp sound than a clinical clean sound, a digital-modelling guitar pre-amplifier is probably the best approach, short of actually miking the amp.

Overdriven Guitar

The direct recording of overdriven guitar is less straightforward, and if an overdrive pedal is patched directly into a recorder, the result will be quite unlike that produced by miking an amplifier. The reason for this is mainly to do with the way in which a guitar speaker and its enclosure modify the electric guitar's sound, effectively acting as a high-cut filter. Guitar speakers generally use a large driver with no separate mid-range units or tweeters, which gives them severely restricted frequency responses. Indeed, if full-range speakers were used, the overdrive sound would be most raspy and unpleasant. The cabinet design also affects the way in which the speaker behaves, and an analysis of the speaker and cabinet combination reveals a complex low-pass filter response. If this is emulated using electronic filters, it's possible to take the output from an overdriven guitar pre-amp or pedal, process it via the filter and record it directly.

The sound produced by using a speaker simulator can be surprisingly close to that produced by a close-miked amplifier, but it isn't exactly the same. That's because most 'speaker simulator' units fail to duplicate the complex distortions that occur when a loudspeaker is overdriven and, apart from those built into digital modelling pre-amps, their design also often fails to take into account the characteristics or positioning of the microphone normally used to record the guitar amp. Even so, a little extra work with EQ and a little added artificial reverb or ambience at the mixing stage can make the differences very small. Indeed, over the past decade, the popular rock-guitar sound has changed significantly, making it more difficult to judge the authenticity of any electronic simulation. Speaker-simulator circuitry is becoming more common in guitar pre-amps and guitar multi-effects units, although the results that can be achieved vary from model to model.

Power Soak

The other popular form of speaker simulator is, in effect, a combined filter and power soak, which is used to replace the speaker in a conventional guitar amplifier. Supplied as add-on boxes, these are available in both active and passive versions and produce either a line-level or a mic-level output from amplifiers rated up to 100W or so. Some have virtually no controls while others may have voicing switches and equalisation, enabling them to simulate many different types of guitar-speaker system. Used with a good valve amplifier, these models produce what many feel is a more authentic basic tone than solid-state pre-amps and effects units, although any effects must be added separately.

The line-output type of speaker simulator may be connected directly to a recorder, but the type with a mic-level output needs to be recorded via a separate mic pre-amp or via the mic input of the mixing console. It can be argued that an overdriven guitar sound is so noisy and distorted that there's little to be gained in bypassing the mixer completely, but ultimately the decision must be taken by the individual engineer. It's certainly worth making a test recording, both direct and via the desk, to determine how significant the difference really is – you may be very surprised. It's common practice to use a compressor after the speaker simulator, and Figure 14.2 shows how a speaker simulator could be connected. (Note that, in the case of speaker simulators that don't include a dummy load,

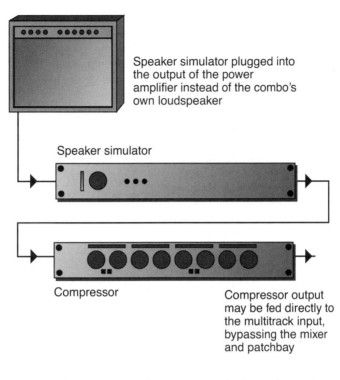

Speaker simulator plugged into the output of the power amplifier instead of the combo's own loudspeaker

Speaker simulator

Compressor

Compressor output may be fed directly to the multitrack input, bypassing the mixer and patchbay

Note: although the use of a compressor isn't mandatory, its inclusion generally produces a more appealing sound by creating a more even tone and enhancing the natural sustain of the guitar

Figure 14.2: Using a speaker simulator

the original speaker must be left connected to prevent the amplifier running into an open circuitry, which could damage it.)

Active Guitars

Active guitars and basses may be plugged directly into the mixing console without any impedance-matching problems, but some form of speaker simulation is still necessary when working with overdriven guitar sounds and basses generally need to be compressed. In my own experience, active guitars tend to be noisier than guitars with passive pick-ups. Given that modelled digital-recording pre-amps are available relatively cheaply for both guitar and bass, it's probably most expedient to use one of these, unless you specifically need an effect that doesn't sound like a miked amplifier.

Keyboards

Keyboard instruments, samplers, drum machines and synth modules can be recorded directly, but most have relatively low output levels, ranging from −20 to −10dBv. This means that it may be possible to plug them directly into a semi-pro machine operating at −10dBv, but the vast majority will have insufficient output to produce a healthy recording level when used with professional tape machines or other recording hardware. Furthermore, some instruments – especially drum machines with multiple outputs – have no proper output-level controls.

Again, the answer is to use an active DI box, which will improve the impedance matching and provide the additional gain needed. As with the electric guitar, it's up to the individual to decide whether it's worth going to the trouble of recording directly or whether recording via the mixer is adequate. The majority of synthesisers still have a disappointing audio specification, and it is arguable whether the trip through a mixing console would make the situation significantly worse. However, as more recordings are now being made with all of the MIDI sound sources played live into the mix from a suitably synchronised sequencer, this question may never arise. In fact, the only keyboard system that must be miked rather than DI'd is the Leslie cabinet, where it's common to use separate mics on the horns and on the bass rotor, although if possible you should use a stereo-mic arrangement on the rotary horns.

Mixer Noise

Even if recordings are made through an analogue mixing console, there are ways to ensure that the signal remains as clean as possible. For example, if the mixer has direct channel outputs or even insert points, a signal could be taken directly from the mixer channel and routed to the recorder, thus bypassing the routing switches, the pan control and the group outputs. Of course, this is only viable when one channel is being recorded to one track; if two or more channels have to be mixed together, there is little choice but to use the desk's normal routing system.

Having said that, there are steps that can be taken to minimise the amount of noise added to the signal on its way to the recorder. Most consoles have an EQ Bypass button, and if no EQ is being added at the recording stage, switching the EQ out of circuit will shorten the signal path slightly.

Muting And Routing

Most people instinctively mute any mixer channels that aren't being routed, and nearly all will set the faders at zero, but this – perhaps surprisingly – doesn't entirely prevent the channel from contributing noise to the mix. Instead, you should ensure that any unused channels are not only muted but also that they aren't routed to any of the group outputs – in other words, ensure that all of their routing buttons are up. Even if unused channels are muted and all of the gain controls are turned down, they will still contribute noise by virtue of their output impedance being connected to the buss via their routing switches.

This is more important when you come to mix, as any unused channel with its left/right routing button down will be contributing a small amount of unnecessary noise to the final mix. To prove this for yourself, route all of your mixer channels to the main stereo output and turn all of the channel faders right down. If you have Channel Mute buttons, set these to their Mute positions and turn up the Monitor Level control until you can hear the console hiss through the monitors. Without changing anything else, go along the console switching the left/right routing buttons up and you'll be surprised by the drop in hiss. The more channels you have on your desk, the greater will be the benefit of careful routing.

Monitor Section

The other danger area is the monitor section of a traditional analogue multitrack desk, which on some models is routed directly to the left/right buss with no means of disconnecting unused channels. On some consoles, the monitor mutes actually disconnect the monitor channels from the mix buss, but on others, especially budget desks with MIDI muting, they mute the signal but leave the monitor routed. Unfortunately, there's not much you can do about this, other than be aware of the problem. Repeating the previous noise test using the monitor Mute buttons will tell you whether they are simply mutes or whether they do switch the monitors off on the mix buss. If the noise goes down as you mute the monitors, you're in luck – the mute switches are really routing buttons.

The same rules apply to auxiliary sends, and many an innocent effects unit has been blamed for being noisy when in fact the mixer has been to blame. Few mixing desks offer the facility to switch individual aux sends off their respective aux busses when they're not being used, but there are several mixers that allow their aux sends to be routed to a choice of aux send busses. This is particularly common in the mid-price market, where a console may have eight aux busses but only four aux send controls that can be switched between them.

Unless all of the aux send busses are in use, one useful trick is to route any unused sends to unused effects busses. For example, if you can route aux 1 and 2 as a pair to either aux busses 1/2 or 3/4, you could designate aux busses 3/4 as being unused and route any unused sends there. This obviously restricts the number of available aux sends, but there are many occasions when a specific effect is required on only one mixer channel, in which case the effects unit can be fed from the direct channel output or insert send point. There's no reason why an effect shouldn't be patched in via the channel insert point, but as most modern effects have stereo outputs, some other method must generally be sought if the effect is to be kept in stereo.

Direct Outputs

Using a channel's direct output as an effects send has the advantage that the send level will be controlled by the channel fader, but unless significant gain changes are planned during the mix, it's possible to get away with using the insert send. Indeed, if the effects returns

can be arranged to come up on an adjacent channel, it should be possible to move the faders together, thus getting around the problem of using the insert send point. Figure 14.3 shows how this is set up.

A more elegant solution is to use the insert send or direct output from the channel carrying the signal to feed the mono input of the effects unit, as before, but this time the channel is not routed to the mix. Its only purpose is to provide an input feed to the effects unit. This arrangement can be connected as follows:

• The two effect outputs are connected to the inputs of two spare channels or to a spare stereo return.

• The effect/dry balance can then be set using the Mix control on the effects unit and the two channels panned left and right to create a stereo effect.

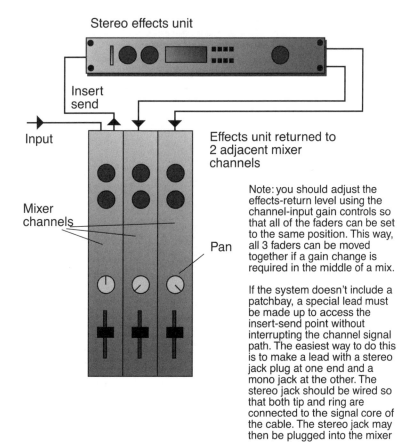

Stereo effects unit

Insert send

Input

Mixer channels

Pan

Effects unit returned to 2 adjacent mixer channels

Note: you should adjust the effects-return level using the channel-input gain controls so that all of the faders can be set to the same position. This way, all 3 faders can be moved together if a gain change is required in the middle of a mix.

If the system doesn't include a patchbay, a special lead must be made up to access the insert-send point without interrupting the channel signal path. The easiest way to do this is to make a lead with a stereo jack plug at one end and a mono jack at the other. The stereo jack should be wired so that both tip and ring are connected to the signal core of the cable. The stereo jack may then be plugged into the mixer insert point

Figure 14.3: Using the insert point as an effects send

• With most effects units, using the mono input will position the dry portion of the sound in the centre of the mix with the stereo effects outputs panned left and right.

This variation is shown in Figure 14.4, the only real restriction being that the dry portion of the sound will always be panned to the centre of the mix, as it appears at an equal level in both left and right channels.

Gain Structure

Finally, all of this effort will go to waste if the gain structure of the mixer isn't set up properly, as below:

• The channel input trims should be set up using the meters in conjunction with the PFL or Solo buttons.

• The mix should be arranged so that the average fader position is around the three-quarters-full position.

• The aux send controls should be set so that the highest one is almost full up. Use the aux send master control or the input-gain control on the effects unit to get the right signal going into the effects processor.

• Don't forget to optimise the level trim on any channels being used to carry effects returns and to turn down any unused sends.

• Always be suspicious if you have output-level controls (or effects-unit input controls) set at

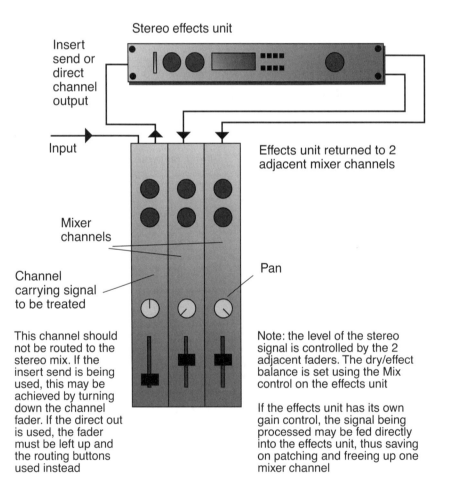

Stereo effects unit

Insert send or direct channel output

Input

Effects unit returned to 2 adjacent mixer channels

Mixer channels

Channel carrying signal to be treated

Pan

This channel should not be routed to the stereo mix. If the insert send is being used, this may be achieved by turning down the channel fader. If the direct out is used, the fader must be left up and the routing buttons used instead

Note: the level of the stereo signal is controlled by the 2 adjacent faders. The dry/effect balance is set using the Mix control on the effects unit

If the effects unit has its own gain control, the signal being processed may be fed directly into the effects unit, thus saving on patching and freeing up one mixer channel

Figure 14.4: Alternate effects patch

minimum. If you use one control to knock the signal level down and the next one in line to build it up again, you're setting up the ideal conditions for unwanted noise. Try to arrange everything so that all gain controls are set in sensible positions.

The measures outlined above may appear unnecessarily complicated, but the few extra moments it takes to set up the console properly will yield a significant difference in signal quality. Eliminating noise at source is infinitely more satisfactory than trying to remove it with gates or dynamic filters at a later stage.

Gain structure must also be observed with digital consoles, particularly at the input stage, where the maximum possible level (without causing clipping) is needed to gain the highest audio resolution and the least noise. Where the internal effects are equipped with on-screen metering, these should be adjusted to receive healthy input levels, just as though they were outboard hardware effects.

15 MIXING

Watching a really skilled engineer at work can be an intimidating experience – the real experts can move along the desk pushing up the faders one at a time, arriving at an almost perfectly balanced mix by the time they reach the end. Somehow they have an instinct for balance, and what they achieve seemingly by magic we have to arrive at by hard work. While technology may have evolved to help out with some aspects of mixing, in particular mix (and plug-in effect) automation, judging balance is still very much a human skill.

It helps before starting the mix to organise logical groups of sounds into *subgroups* so that the mix can be handled with fewer faders. Most recordings have the drums spread over several tape tracks, and life is far easier if these are routed to a pair of adjacent group faders in order to form a stereo subgroup. Similarly, backing vocals can be assigned to subgroups, along with any other sections that seem logical. Most analogue and digital consoles designed for recording can handle subgrouping, the master level control being the group fader (or often a left/right pair of group faders). If you're working with a computer-based system such as Pro Tools, Cubase or Logic Audio, their virtual mixers can also be used to create subgroups, although as methods of doing so vary slightly from program to program you'll need to consult your manual to find the best way of doing this.

A Question Of Balance

If the basic tracks have been recorded properly, it should be possible to set up a reasonable initial balance without resorting to EQ. Effects need not be added right from the outset, but it helps to have the necessary effects units patched in and ready for use, especially some vocal reverb, as this helps provide an impression of how the mix will sound. Switch the EQ to bypass on all channels where it isn't being used, and with an analogue mixer ensure that any unused mixer channels aren't only muted but are also unrouted – in other words, all the routing buttons should be in their up positions. This will prevent the channel from contributing to the mix-buss noise of the console and will help achieve a quieter final mix. All unused aux sends should be set to zero, and the loudest sends should be between three-quarters and full up, which will again help to reduce noise. All console inputs should be trimmed using the PFL metering system (if your console allows trim on mixdown). Likewise, all of the effects units should be checked to make sure they're at the correct input levels. If it's possible to route unused sends to an aux buss that isn't being used, this can reduce mix noise considerably, while any effect intended to process a single channel will produce the best audio quality if connected via the channel-insert point.

Having attended to these basic niceties, my own way of working is to sort out the drum-and-bass balance first, but this shouldn't be refined too much as the apparent balance will change once the rest of the instruments and voices are in the mix. Once the rhythm section is sounding good, the remaining faders can be brought up one at a time until a reasonable overall balance has been achieved. It's only when all of the instruments are in place that you should start to worry about the finer points of EQ and balance, because things sound so different when they're heard in isolation.

Of course, some engineers and producers insist that the only possible way of working is to put all the faders up to start with and then adjust for a balance.

Don't be put off by this, though, because I've spoken to many well-regarded engineers and producers who admit that they don't have this natural gift for balance – they have to work just as hard as the rest of us! After a little practice, you'll discover which approach works best for you.

Stereo Positions

Once a reasonable balance has been achieved, you can start to work on the effects being used and on the stereo positioning of the different sounds. Bass drums, bass guitars and bass synths are invariably panned to the centre to anchor the mix and to spread the load of these high-energy frequencies over both speakers. Similarly, lead vocals are usually positioned centre stage because that's where we expect the vocalist to be.

The position of backing vocals is less rigid, however, and can be split so that some are left and some are right; they can be spread around the centre, or they can all be grouped in one position off-centre. I like to hear different backing vocal lines coming in from different sides, but this decision is purely artistic – there is no absolute right and wrong. If recorded vocals exhibit any sibilance problems, a de-esser should be patched in to deal with it before proceeding.

Once the mix is almost there, it can be very helpful to listen to the balance from an adjacent room with the adjoining door left open. Although I can find no logical explanation for the phenomenon, any slight balance problems really show up when a mix is auditioned in this way, and most engineers and producers who've discovered this way of checking a mix use it regularly. Figure 15.1 shows a typical panning arrangement for a pop song, but other than the general rule of keeping lead vocals and bass sounds in the centre of the mix, there's no reason why you shouldn't experiment with this.

Level Adjustments

A good mix will almost 'fly' itself, but some parts invariably need level corrections throughout the mix. Obvious examples are instrumental solos and changes in effects levels, but even on vocals with heavy compression it may still be necessary to adjust the odd vocal phrase by a decibel or so, using the mixer fader to make it sit properly. If the mix is being conducted manually, responsibility for the various fader adjustments can be devolved amongst the various band members. The level settings should be marked clearly with wax pencil and each person should have a note of the various tape-counter positions at which levels have to be changed. Of course, if an automated mixing system is available, these changes can be handled quite automatically and the mix refined over several passes.

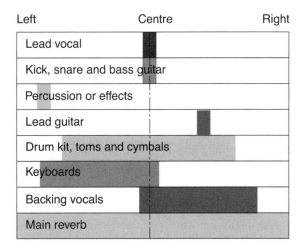

Figure 15.1: A typical stereo-panning scenario

If a track requires a fade-out ending, this may be performed manually or with an autofader, but it's invariably better to leave fades until the mastering stage. Fades are seldom shorter than 15 seconds and may be as long as 30, so it's important to ensure that there's enough recorded material to cover the duration of the fade. If you know in advance that the album is going to be compiled using a hard-disk editing system, you should definitely leave the fades until the final editing stage, where they can be controlled more precisely and will fade into true silence.

I've already covered some of the console settings that affect noise, but it's also important to consider noise that's part of the recorded sound, including breath noise from singers, hum and hiss from guitars and digital background noise from synths, samplers and drum machines. If sequenced MIDI instruments are being used, it's often possible to program level changes via MIDI, but it's vital to be careful, as some instruments put out a more or less constant level of unwanted noise, regardless of the level of the voice currently playing. You should always strive to use these machines as close to their maximum volume setting as is practical, as this will usually give the best signal-to-noise ratio. Likewise, it's possible to mute instruments via the sequencer, but this just stops the sequenced parts from playing and doesn't affect the background noise in any way.

Gates And Mutes

Gates or expanders are very effective in cleaning up electronic instruments, although care must be taken to match the release time of the gate to the sound being processed. In some cases, it may be possible to use a pair of gates over a stereo subgroup, offering the advantage that fewer gates are needed. It must be remembered, though, that gates can only keep the noise down during pauses and can do nothing when a signal is present.

Perhaps the most dramatic effect of automated muting or gating can be noticed right at the beginning of the song, where perfect silence reigns until the first note is played. It shouldn't be necessary to mute every short silence, but it's a good idea to mute the vocal track during instrumental solos or bridge sections and to mute the lead-guitar track both before and after the solo. Again, though, if the mix is going to be mastered, silencing any unwanted sound prior to the start of the song is a simple matter at the editing stage, so you needn't worry about cleaning it up at the mixing stage. Indeed, many of the de-noising programs used in mastering work learn a short section of noise, usually taken from immediately before the track start, so if you clean this up, the mastering engineer will have no way to take the necessary noise 'fingerprint'.

Automated console muting can be very useful for dealing with source noise, and although it may take a little time to set up, the results are usually well worth the trouble. It's necessary to go through each tape track and set up the mute points individually, but once they're right, they'll be right every time you run the mix. If you can arrange muting and unmuting to occur immediately before and after beats, it may help to disguise any discontinuity or change in noise level.

The mutes on most automated desks are very quiet in operation, but I know that on some older models there is an audible click if many mutes are switched at the same time. If this is the case, it should be possible to work around the problem by using the mutes on the subgroups or master-output faders rather than attempting to switch on all of the channels at once.

Mix Automation

At one time, automated consoles were hugely expensive and found only in top studios, but today virtually all digital mixers and computer sequencers with audio capability include the ability to dynamically automate mixes.

Automation first appeared on analogue consoles, the two main systems being either motorised faders or VCAs (Voltage-Controlled Amplifiers) controlled by standard manual faders. In the VCA system, no audio passes through the faders – the VCAs control a DC voltage that is read by the automation computer to determine the fader position. In contrast, most moving fader systems route the audio signal through the faders, as with a manual analogue mixer.

VCA systems originally had the advantage of being

cost-effective (early motorised faders were very costly) and of avoiding the crackle produced by dirty faders, but the main disadvantage of these models is that, as the faders don't move while the mix is playing back, you have no visual feedback of the actual levels, unless you use a system to which a computer monitor screen can be connected.

A typical VCA system connected to a monitor will show both the physical positions of the faders and the virtual fader levels corresponding to the VCA gain setting, which may well be different. Where edits need to be made to the mix data, the screen may be used to match up the actual fader levels to their virtual values, although on systems with no monitor facilities a system of LEDs is often used to tell the user which way to move the fader in order to match the VCA level.

Early VCAs also compromised the sound and the headroom of the console to some extent, although modern VCAs can be almost as good as a fader-operated system, with the added benefit that they don't go scratchy with age or dust.

Moving-fader systems are far superior from a visual feedback perspective because the physical fader position always relates to the actual gain setting of the channel. However, their main disadvantages, in analogue consoles, are their cost. The mechanical noise of moving faders can also be distracting when you're mixing.

Virtually all analogue mixers that offer fader automation also have a system for automating channel mutes and sometimes effect-send/-return mutes as well. Mutes may also be used to remove recorded parts that are no longer required in a particular section of the song for artistic reasons in order to kill noise during pauses in the music.

The vast majority of digital consoles now use moving faders, partly because motorised faders have come down in price but mainly because digital mixers use one set of faders to control multiple banks for settings, and so non-moving faders would be too confusing. For example, a typical mixer may have 16 physical faders used to control maybe 24 tracks of audio, eight group-output levels, the master effects-send and -return levels and maybe the aux send levels as well. These functions are arranged into banks, and

as soon as you switch to a new bank, the faders change position to match the values relevant to that bank.

Automated Mix Data

When a mix is being set up, the data generated by manual fader movements is stored in a computer. The automation system must also be synchronised to the multitrack recorder so that it knows whereabouts in the song it is at any time. When analogue tape was the main multitrack media, this invariably meant sacrificing a tape track to SMPTE time code, where a separate piece of synchronising hardware was used to read and write the SMPTE code to tape. Although SMPTE is still used on some applications, most project studio systems are synchronised via MTC(MIDI Time Code), which carries the same timing information as SMPTE and supports the same frame formats but, in many cases, is generated directly by a digital multitrack recorder – or, in the case of ADATs, by means of a BRC (Big Remote Control) controller.

Most automated mixers include the automation computer, which will either be integral to the mixer or in the form of an external hardware box. However, there are mixers that rely on a separate desktop computer for handling the automation data. The ease with which it's possible to edit the mix data will depend on how sophisticated your sequencer is. You may also have the facility to store multiple mix histories, allowing you to return to any point in a project, or you may have only one mix, which is constantly updated. In this latter case, saving some interim versions to disk can be helpful.

Once a rough mix has been written, the mix data on individual mixer channels may be replaced or modified, much like doing a punch-in on a multitrack tape recorder. This is how a mix is fine-tuned until everything is exactly right. Only then is the mix run to the master stereo recorder.

Fader Groups

With a manual analogue mixer, it's necessary to use the desk's routing busses if you want to subgroup a set of channels while mixing. However, an automated desk, whether of the VCA or moving-fader variety, can generally handle automated fader grouping without the need to involve the group busses. Once a number

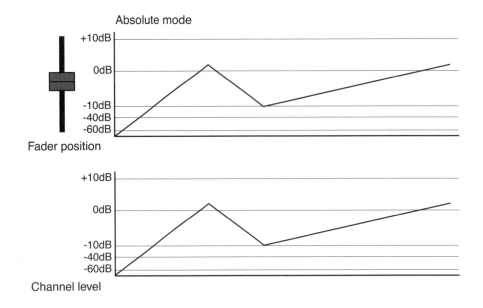

Figure 15.2: Response of channel gain in Absolute mode

of faders have been assigned to the group, operating one of the faders in that group causes the levels of the entire group to be adjusted, maintaining any relative level differences that may have been set up. All of the faders in the group will move when the controlling fader is moved, and all the faders will be scaled so as to reach the bottom of their travel at the same time, regardless of their relative positions at the start of the fade. This provides the same characteristic as a true master-buss fader.

Fader Modes

The process of recording mix data is known as *writing*, and a typical automation console has a number of write modes for different stages of the mixing operation. When you first write a set of mix moves, it's normal to use Absolute mode, where the fader values are written directly into memory for any tracks that are set to Write mode. Figure 15.2 shows how the channel gain responds in Absolute mode.

Once the initial mix been written, either all in one take or a few tracks at a time, you'll almost certainly need to make further adjustments. This is where Trim mode is useful because, although you can completely replace unsatisfactory mix data in any track using

Absolute mode (again much like punching in and out on a tape recorder), it may be that the dynamic changes you wrote the first time were largely OK but you just need to nudge the levels up or down in places. In Trim mode (sometimes also known as Relative or Offset mode), new mix moves don't replace the existing data but rather add to or subtract from it, depending on how you move the fader from its original position. For example, if you push the fader up by 3dB, all of the existing mix data will be increased in level by 3dB. Figure 15.3 shows how levels behave in Trim mode.

Yet another useful feature offered by some automation systems is Write To End mode. This allows a fader or control setting to be continued from the current position to the end of the mix without you having to play the track all the way through. In fact, a number of different strategies are in place to determine how the automation system behaves when you take a track out of Record mode when that track previously contained mix data. If the value were to immediately jump to the old stored value the moment you stopped recording, there could be an audible click or glitch in the audio, so many systems allow the user to set a fade time so that the new information will merge smoothly into the old information at the end of

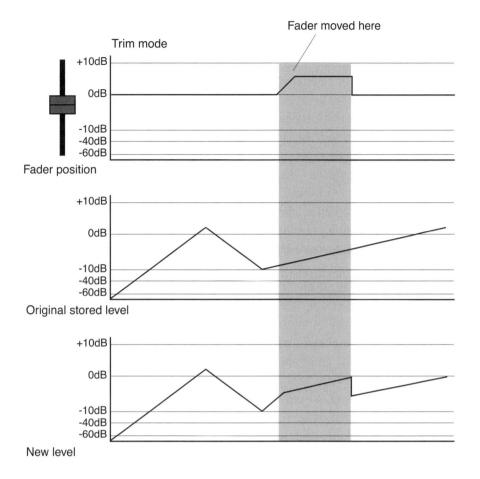

Figure 15.3: Behaviour of levels in Trim mode

an edit. Other options include the ability to hold the last recorded level for the duration of the song, which is sometimes called Latch mode.

Read And Write

Recording and updating mix data is done using one of the available write modes, but when you come to play back your mix data the console must be set to Read mode. In Read mode, the computer moves the faders according to the stored mix data, as it does if you're updating a mix but haven't punched into Write mode yet.

Some consoles also have a mode that automatically flips the channel from Read to Write mode if you touch the fader during a mix playback, provided that that particular channel is 'armed' in a

write-ready mode. When you release the fader, the channel goes back to Read mode. This system is also adopted by some of the moving-fader controllers developed for use with computer-based recording systems and they work by having circuitry that detects the capacitance of your fingers as they touch an electrically conductive fader cap.

If your faders aren't touch responsive, there may be a button associated with each channel that is the equivalent of the Record Select button on a multitrack recorder. Of course, no two automation packages are identical, although most have a straightforward Read mode and at least Absolute and Trim write modes. It's also common to have an Automation Off mode, where the fader is disconnected from the automation system, enabling you to control it manually.

Snapshots

The *snapshot* or *scene-based-automation* feature is common not only on mixers that don't feature full dynamic automation but also often as an additional feature on more sophisticated mixers. A snapshot is, in effect, a complete set of information that defines the status of the console at the point in time at which the snapshot was created, and it will include all levels and mutes at the time the snapshot was stored. On a digital console, the snapshot may also include the pan, EQ, aux, effects and dynamics settings as well as any routing settings. When you're working on a mix that requires a lot of changes to happen instantaneously, it's often easier to create a snapshot and then call it up at the appropriate time (under control of the automation) than to try to change everything at once using the dynamic controls.

Most automated desks can store a number of automation snapshots that may be called up at any time during a mix (at a specified time-code location) and some systems include the ability to merge or morph between snapshots to provide smooth transitions.

If you have a digital console and you're using only the built-in effects, you can use snapshots to recall an entire project (with static mixes only, of course) and know that everything is set exactly as you left it. Similarly, you can store your clients' projects so that, when they return after a few weeks to do the inevitable remix, you don't have to waste time trying to recreate the original mix.

Digital Console Extras

While it's unusual to find an affordable analogue console that offers more than fader or mute automation, digital consoles can be designed to automate pretty much everything, apart from input pre-amp gain trims. This includes recalling settings of effects and processors, perhaps dynamic changes to the effects settings made during a mix, or all of the aux and EQ control settings. Because it's now relatively cheap to build an automated digital console, compared to the cost of doing the same thing using analogue circuitry, most of the automated mixers available to project studio users are either in the form of a digital hardware console or a computer-based system controlled by a moving-fader interface that provides a mixing experience similar to using a hardware digital console. In the case of hardware interfaces working with a sequencer, the mix data will be stored as part of a sequencer song, whereas with a hardware mixer the mix data will usually be saved to internal memory, after which it can be backed up to a disk drive or a computer, often via MIDI.

Automation Practicalities

Using an automated mixer for the first time can be confusing, although the basics of setting up a mix are the same, regardless of the system you're using. Even if you're using a software audio package with no user interface other than a mouse, the only significant difference is that you can't move more than one virtual fader at a time.

Before even thinking about automation, you should try to find a static balance that sounds as good as you can get it, and that includes setting pan positions, EQ and effects. If you're using a console with on-board dynamics or an audio software program that supports plug-ins, you can also set up such compression as is necessary for the main parts, and fader groups can also be set up at this stage. If the vocal part is to be 'comped' from various takes, you can do this either by copying the wanted sections to a single track or by using the automation system's mutes to play back only the required phrases from each vocal track. Other than using the automatic mutes to assemble your best vocal track from several takes, the process so far is much the same as the first stage of a manual mix, but now you can go on to refine the mix using the automation system.

Perhaps some notes, words or phrases are a little too loud or too quiet. There may also be parts playing throughout the mix that you'll want to take out in some places. Perhaps the best place to start is with the mutes, where you can silence any sections where nothing is playing but where spill or other background noises may be present. If you take your time getting this right you'll be rewarded with a cleaner mix.

The next stage is to listen to the mix you have in order to identify what needs fine-tuning. Are some vocal phrases too loud? Do some sink back into the mix, even after compression? If so, use the fader automation to get them right. You may also find that you'd like to make small changes in level for artistic reasons – for example, dropping an instrumental part by a decibel or so during the vocal or pumping up a support part slightly during a solo.

In most cases, it's best to work on one fader at a time until the balance is as you want it all the way through the song. The first pass of fader moves is done in Absolute mode, but if you need to go back and refine your moves further it's often best to use Trim/Update mode, as this doesn't overwrite your pre-existing mix data; it simply allows you to add or subtract from what you've already done. However, if you need to completely redo a section of automation, Absolute mode is probably more appropriate as it completely overwrites earlier information recorded to that track between the Write in and out points.

As a general note, just as with any another software-dependent process, you should save your mix at regular intervals just in case you suffer from a system crash.

Refining The Mix

When your mix is automated to the stage at which there are no further balance problems that need addressing, listen to what you have to determine if there's anything creative that automation can help. For example, do you want to bring up an echo-send level at certain points in the song to add repeat echo? Do you want the reverb level to change in the chorus? Would you like to change some aspect of the EQ during a particular part of the song?

You can automate pretty much anything you like, but for some this degree of freedom can lead to over-indulgence and, as with any other stage of music production, overdoing something can ultimately ruin it. If you always remember to put the needs of the song first, you won't go far wrong. Also, keep in mind that, whatever else you automate, it's generally best to keep the rhythm section at a more or less constant level, or it will sound as though someone's playing with the faders! In a typical mix, it's likely you won't need to automate all of the channels; once a basic balance has been set up, you may need to automate only two or three parts in order to get the effect you

need. Fine-tuning an automated mix so that every little detail is taken care of is a time-consuming process and requires a lot of concentration, and you'll probably find that the job takes you rather longer than it did when you mixed manually. However, I firmly believe that the proper use of automation allows the creation of much better mixes than was ever possible by manual means. It won't necessarily make you a better mix engineer, but it will allow you to hear what your mix sounds like without having to split your concentration so that you can move the faders manually.

When you're done setting up the mix, listen carefully to the mix running under automation. If you're still happy, run off a DAT, cassette or CD-R (CD-Recordable) copy to check it on other sound systems to see if your mix 'travels' well. It's also a good idea to check the mix over headphones, as these often show up problems that aren't obvious over loudspeakers, such as unwanted background noises due to missed mutes or distorted signal peaks. If you've saved your mix data, you can always come back to it if there are problems, but if you're using an analogue mixer, keep in mind that there are lots of mix controls that probably aren't automated (pan, EQ, aux sends and so on), not to mention any external effects and signal processors that you might have patched in. In such cases, a cheap solution is to use a pocket mini-cassette recorder to record the settings of each mixer channel, all of the send/return settings and all of the outboard equipment settings. Also, if you dictate notes on any special patchbay connections, the next time you come to recreate the mix you can play back the cassette and adjust the controls as the settings are read out to you.

Advanced Automation

Most digital consoles allow you to copy and paste automation data in much the same way as sequencers copy and paste MIDI data. This can be useful if, for example, you want to copy the automation data from one chorus to all the choruses in a song. It's also often possible to edit individual automation moves in an edit list, and this can be useful if you want to move the positions of mutes that are set too early or too late. In many instances, however, it's quicker and easier to redo the automation moves than to edit the old ones.

The mixing process in the virtual studio is conceptually similar to mixing using a hardware digital mixer, except of course you can change only one parameter at a time, unless you have a hardware fader controller. Rather than mute unwanted sections, I generally use the sequencer's edit tools to silence longer sections, as these are very obvious on the Waveform display and easy to locate. Short gaps or pauses within the remaining sections can then be cleaned up using the Silence function (which is a destructive edit) on the selected regions, or you can simply pull down the channel gain briefly to mute shorter pauses. If a Graphical Automation edit mode is available (ie the type where you can draw and manipulate automation envelopes), this latter system can work very well, and it also has the benefit of being non-destructive.

Dynamic Noise Filters

While it's true that mix automation solves a lot of problems, it obviously can't solve them all, and one common problem is that of audible noise that occurs during a recording rather than just showing itself during pauses, where it could easily be muted. In such cases, where some sound sources are unavoidably noisy, it might be practical to use a single-ended noise-reduction unit to minimise the noise. These devices are essentially dynamic filters that progressively filter out higher frequencies as the sounds being processed fall in level, and if they're used carefully they can bring about a dramatic decrease in noise without affecting the sound of the wanted signal to an unacceptable degree. However, they do tend to affect the tail ends of long reverbs or other sounds with long decays, so it's probably prudent to assign all of the noisy sounds to a stereo subgroup and process just this group rather than the entire mix, ideally before adding reverb. This leaves the higher-quality sounds and effects returns unprocessed, which will give a more natural result. Although very limited in comparison with digital de-noisers, single-ended noise-reduction systems are still very effective in cleaning up electric-guitar, bass and synthesiser tracks that suffer from moderate high-frequency noise contamination.

Mix Processing

Producers tend to be divided when it comes to applying further processing to the overall stereo mix. The more puritanical might say that there's no need to process the mix once you've got it right, while others will insist on putting it through their favourite compressor, equaliser or exciter. There can be no definitive right or wrong answer to this question; in pop-music production, the end always justifies the means (as long as the means are within budget!), but you should never apply processing that could be better used during mastering as you may prevent the mastering engineer from being able to do the best possible job on your music. However, it's still a good idea to explore some of the implications inherent in post-mix processing, some of which are discussed in more detail in Chapter 16, 'Editing And Mastering'.

Overall Compression

Compressing a complete mix reduces the difference between the quietest parts of the mix and the loudest. If the highest levels peak at around the same value as they did before compression, it follows that the average level must be higher, and this is reflected in a subjective increase in musical energy. However, a sound will only appear to be loud if it has a quieter sound to contrast with, so there's a danger of making a piece of music sound quieter by compressing it too much.

When compressing a mix, the attack time of the compressor is usually extended slightly to allow transient sounds such as drums to punch through with more power, although the best setting can be determined only by ear, as every piece of music is different. It's also true that some compressors perform disappointingly when used on complete mixes whereas others produce results that appear to be little short of magic. As a very general rule, soft-knee compressors produce the most subtle results.

Multiband Compression

Most mastering facilities make use of multiband compressors, the operation of which is described in Chapter 12, 'Dynamic Control'. Because these treat each band of frequencies separately, there's less chance of loud bass sounds causing unwanted gain reduction at high frequencies, making it possible to compress more heavily without producing undesirable side-effects. It's also possible to use different compression settings in each of the three bands in order to suit the material being mastered, which provides a powerful means of controlling both tonality and dynamic range.

Overall EQ

Equalising the whole mix might seem unnecessary if the mix already sounds good, but some equalisers seem to improve the sound noticeably even when very subtle settings are used. Music can be made to appear louder by cutting the mid range slightly, as this emulates the response curve of the human ear. It may also be necessary to equalise a mix if it has been made in a studio with an inaccurate monitor system. Indeed, there are so many inaccurate control rooms around that, when a master tape is sent to the cutting room to be prepared for record or CD mastering, it's very common for the engineer to apply a degree of corrective EQ at that stage.

In my view, overall EQ should be left to the mastering stage, as it's very difficult to undo the effects of an inappropriate EQ setting later in the process. A commercial mastering house will invariably have nicer-sounding equalisers than you anyway, and the monitoring system will be designed to be as accurate as possible. Of course, many project-studio owners do their own mastering, but this should still be treated as a separate stage and, in any event, should be done some time after the mix to give you chance to stand back and appraise what you've done.

Enhancers

It's not uncommon to treat a whole mix with an exciter or a dynamic equaliser. These tend to emphasise certain parts of the frequency spectrum in a way that is related to the dynamics of the signal so that transient sounds are given more definition. This increases the perceived sense of loudness, which helps a record stand out from the competition on the radio or on the dancefloor. The exciter actually synthesises harmonics based on the existing programme material and so may be more suitable for dealing with a mix that is insufficiently bright. The dynamic equaliser creates no new harmonics but, in effect, redistributes what's already there and so may give a smoother sound. Dynamic equalisers can also be used to add power at the bass end, whereas most exciters simply work at the very high-frequency end of the audio spectrum. Newer models, however, increasingly address the bottom end of the frequency spectrum by offering some type of bass enhancement. At the risk of repeating myself, don't add enhancement during the mix if you're going to master the material later. As with EQ, trying to undo inappropriate enhancer treatment is virtually impossible.

Monitoring Alternatives

Before a final mix is approved, it should be checked on different speaker systems, including car systems and domestic hi-fi. Large studio monitoring systems can be very misleading, and it is essential to test the mix at a moderate listening level on a pair of small speakers. Avoid the temptation to mix at too high a volume, as this will only serve to adversely affect your hearing judgement. Ultimately, the best test is to listen to your mix at the same level at which you'd expect the end user to listen.

The Master's Format

Although DAT recorders are in danger of going out of production in the near future, DAT is still a standard mastering medium, even though it's still, strictly speaking, only a semi-pro or domestic format. If you have the choice, you should make the master at a sampling frequency of 44.1kHz, as this means that you won't need to have the sample rate converted when you make a CD master. With any form of digital recording, you must keep a very close eye on recording levels because there's no leeway above 0VU; the sound immediately clips and distortion is usually audible. Try to arrange your levels so that the peaks reach between −3VU and −6VU on the DAT machine's meters, which should provide an adequate margin of safety while still giving a good signal-to-noise performance.

Once the master tape has been recorded, it must be backed up, particularly if it's on DAT, as, contrary to some expectations, DAT isn't 100 per cent reliable. If you want to back up data from one DAT to another, make a clone by connecting the machines via their digital-audio links. It's safest to leave at least ten seconds of unrecorded tape at the beginning of a DAT cassette – if trouble is going to occur, it usually occurs here – and the back-up should be clearly marked and stored in a safe place.

It's also worth backing up DAT masters to open-reel analogue tape if you still have a decent analogue two-track recorder in working condition. Interestingly, in many cases, the analogue copy sounds subjectively better than the DAT, due to the many small technical imperfections of analogue recording that contribute to its alleged warm, comfortable sound. Making CD-R back-ups of mixes is also cost-effective and convenient, especially for users with computer-based studios.

Labelling

All session tapes should be labelled clearly, as should any unused mixes and out-takes that you wish to keep. Further information on the subject of labelling is included in Chapter 19, 'Media Matters', but for now be sure to include such information as the following:

- The track format;
- The tape speed;
- The noise-reduction system used;
- Track titles;
- Track start times and end times;
- Track durations.

Stereo Masters

If you're working with analogue tape, record a set of calibration tones at the start of any analogue masters or back-ups. At the very least, record a 1kHz tone at a meter reading of oVU. Although calibration tones shouldn't be necessary with DAT, tape duplicators and mastering houses like to have a 1kHz tone recorded at the start of a tape, usually around 20 seconds in duration and at a level of –10VU. The actual level is less important than writing the actual level on the box!

If the master tape is intended to be used in album production, the individual tracks must spaced apart by the required duration of silence. With analogue tape, this was achieved in the past by splicing lengths of plastic leader tape or blank recording tape between

the individual songs, the actual length of which depended very much on how the previous song ended and on how the next one started. For example, the space required after a song with a fade-out ending might need to be only a couple of seconds; on the other hand, if one songs ends with a bang and the next starts equally as abruptly, anything up to five seconds might be needed. There are no hard-and-fast rules about this, but you can instinctively feel if a gap is more than half a second too short or too long. Today, this method of editing has been largely consigned to the history books and it's far more likely that the finished analogue recordings will be transferred to a digital editing system which can handle gap spacings, level changes and fades much more easily.

Track Spacing

Spacing songs on a DAT tape is far less straightforward than doing the same job by splicing analogue tape because you can't stop and start a DAT in the same instant way as you can with analogue machines. Using two DAT machines, it's possible to make a reasonable job of compiling an album simply by using the Pause button on the second machine to start and stop it, but in this way it's difficult to obtain gaps to an accuracy of better than one second. Again, it's much better to use a hard-disk editing system, where the gaps can be timed to millisecond accuracy and where unwanted noise before and after songs can be cut out with surgical precision. Given that almost any modern computer can run basic stereo editing software, there's little reason to struggle with the older and less satisfactory methods of album compilation.

Level Matching

Getting the different tracks on an album to sit well together is an art, not a science, and simply making all of the tracks the same level won't provide the required results. Imagine a heavy rock track and a soft ballad, both mixed to the same level. If heard right next to each other, the ballad will sound far too loud, so your job is to adjust its level downwards so that it balances naturally with the tracks on either side of it. Listening to the relative voice levels between tracks provides a clue, as does listening to the drum parts.

Stereo-Width Manipulation

When it comes to stereo, most of what's done in the recording studio is out-and-out fraud! In real life, our hearing systems establish the direction of a sound source by evaluating a multitude of parameters, including phase, amplitude and spectral content; in the studio, engineers cheat and use pan pots. It's true that using proper stereo-miking techniques can capture many of the nuances of a real-life soundfield, but when it comes to producing pop music sound engineers inclined to rely on pan pots to change the balance between the left and right speakers, effects with synthesised stereo outputs and electronic musical instruments whose stereo outputs are artificially created by routing different mixes of signal to the left and right outputs.

Even so, there are some simple but effective processing techniques that can be used to create the illusion of stereo, even when the signal being treated is in mono. In multitrack recording, such processing is very useful and could have been a life-saver back in the days when four- or eight-track recorders were popular and where parts often had to be bounced into mono to conserve track space. Today, even with the generous track allowances of current recording hardware and software, these tricks can still be useful.

All In The Mind

Sophisticated though the human hearing system is, it would appear that it's far easier to fool than, for example, our vision. Digital reverberators create the illusion of stereo simply by using different sets of delay taps on the left and right channels, giving rise to two sets of reverberation patterns, which, although similar in their overall parameters, differ in their fine detail in essentially random ways. It seems that our hearing systems are so keen to make sense of the world around us that they eagerly accept this random information and use it to construct an imaginary, auditory world in which the processed sound exists.

This provides one very simple way of turning a mono sound into something that sounds like stereo: adding reverb to it. The trouble is that you might want the sound to appear to be in stereo but don't want to add any noticeable amount of reverb. In that case, choose a reverb setting that provides an early-reflections pattern but without the following reverb. Such settings add a relatively small number of closely-spaced reflections to the sound with different patterns in the left and right channels. The result is that the sound takes on a sense of space but with no apparent reverberation.

By using a less sophisticated reverb, a similar effect can be achieved by selecting a very short, bright reverb setting (around half a second decay or even less) and then increasing the mix of the reverb until the sound takes on the required extra dimension. If the reverb allows the density to be edited, set a low density value to further emphasise the early reflections. If the reverb time is set short enough, the effect is not dissimilar to that created by an early-reflections-pattern setting, although with some of the cheaper reverb units short settings might tend to sound a touch 'ringy', especially if percussive sounds are involved.

Delay

There are lots of tricks that you can pull with a simple delay unit that have the effect of widening the stereo image, but you must be aware that most of these aren't completely mono compatible, so keep pressing the Mono button on your mixer or power amplifier to see if what you've done has unacceptable side-effects. This is particularly important for broadcast material, as there are still many people listening to mono radios and mono TV sets, but insisting on absolute mono compatibility does place severe restrictions on what you can do – after all, real life isn't actually mono compatible, when you come to think about it!

The simplest trick is to pan your mono signal to one side of the stereo field and pan a delayed version of the same sound, at the same level, to the other side. The delay should be very short, so as not to produce an obvious echo – between 2ms and 20ms will work.

You'll notice something very interesting when you try this: even though the level of signal in both speakers is equal, the sound will appear to be coming from the speaker that's receiving the undelayed sound. At the same time, it will sound wider that a straight mono source. The reason for this is tied up with the way in which our brains process sound: if a sound

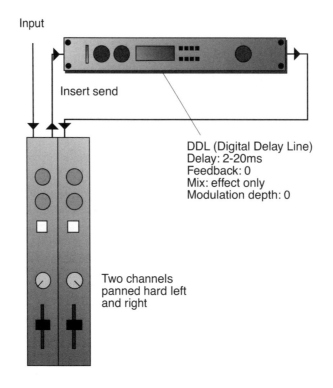

Input

Insert send

DDL (Digital Delay Line)
Delay: 2-20ms
Feedback: 0
Mix: effect only
Modulation depth: 0

Two channels
panned hard left
and right

Figure 15.4: Using a DDL for panning delay

comes from our left, it will reach the left ear before it reaches the right ear, and this small time difference is one criteria with which the brain works out the direction in which a sound arrives. In recording, this is known as the *precedence effect*. Figure 15.4 shows a simple way of setting up this process using a basic DDL and a mixer with channel-insert points. The DDL should be set with a delay time of between 2ms and 20ms, with no modulation and no feedback, while the mix control should be set to give only the delayed sound and none of the direct sound. On a manual unit, this usually means the fully clockwise setting of the mix control.

Another effect that can be produced by using the same set-up is *stereo chorus*. This is something I discovered back in my serious gigging days, at a time when stereo chorus units didn't exist. I used to have two guitar amps, one fed from the straight guitar sound and the other fed through a mono chorus pedal. I noticed immediately that this combination created the illusion of movement between the speakers, and from the normal listening position it wasn't easy to tell which speaker was producing the straight sound and which one had been put through a chorus. When I got into home recording, I took this technique into the studio and found it incredibly useful for creating really wide, dynamic chorus effects for guitar and synthesiser. Even though stereo chorus units then started to become available, I don't think any of them ever sounded wider than my simple set-up, which is shown in Figure 15.5. By feeding the effect from a post-fade aux send, you can add different amounts of chorus to different instruments in a mix. The only limitation here is that, in order to get the full effect of the stereo spread, all of the sounds being processed should be panned more or less to one side of the mix and the output from the chorus unit to the other. To achieve a suitable chorus setting using a general purpose DDL with modulation capabilities, you should do the following:

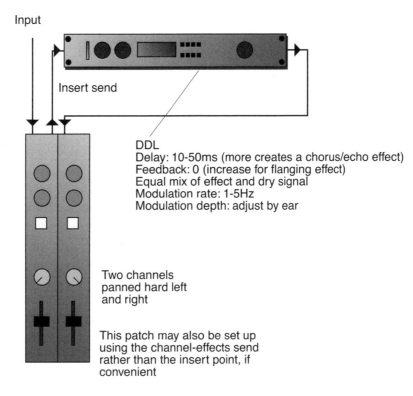

Input

Insert send

DDL
Delay: 10-50ms (more creates a chorus/echo effect)
Feedback: 0 (increase for flanging effect)
Equal mix of effect and dry signal
Modulation rate: 1-5Hz
Modulation depth: adjust by ear

Two channels
panned hard left
and right

This patch may also be set up
using the channel-effects send
rather than the insert point, if
convenient

Figure 15.5: Pseudo-stereo chorus

- The DDL should be set with a delay time between 10ms and 50ms with a modulation rate of between 1Hz and 5Hz.

- The modulation depth should then be brought up slowly until the required chorus effect is created.

- The mix control should be set at 50 per cent delayed sound to 50 per cent direct sound, which is generally the centre position on a manual unit.

True chorus uses no feedback, but some feedback may be added to create an effect somewhere between chorus and flanging, if preferred. As a rule, when setting up modulated-delay effects, the longer the delay time, the less modulation depth is required.

An interesting variation on this effect is to pan the dry sound to the centre and then use two different chorus effects, one panned to each side. This creates a rich, layered effect that may sound nicer than the out-of-the-tin effect presented by multi-effects units. To achieve this:

- Pan the chorused sound to one side.

- Pan the same chorused sound processed via a channel with the Phase button depressed to the other side.

This also gives a wide stereo spread and should be reasonably mono compatible, but always remember to check mono compatibility when adding any stereo effect.

Width Enhancement

One effective but decidedly artificial method for making mono appear to be in stereo was devised back in the early days of stereo recording, when old mono records were frequently reprocessed to sound wider in stereo. This particular technique employed a stereo graphic equaliser, with the input signal being split to feed both channels of the equaliser. The idea was to set the two channels differently so they'd emphasise different parts of the mix, which could then be panned left and right. The method outlined in Figure 15.6 is a refinement of this idea and has the additional benefit that it can be accomplished with a single-channel equaliser. In general, the more bands you have to EQ, the better, but you can get a useful result from just about any graphic equaliser. The patch may be set up either by using a Y-lead to split the output from the graphic equaliser or by using the channel-insert sends as shown. Here's how:

- Feed the original signal directly to a mixer channel and pan it dead centre.

- Take a feed from that channel's insert send and then feed it into the graphic equaliser.

- Split the output of the equaliser into two by using

a Y-lead and feed the signal into two more mixer channels, one panned hard left and the other hard right, depressing the Phase Invert button on one of these two channels (it doesn't matter which one).

- To create the stereo effect, the equaliser needs to be set so that it produces a number of bumps and dips in the audio spectrum, and although just about any setting will produce a useful result (for example, setting the faders alternately up and down) it's more productive to try to identify specific areas of the spectrum in which certain things are going on – guitars, keyboard pads and so on – and then home in specifically on these.

So how does it work? Assuming that the channel panned to the right is the one with the phase button depressed, the left signal will be a sum of the direct signal (centre) and the equalised signal (left). The right-hand signal, on the other hand, will be the difference

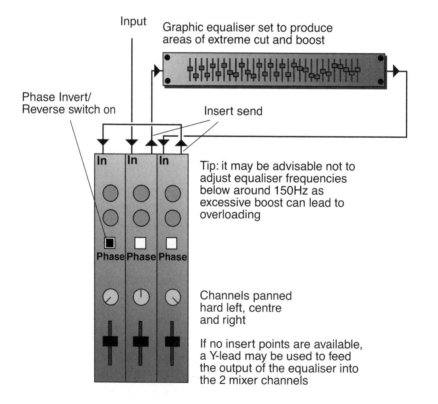

Figure 15.6: Psuedo-stereo chorus via a graphic equaliser

between the direct signal and the equalised signal because of the action of the Phase Invert button. This means that what constitutes an EQ peak in the left channel will manifest itself as an equal and opposite dip in the right channel, and vice versa. The neat thing about working in this way is that, if the signal is heard in mono, the contribution of the equaliser cancels itself out, so you're left with just the original mono signal. However, don't assume that the process is 100 per cent mono compatible, because the subjective level appears to drop when the left and right components are cancelled out. The seriousness of this problem will depend on how much of the equalised sound is added to the direct sound.

It's important to get the levels of the two channels fed from the equaliser as similar as possible. The easiest way to do this is to mute the direct signal using the channel mute and listen to just the two channels fed from the equaliser. If these are (temporarily) panned to the centre, the signal will cancel completely when both are exactly equal in level. Once this has been verified, they can be panned back to their respective sides and the direct signal turned back on.

The result of this processing trick is quite interesting in that the stereo image takes on an extra dimension, but you can't actually pick out where the sounds are supposed to be coming from. In that respect, it's rather like reverberation – the illusion of space is created, but no real directional information is provided.

Although it's no substitute for true stereo recording, this trick and others like it make it possible to produce a wide and interesting stereo image when working on a four-track system, where several musical parts have to be bounced into mono. Interestingly, this old effect has recently enjoyed a resurgence of interest in the plug-in effect market, as emulating this in software form is relatively simple.

Width Expansion

Here's a simple but nevertheless effective technique for making the stereo spread appear to be wider than the spacing of the stereo loudspeakers. This particular trick has been used in ghetto blasters for many years and simply involves taking some of the right-hand signal and feeding it, out of phase, to the left hand

channel, and vice versa. The phase effects introduced in this way appear to push the sound out beyond the boundaries of the speakers. However, if too much of the out-of-phase signal is added, the stereo positioning actually appears to swap sides. For this reason, it's vital to make sure that the unprocessed stereo signal remains the loudest part of the mix. Too much out-of-phase component also makes the mix sound 'phasey', and although different people perceive this in different ways, I find it physically uncomfortable. Try it yourself by setting an equal mix of direct and out-of-phase sound and standing exactly between the speakers.

Ideally, you need to mix the out-of-phase sounds low enough to avoid this effect. Although it's no substitute for Roland's RSS 3D sound system or Q-Sound processing, this simple trick can be usefully applied to individual subgroups within a mix or to stereo effects returns to add an extra dimension to a mix. Also, as the added components are equal and opposite, they cancel completely when the signal is summed to mono, so the only changes will be changes in perceived level. Figure 15.7 over the page shows how this trick works.

At least one mastering processor provides this type of width expansion in a split-band form, which I feel is very useful. Manipulating the phase of bass sounds can be problematic, but with multiband width expansion it's possible to keep the bass end unchanged while expanding the mid- and high-frequency sections of the audio spectrum.

Difficult Mixes

If you can't get a mix sounding right, try to get an initial rough mix without using EQ or effects and then work from there. Also check that the mix sounds OK in mono, then check the following points:

- Is there too much going on at once? Do you need all those parts and, if so, can you afford to have some of them lower in the mix?

- Are mid-range sounds cluttering up the mix or overlapping with the bass sounds? If so, try using EQ to thin out the sounds. They might sound odd in isolation, but they're more likely to sound right in the context of the mix as a whole. Try shaving

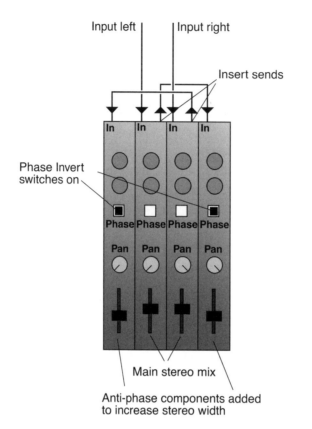

Figure 15.7: Stereo-width expansion

some bottom end off a pad-synth part or acoustic-guitar rhythm line to clean up the low-mid region of the mix.

- If you're still having difficulty, balance up the drum and bass sounds first and then add the vocals and main instruments. You'll probably find that the mix sounds 90 per cent there with just the drums, bass, chords and a vocal line.

- If you're working with a sequencer, try using alternative pad or keyboard sounds if the sounds you've chosen appear to be taking up too much space in the mix.

- Use effects sparingly, adding reverb where it sounds good, not simply where you feel it ought to be. Very often, the restrained use of effects produces the best result.

- Pan the instruments and effects to their desired positions.

- There may be some benefit in adding a little compression to the complete mix, although this isn't compulsory. A compressor with an auto attack/release feature may cope best with the shifting dynamics of a real mix, and a soft-knee expander will usually provide the most transparent results.

- Valve compressors often give the most flattering sound, and many top engineers like to pass their mixes through their favourite valve compressor, more for the benefit of the valve coloration than for the compression it provides.

- Subtle use of an enhancer such as an Aural Exciter will also help separate the individual sounds and emphasise detail.

Mix Recorders

Originally, a mix was invariably recorded on quarter-inch analogue tape on an open-reel machine running at 7½ or 15 inches per second, and even today a well-maintained analogue tape machine can give fantastic results, although now they compete with DAT, MD, CD-R, CD-RW and hard-drive recording as repositories for your previous mixes. Before you can decide which one is best for you, you'll need to know the strengths and weaknesses of each format. Furthermore, if you're handling a project that needs to move between studios, you'll need to know that your chosen medium can be supported by all of the studios involved in the production process.

DAT As A Master Format

Although specialist 24-bit models are still being produced, most DAT recorders are designed to work at 44.1kHz and 48kHz, recording 16-bit uncompressed audio, which gives them the ability to record audio at the same sample rate and bit depth as that used by commercial CDs. Recording your final mix in a 16-bit format is fine if it's your final mix, but most of the time you'll need to do some post-mix mastering, even if it's only adjusting levels or adding a bit of EQ and compression. Every time you process digital audio, a small amount of resolution is lost due to errors incurred by scaling or rounding data up or down, so in an ideal world it's better to record at more than 16 bits and then dither down to 16 bits at the very end of the mastering process.

When digital data is subjected to a loss of resolution, the effects are most audible at very low levels, where fewer bits are being used to represent the signal. Classical or acoustic music with a very wide dynamic range is most at risk while pop music, with its limited dynamic range, is least likely to be affected audibly. Fades should be done at the mastering stage, not when you mix down to DAT, otherwise subsequent processing could cause the tail end of the fade to sound a little grainy.

If you need more mastering resolution, you could choose one of the specialist, 24-bit DAT recorders, although you could also use two tracks of a modular digital multitrack recorder, most of which work at 20- or 24-bit resolution. However, you may need a suitable digital interface to make the best of their resolution, as their internal analogue-to-digital converters may not be as good as those used in mastering. You'll also need to be sure your soundcard/mixer is able to support 20- or 24-bit data transfer, or you might find your signal truncated to 16 bits anyway. Another advantage of using a multitrack recorder for mixing is that there are enough tracks to accommodate surround mixing (the 5.1 format needs six tracks) and an eight-track machine neatly accommodates a surround mix plus a regular stereo mix.

The disadvantage of any digital tape format is that the machines need to be well maintained and properly aligned in order to avoid problems, and even in the best-run studios, machines sometimes damage tapes! For this reason, keeping back-ups is essential.

Mastering Analogue Tape

Analogue tape is full of technical imperfections, but there's no denying that it has a 'sound'. For this reason alone, some engineers are willing to risk wow, flutter and less-than-immaculate noise performance in the quest for warmer-sounding masters. If you're thinking of using analogue tape, choose a machine that can run at 15 inches per second and clean the heads before every recording. Then make some test recordings to find out how far you can push the recording levels before warmth gives way to audible distortion. You should consider using one of the newer high-energy tapes for a better signal-to-noise performance, although this will mean that you'll have to get your machine realigned in order to match the new tape. Your machine alignment will also need to be checked at regular intervals, using a test tape.

If you do mix to analogue tape, it's likely that you'll still edit and master the recording digitally, so your digital system will need to be fitted with high-quality, 24-bit analogue converters if quality is to be maintained. Software de-noising can be used to reduce the effects of tape hiss without introducing noticeable side-effects.

Analogue tape is now quite expensive and has to be kept in a stable environment, and tape machines also require regular maintenance and alignment. On the plus side, analogue deterioration is progressive and therefore easier to detect than digital media problems.

MiniDisc

MiniDisc is a cheap format, in terms of both recorders and media, which makes it a very tempting option for the home recordist, and the discs are also reasonably robust. The sound quality that they reproduce is also surprisingly good, given that the data compression they employ means that the signal is squeezed to less than a quarter of the storage space of an equivalent-length CD, and if you're working on a PC-based system with a budget soundcard and you're recording pop or dance music for private release, MiniDisc should be perfectly adequate. However, while CDs and CD-Rs can be cloned with no appreciable loss of quality, attempting to clone a MiniDisc to another MiniDisc will entail a further round of data compression, so there's no way to make a perfect copy.

If you decide that MiniDisc is OK for your needs, you'll obtain the best results by using the digital input, as the converters on the cheaper machines are less than optimal.

.mp3

Some low-end multitrackers use the .mp3 format or some similar form of aggressive data compression to allow you to make audio recording onto Smart Media Flash memory cards. The sound quality from such systems depends to a great extent on the type of sound being recorded, and complex sounds with lots of frequency components tend to suffer the most. Used with care, these machines can produce surprisingly good results that are far cleaner than could ever be achieved with cassette tape, but this is due in part to the fact that any effects added after recording help to hide the artefacts of compression. Reverb is particularly useful with this format as it replaces some of the missing low-level detail. However, it is not a good idea to use these machines for capturing the stereo mix as the music will suffer a further stage of data compression. Instead, you should either master to an uncompressed digital format or mix directly into a computer editing system, where available.

CD-R/CD-RW

Stand-alone CD-R recorders are affordable and the media is cheap, making them an attractive option. However, if you make a mistake when recording to a CD-R, the disk is wasted, and although CD-RWs are now very affordable, going through the process of erasing an unwanted recording is a time-consuming process. Erasing tracks can usually be done only from the last to the first, in order – but then again, at least it's possible. In the real world, you often need to go through a mix several times before everything's right (unless everything in your mix is fully automated), so retries are a fact of life.

The audio-data format used by CD-R is identical to that of pressed audio CDs, and most machines are provided with both analogue and digital inputs and often equipped with integral sample-rate conversion. However, they don't allow you to record at a higher bit depth and then dither down later, so you're no better off than mixing to DAT, and in many ways DAT is still easier to use.

If you choose a CD recorder that can burn Red Book-compatible disks in Disk-At-Once mode, you may also be able to use it to record album masters from your computer after editing, although you'll need to have the complete album edited and able to play in the right order without breaks. To make a CD album master, the whole disk must be recorded in one pass – pausing between tracks causes data errors, which are not acceptable.

Most computer systems now come with CD-burning capability, and Red Book CD compilation and burning packages such as Roxio's Jam for Macintosh do the job perfectly well without recourse to external hardware. My own view is that, if you have a computer system, it's easier and better to record stereo mixes directly into the computer at 24-bit resolution (even if that means recording back to a spare stereo audio track on your sequencer) than to go via a 16-bit CD-R (or DAT) machine. CD-R is perhaps a better bet for those people who don't use computers, but be warned that not using a computer makes editing and compiling albums very difficult, and tracks recorded one at a time to CD-R can't be used as commercial CD masters unless they're later copied to another machine in Disk-At-Once mode.

CD-R and CD-RW disks vary hugely in quality, so cheap, unbranded disks aren't the best bet for anything you want to archive (they tend to have a shorter lifespan), and their error rate also tends to be higher than that of quality, branded disks.

Mixing Directly To Computer

Mixing directly to the hard drive of your computer now makes a lot of sense because, if you have a computer, you'll need to get the audio in there at some stage for editing, anyway. Some users rely entirely on virtual instruments and effects, so creating a mixed file can be achieved entirely within the sequencer software, without recourse to an external mixer. In most cases, however, there will probably be some external MIDI devices involved and, although it's possible to record these back into the sequencer as audio sequencer tracks, the most common option is still to use an external mixer to combine the computer audio interface outputs with those from the hardware MIDI instruments. In this case, the stereo mix from the mixer's main output would be fed back into the computer via the analogue audio inputs (or possibly the S/PDIF inputs, if a digital mixer is being used) and recorded into the sequencer as the mix is played back, ideally as an interleaved stereo sound file on a stereo audio track. Common audio-file formats are .WAV, .AIFF and .SDII, and it's common for the better stereo editing and CD-mastering/-burning programs to support the import of all these file types, with .WAV being the standard for PC users and .AIFF or .SDII being more commonly used on the Macintosh platform. However, software supporting the importing or exporting of Sound Designer II regions will do so only with .SDII or .WAV files, not with .AIFF files. Note that you may need to disable input monitoring when recording computer mixes to new computer tracks, or you may set up a feedback loop.

Summary

The requirements of mix recording have changed considerably in recent years and may do so again if surround sound becomes more widely adopted within the consumer-audio market. It's now generally accepted that recording and mixing should be done to a greater bit depth than the delivery medium, although there is some argument concerning whether it's best to record at a high sample rate and then convert down to 44.1kHz at the end or whether to work at 44.1kHz throughout. My own approach is to work at 44.1kHz throughout a project, but as the jury is still very much out on this, I'll try not to influence your decision one way or another.

Mixing into your computer at 24-bit resolution is probably the best way to maintain signal quality if you run a computer-based studio, but making 16-bit CD-R back-ups would also be prudent and, unless you're recording music that has a wide dynamic range in a very fastidious way, you're unlikely to hear any appreciable difference in the end result, should you need to work from a 16-bit CD-R or DAT.

For those not using computers, hardware recorders that use an uncompressed audio format provide the best results, and CD-R has the advantage that you can make copies of your work to pass on to record companies or friends, who can play your music just by plugging the digital out of a regular CD player into the digital input of the CD-R machine. More dedicated machines, such as the Alesis Masterlink – which combines hard-disk recording and CD burning with 24-bit/96kHz recording capability – have the advantage that they can be used to mix, edit and master CDs without the need for a computer. MiniDisc and other compressed media are best avoided for work intended to end up on CD but are fine for serious demos, independent releases of some types of pop music, and of course for mixing music intended for distribution over the internet.

16 EDITING AND MASTERING

Just a few years ago, hard-disk recording and editing systems were expensive and tended to be used only by professionals. Today, the situation is reversed and software recording and editing is the most cost-effective way of doing the job. All of the major sequencer packages can handle audio recording, which means that they can also be used for basic stereo editing, but dedicated stereo-editing software such as Bias Peak, Sound Forge, WaveLab and TC Spark is generally more suitable as these programs include additional tools specifically designed for editing, such as facilities for fine-tuning the timing of edit points. Both sequencers and editors are generally able to run plug-in software, the most popular being the VST format introduced by Steinberg and then subsequently opened up to third-party development and support.

There are two main musical areas in which hard-disk editors really make life easy: one is in the compiling of albums from a stock of individual tracks, and the other is when editing a song with a view to changing its arrangement. Musical data can be recorded directly onto a computer-based editor via the audio interface used for performing routine sequencer work, provided that your computer has driver support for your editing software. The ASIO driver format is commonly supported by the major software and hardware manufacturers, although Apple users may find that, with Mac OSX, software support is also included for Core Audio (the audio capabilities embedded within OSX).

The only requirement of the hard drive being used to record audio is that it has adequate capacity – all modern drives are fast enough to record multichannel audio, so stereo material presents few challenges, even at higher sample rates and bit depths.

As a rule of thumb, stereo material sampled at 44.1kHz (the same as CD) occupies around 10Mb of disk space for each recorded minute. It therefore follows that, to put an album together, you'll need in excess of 600Mb of disk space available. Allowing for undo files and unused tracks, 1Gb per album is a reasonable estimate.

Material Transfer

Material may be transferred onto disk in real time either from a digital recorder – via the interface's digital input, if it has one – or fed in as a conventional analogue, stereo signal. If the transfer is digital, the recording is an exact clone of the original and there's no need to worry about recording levels. However, when the analogue inputs are used, metering is usually provided for the setting of levels. A third method of getting audio into a computer for editing is to import it from audio CD-R, which may be supported directly by your editing program or may require a third-party audio-extraction program.

There is just one area of concern when transferring from a recorder (such as DAT or MiniDisc) in the digital domain: any errors caused by interference picked up via the cable can give rise to seemingly inexplicable clicks or glitches on the finished master. It's therefore imperative that you use good-quality cable and connectors and that the cable is kept as short as possible. It's also wise to use a mains filtering system to avoid mains-borne interference, which can also cause data corruption.

Where the source audio files already exist on the hard drive or on a CD-ROM (because they've been produced within a sequencer or other multitrack audio-recording package), it's generally possible to import them directly, provided that they're in one of the common audio-file formats such as .WAV, .AIFF or .SDII. Where sample-rate conversion is needed (as would be the case when recording a 48kHz sampled source for use in CD production at 44.1kHz), this may be available in the editing software either as a real-time or offline process. As a rule, offline processes produce the best results, even though they take a little longer. Alternatively, a hardware sample-rate-conversion device may be placed between the recorder and the input to the computer interface. However, where sample-rate conversion isn't available in any form, you'll have to load the audio via the interface's analogue inputs with the sample rate set to whatever final sample rate is required.

Random Access

As you're probably aware, unlike recordings made onto tape, any part of a hard-disk recording can be accessed very rapidly without the need to rewind. Even sections of a recording that are, say, half an hour apart can be accessed in an instant and, with the addition of a little buffer memory to ensure an unbroken flow of audio data, it's possible to select sections from anywhere on the disk and replay these seamlessly, in any order, without making any changes to the original data. This so-called *random access* is fundamental to hard-disk recording and editing, and it makes it possible to employ editing procedures that are quite unthinkable by conventional, traditional methods. As the originally recorded data need never be erased or altered, this form of editing is said to *non-destructive*.

The way in which a hard-disk editing unit handles data will be more readily appreciated by those who have had some experience with MIDI sequencers. A sequencer allows a composition to be built up by combining various sections or patterns into some kind of order, and there's no restriction on how many times the same pattern can be used – for example, a chorus section can be recorded once and then called up whenever a chorus is required. Not only that but hard-

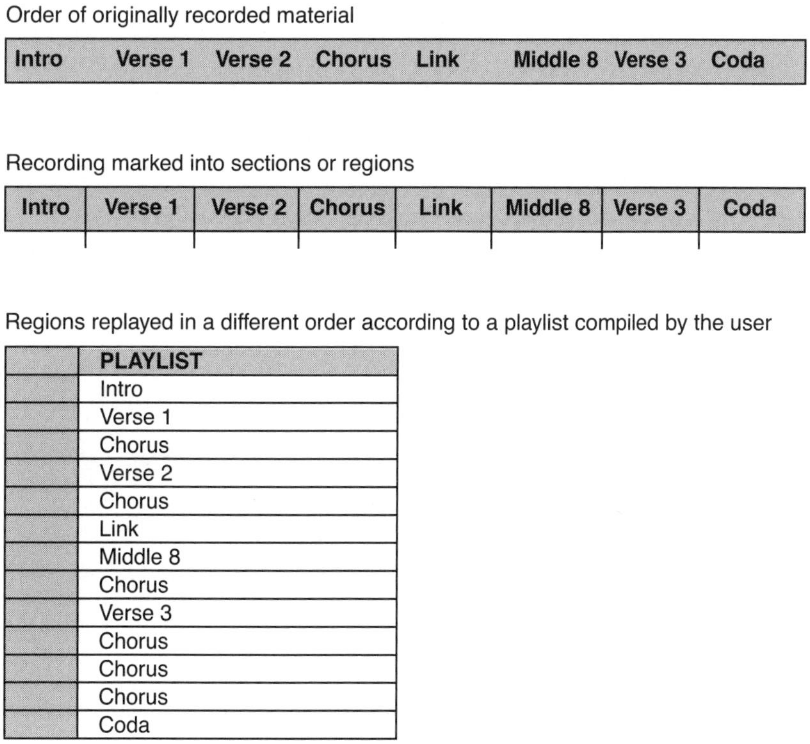

Order of originally recorded material

Intro	Verse 1	Verse 2	Chorus	Link	Middle 8	Verse 3	Coda

Recording marked into sections or regions

Intro	Verse 1	Verse 2	Chorus	Link	Middle 8	Verse 3	Coda

Regions replayed in a different order according to a playlist compiled by the user

	PLAYLIST
	Intro
	Verse 1
	Chorus
	Verse 2
	Chorus
	Link
	Middle 8
	Chorus
	Verse 3
	Chorus
	Chorus
	Chorus
	Coda

Figure 16.1: Random-access editing

disk editing allows you to do exactly the same with audio data – songs can be divided into sections such as verses, choruses, intros, links, bridges, solos and so on, and then rearranged to produce a longer or more interesting version of the song. (Again, if you already use a sequencer with audio capabilities, you'll be aware of this incredibly useful feature.)

Compiling Albums

When compiling an album, the required songs are recorded into the system either via the analogue inputs or via a direct digital S/PDIF link from a hardware recorder, such as a DAT machine. The songs may be recorded one at a time or the whole album may be recorded as one long audio file, in which case editing is accomplished by dividing the recording into marked sections which can then be compiled into a playlist. Where songs are recorded individually, they

need only be 'topped and tailed', a term meaning that any unwanted noise or count-in clicks are removed from the start and the end is either cleaned up or faded, as appropriate, so that all that remains is the audio that will comprise the finished track. Indeed, many so-called extended remixes are accomplished by using these basic techniques. Figure 16.1 shows how the sections of a song can be rearranged in a hard-disk editor.

Any decent stereo editor will allow you to mark cue points 'on the fly', making it very easy to mark a song at exactly the right place while playback is taking place. Then, if you can tap along in time with a song, you can mark an accurate edit point! These edit points can subsequently be fine-tuned to perfection. This degree of precision is very useful when it comes to joining two sections of audio that need to flow seamlessly from one into the other.

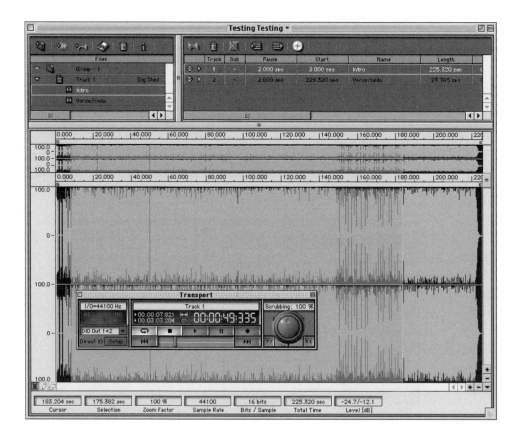

Figure 16.2: TCWorks' Spark editor

If the individual songs don't need to be edited in any way, they simply need to have their start and end points marked so that they can be arranged in the correct order with the required gap between each, usually in a part of the editor known as a *playlist*. Alternatively, the regions can be exported into a CD-burning program such as Roxio's Jam for Macintosh, where the appropriate gaps can be set and track levels changed (in Jam's own playlist) before burning a master audio CD.

Most systems provide some form of visual display that shows the audio waveform of the material being worked on, making it easier to locate the starts and ends of songs and to spot clicks and glitches. It's normally possible to audition the transition between one song and the next, and if the gap is too short or too long, it can easily be modified. Fade-outs at the ends of songs can be handled automatically by marking the start and end of the fade and then by applying either a destructive edit (ie one that permanently changes the data) or a non-destructive edit, depending on the way in which your specific editor handles fades. A typical editor will offer destructive cut/copy/paste, reverse, gain change, normalisation and fade in/out functions, in addition to its non-destructive capabilities. Figure 16.2 illustrates the main page of the TCWorks' Spark editing program, showing the waveform display.

Normalising

All hard-disk editing systems provide the facility to normalise audio files or sections of files. In this process, they simply identify the highest peak in the selected region and then increase the gain of the whole region by exactly the right amount in order to ensure that this peak is at the maximum digital level (or some lower level, if specified). In other words, normalisation lets you get a song as high in level as possible without clipping occurring. It sounds great, but there are a couple of points to watch out for.

Firstly, it's usually best to normalise after you've done all other processing, otherwise other processes such as EQ may increase the signal level further and lead to clipping. Even an EQ setting that produces only cut can increase the signal level slightly, simply because you may end up reducing the level of some frequency components that were previously helping to cancel out peaks at other frequencies. (This is also true of sample-rate conversion, because of the filtering involved.) Secondly, even if you've done all of your processing, it may still be best to normalise to a decibel or so below the maximum peak level in order to avoid causing clipping in some types of over-sampling digital-to-audio converters (as used in commercial CD players).

Processing

Separate sections of audio may be processed using plug-ins, either destructively or in real time. If you have a system that uses VST plug-ins, or indeed any of the other plug-in standards that offer real time MIDI control, these can be automated, which means that, if you need to make an EQ change at some point in a song, you can simply record the control changes once and they'll then occur every time you play back the song. Such facilities can be invaluable when compiling songs from different recorded versions where the tonality and level may not match exactly. (The rearranging of songs is discussed in more detail later in this chapter.)

Compiling albums is pretty routine stuff for a digital editing system, but these devices offer far greater precision than can be obtained with manual editing methods, and once the songs have been marked and named, it's easy to compile several alternative running orders, as might be necessary when producing masters for CD, vinyl and cassette releases of the same album. Any CDs destined for commercial production should be burned in Disk-At-Once mode using software that supports 'Red Book audio', the standard for commercial CD manufacture.

Red Book Audio

The term *Red Book* describes the data format used to manufacture commercial CDs. In addition to audio data, a CD also includes information concerning the start and end times of each track, the number of tracks, the total playing time and so on, and all of this is stored in a TOC (Table Of Contents), which is accessed before the audio starts. If a CD-R is to be used as a production master, it must have all of this data in place in such a way as to comply with the Red Book protocol. Some software produces audio CDs that will play on a regular

CD player, but they don't include all of the necessary information for Red Book compliancy. You should be aware that production-master CD-Rs should be burnt in a single session (ie in Disk-At-Once mode), as recording in multiple sessions creates errors between the tracks, which a commercial CD production system might reject. It's also important to use good-quality CD-R disks for mastering as low-cost media may have an unacceptably high error rate. Unfortunately, there's no easy way to tell what this error rate is, as this requires specialised equipment, so it's best to play safe and use reputable media.

Rearranging

The real power of a digital hard-disk editor becomes apparent when it comes to editing individual songs. Provided that the recorded material is accurately marked off into sections, these sections can be strung together without the slightest trace of a glitch between them. A straight butt joint between sections is often satisfactory, but better editors offer a crossfading facility to join sections for those occasions when this is more appropriate. It's normally best to choose edit points that coincide with drum beats, as this will make timing easy to handle and will hide any discontinuities that might occur when joining two sections that weren't originally consecutive.

The way of fine-tuning edit points with a hard-disk editing system is to loop around the edit continually so that you can hear any changes as you make them. For instance, it would be normal to set a few seconds of pre-roll before the edit and a few afterwards so that you could get a feel for the pace and rhythm of the music as the edit passed by. Small changes in timing can then be made, often using simple nudge buttons, which can be set for a user-definable number of milliseconds, and then, when the timing matches up, all that you need to do is apply a crossfade if the join isn't already smooth enough.

Problems to listen out for here include things like the end of a sustained note appearing directly after an edit because the original part preceding the edit included the note. If the new preceding part doesn't end with the same note, the 'orphan' note decay will sound unnatural. Moving the edit point forwards or backwards by a whole number of beats can sometimes help, as can using a longer crossfade time, but in some instances no satisfactory solution is possible. With a good edit, even the engineer who performed it shouldn't be able to notice it.

Corrective Measures

Most serious computer-based editing programs – for example, Sound Designer II, TCWorks' Spark, Wavelab, Bias Peak and Sadie – allow the operator to zoom in on a tiny section of the musical waveform, where flaws such as interference clicks can be identified quite easily. These can usually be 'drawn out' using an on-screen drawing tool to replace the damaged section of the waveform with something smoother or, alternatively, a similar section can be copied from elsewhere in the song and pasted in place of the damaged piece. If the software includes an automatic smoothing facility, this should be enabled when drawing out clicks or some discontinuity may still be audible. Once a song has been put together from various sections and you're sure it sounds OK, the next option is to save it as a new sound file so that it can be added to your album along with the other songs.

Backing Up

While disk-based systems offer faster and more flexible editing than analogue tape, razor blades and splicing tape, the finished work has to be backed up both to free up the disk for the next project and to provide security copies. At one time, backing up was very a time-consuming process – everything had to be done in real time – but today you can back up over 70 minutes of stereo audio onto a CD-R costing only a few pence. Larger projects can be backed up to DVD-R, but CD-R is generally fine for stereo work. Where the audio is being backed up at a 16- rather than 24-bit rate, it should be backed up as data files rather than as audio. 16-bit projects may also be backed up as data, the advantage being that you also store all of the session details, such as cue points.

It's tempting to think that, once you've mixed a few stereo tracks, all you need to do is put them on CD and you have an album. Certainly the low cost of CD-R disks makes this an attractive proposition, but there are several processes that need to be carried out before you're ready to record a master DAT tape or burn a CD that can be used as a master for commercial production. These stages tend to come under the umbrella title of *mastering*, because the ultimate aim is to produce a master that can be copied for commercial production.

The editing aspects of mastering were covered earlier in this chapter, although a professional mastering engineer will also often use his skill to enhance the quality of the source stereo recordings using a variety of signal-processing techniques and may even rearrange the various elements within a song – for example, removing an unwanted verse or chorus.

Signal Processing In Mastering

Some people think that mastering simply means compressing everything to make it sound as loud as possible, but although compression can play an important role in mastering, it's only one piece of the puzzle. The most important tool by far is the ear of the person doing the job, because successful mastering is all about treating each and every project individually. There is no standard blanket treatment that you can apply to everything to make it sound more 'produced'.

Project studios often have less-than-optimum monitoring environments, resulting in mixes that may need further tonal adjustment during the mastering process. To do this job successfully, you'll need at the very least a good parametric equaliser, a compressor (ideally a multiband model) and a monitoring system that you know to be accurate and with which you're used to working. When mastering in a private studio, the processing will probably come from plug-ins or from a dedicated hardware mastering processor such as a TCWorks Finalizer or Drawmer 2476. The top professional mastering houses use a lot more than this, including some very specialised equipment, but if you take care you can achieve excellent results using relatively simple equipment, especially if you have access to some good software processing plug-ins.

The majority of mastering is carried out in the digital domain, but there's no reason not to use an analogue equaliser if you have one that sounds especially musical. Bear in mind the consequences of transferring data to the analogue domain and back again, though, as this may outweigh any benefits offered by your analogue EQ, unless your system has especially good converters.

Common Issues

The most serious errors in tonal balancing tend to occur at the bass end of the spectrum, where project-studio systems are invariably least accurate. The practical outcome is that the master recording will have either too much or too little bass. Additionally, many mixes suffer from a slightly congested sound with a lack of detail.

If you attempt to turn up the high end using a shelving equaliser, you'll also bring up any noise present in the recording and this can also produce a harsh tonal quality. A better approach is to identify the high-frequency sounds that need help and then use a parametric EQ or sweep mid to lift these slightly. One popular mastering technique is to add a sense of 'air' to a recording by applying a very wide boost (using a parametric EQ set to a bandwidth of around one octave) at around 14kHz. This is too high to produce tonal harshness but lifts out high-frequency detail in a very smooth and musical way.

Similarly, bass problems should be addressed by concentrating on the problem area rather than by applying global bass boost. For example, most kick-drum problems occur between 70Hz and 100Hz, so there's little to be gained from using a setting that also boosts the 40Hz region by a significant extent. Meanwhile, a congested mid range can often be addressed by using gentle mid-range cut centred at around 1kHz, but be sure to keep this fairly wide and only cut by a decibel or two.

Dynamics

Some producers like to compress their finished mixes while others claim that this always makes things worse. The truth is that it all depends on the type of material you're working with, and if you want to maintain a high-energy feel, a few decibels of compression can help knit together the various component sounds within a mix. Soft-knee compressors seem to give the smoothest results on complete mixes, and a model with an Auto mode will deal best with changing dynamics.

At the mastering stage, the use of multiband compression (see Chapter 12, 'Dynamic Control') is common, because it allows the engineer more control over the separate parts of the audio spectrum. With a regular full-band compressor, high bass energy will also cause high frequencies to be compressed, but by using separate compressor circuits for each of three or four frequency bands, such side-effects are largely avoided – for example, you could use a higher compression ratio at the bass end to increase the density of the bass sounds without affecting the mid range or high end. Each band also has its own gain setting, allowing you to compensate for any tonal imbalance caused by compressing one band more than another.

I've used this type of compressor for mastering for several years now and find that one of the most effective strategies is to set a very low threshold (around –30dB) and a low compression ratio (1.1:1 or maybe 1.2:1). This results in the whole dynamic range being compressed gently rather than just the top few decibels being compressed hard, which is what happens when you use a high threshold and high ratio. Subjectively, the mix becomes more solid and apparently louder but without sounding obviously compressed. Small increases in ratio can be applied to any band that needs more assertive treatment – to increase the density of bass sounds, for example.

Limiting is also a vital tool at the mastering stage because very often you'll have a few really high-level, short-duration peaks that force you to keep your average signal level low in order to avoid clipping. Because these peaks are usually very short, they can often be limited quite severely before any audible difference is evident, but you'll need a limiter designed for mastering, set with a very fast attack time and a fast release time. A good mastering limiter will let you trim at least 4dB or more from peaks without producing any audible side-effects, which means that you can lift the level of the whole track by the same amount, making it louder. Producers argue the relative merits of using mastering to make tracks sound louder, but the sad fact is that, if you don't use limiting to get your track as loud as possible, it will sound very quiet when played next to a commercially produced pop CD, and the client will normally perceive this as a fault.

The real skill comes in being able to maximise level without introducing unacceptable side-effects.

Mastering Hardware

Stand-alone mastering processors generally feature both digital and analogue I/O (In/Out) and also tend to include parametric equalisation, limiting and multiband compression alongside other functions such as tube emulation, dynamic equalisation, de-essing and stereo balance/width control. The best of these units split the audio into three or more frequency bands before any form of dynamic control is applied.

Other facilities may include a choice of noise-shaped dither options for reducing the bit depth of high-resolution recordings (for example, reducing a 24-bit recording to 16 bits) while retaining as much of the original dynamic range as possible. Dithering works by adding a tiny amount of mathematically calculated 'pseudo noise' to the audio in order to avoid the severe distortions that occur at extremely low signal levels. Instead of the last bit simply switching off at the end of a fade (which sounds like gated distortion if heard at a very high level), the signal fades down into the background noise, much as it does with analogue tape. Because the noise is added at frequencies to which the ear isn't very sensitive, the perceived signal-to-noise ratio is not significantly changed.

Some processors also include an automated facility for the creation of fade-outs, although personally I prefer to handle fades on the computer after all other processing has been carried out, if at all possible.

The Resolution Revolution

Every time you manipulate the level of a signal in the digital domain or apply any form of processing, some resolution is lost because the resulting data has to be scaled down again to fit into the original number of bits. After multiple stages of processing or changes in level, low-level detail may suffer.

This problem may be avoided by recording and mastering using more bits than you intend to end up with, which is why 24-bit mastering is sometimes used for CD production, even though CDs only have a 16-bit depth. Once all the processing is complete, you'll still have audio with better resolution than the 16 bits you'll be using for your CD master, so the final stage is to use noise-shaped dither to reduce the bit depth from 24 to 16. A number of software editing packages include dither as standard.

Noise Removal

The use of budget effects, noisy synths and the contribution of ground-loop hums in home studios invariably mean that most recordings will have some audible noise on them during pauses or quiet passages. Topping and tailing the tracks helps, as the track remains completely silent until the music starts, but the noise will still be there in the background all the time the track is playing. If this is a problem, you can try using noise-removing software. Don't use gates or expander, because these can help only during pauses in the music, and even dynamic noise filters (sometimes known as single-ended noise reduction systems) are too limited for serious mastering.

Noise-removing software splits the audio into hundreds of separate frequency bands and then treats each individually. When the signal in a particular band falls below the noise threshold, an expander attenuates the signal, but because this happens over many independent frequency bands, it's quite possible to expand the noise in one part of the spectrum, leaving other parts unprocessed. Obviously, you don't have to set the threshold for each of several hundred expanders manually!

Most systems set their own thresholds by analysing a section of noise-only recording from immediately before the start of a song (sometimes called a *noise fingerprint*), and so for these to work it's essential that the songs have not yet been topped and tailed. The resulting noise spectrum is then used to set the threshold for each of the expander bands, although the user can usually alter these parameters to some extent. Over-processing can cause the background noise to take on a ringing or chirping character as frequency bands in different parts of the spectrum turn on and off, but better software uses intelligent linking between the bands to avoid this. Although side-effects can be audible if the amount of noise contamination is very high, most realistic situations can be dealt with very effectively.

More advanced noise-removing software, such as that developed by Cedar Audio, continuously evaluates the noise in the presence of signal, which is better in situations where the level and character of noise may change during a mix, as it often does if faders are being adjusted and tracks muted. These generally allow a much greater improvement in signal-to-noise ratio before side-effects become evident. Nevertheless, provided that the noise isn't excessive, a 'fingerprint' system should produce worthwhile results.

Artistic Decisions

When compiling an album, there are artistic as well as technical decisions to be made, not least in terms of setting the relative levels of tracks. If you were simply to normalise all of the tracks on an album individually, quiet ballads would sound unnaturally loud next to heavier-sounding tracks. Your judgement of what's right is all you have to go by, but a good guide is to make sure that the vocal levels are subjectively similar from track to track. The trick of listening from outside the room as one track plays into another will help you pick up any problems with level.

Similar problems arise if you're using tracks recorded at different sessions or even in different studios as these may differ in timbre as well as in level. You'll often need to apply parametric EQ so that they sit well together.

Judging the lengths of the gaps between songs is another subjective area. The usual inter-track gap is between two and four seconds in length, but much depends on whether the previous track has an abrupt stop or a fade-out and on the difference in mood between the two songs. The abrupt end usually needs more of gap than does a gentle fade-out. Fortunately, the correct gap is usually pretty evident, and I've found that, even when several people are involved in a session, the chances are they'll agree on the optimum gap length to within half a second. For my own projects, I edit and master individual tracks within my editing software before exporting the finished tracks into an audio-CD-burning program (Roxio's Jam is a good choice for Mac users) and input the gap lengths there. It's also possible to adjust levels in Jam, but it's best to do this before dithering so as not to make the task pointless. Figure 16.3 shows Jam's very simple playlist structure.

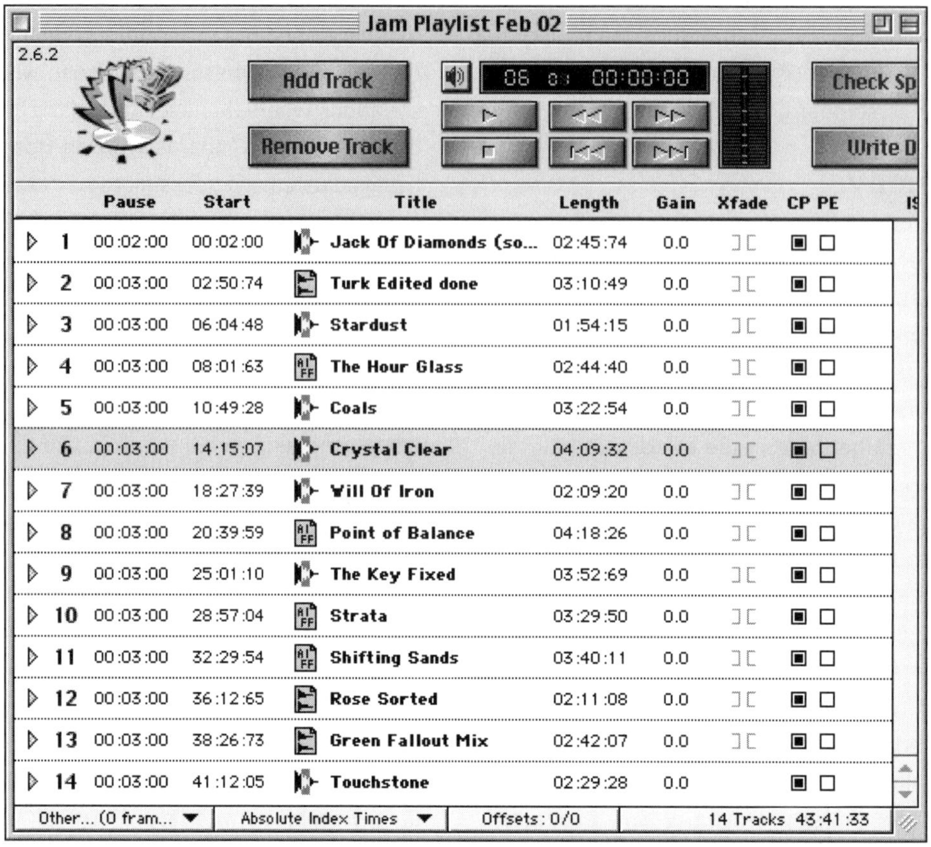

Figure 16.3: Roxio's Jam playlist

Avoiding Pitfalls

Most mixing and mastering mistakes are the cause of over-processing, so don't feel that you have to process a piece of music just because you have the tools. Here are some tips that might help if you're new to mastering.

• Where possible, handle fade-out endings in the computer editor rather than using a master tape that was faded during the mix. Not only will the computer provide more control but it will also fade out any background noise along with the music so that the songs ends in perfect silence. Ideally, fading out should be the last thing you do before dithering down to the final bit depth.

• Once you've decided on a running order for the tracks on your album, you'll need to get the levels to match. As stated earlier, this doesn't just mean making everything the same level, as this will simply make any ballads seem very loud when compared to more powerful songs. The vocals often give you the best idea of how well matched songs are, but ultimately you have to rely on your ears. In particular, pay attention to the levels of the songs on either side of the one on which you're working, as it's in the transition of one song to the next that poor level-matching shows up most.

• If tracks were recorded at different times or in different studios, they may not sound consistent enough to sit together comfortably on the album without further processing. Although this incompatibility can be ascribed to various factors, including the types of musical arrangements employed, it's generally possible to make a significant improvement by using equalisation alone. You'll need a good parametric equaliser (either hardware or plug-in), however, as poor equalisers can really mess up a sound.

Listen first to the bass ends of two adjacent songs to determine how each differs and use the EQ to try to even things up – for example, one song might have all the bass energy bunched up at around 80–90Hz while another might have an extended deep bass that goes right down to 40Hz or below. By rolling off the sub-bass and peaking up the 80Hz area slightly, you might be able to bring the bass end back into focus. Similarly, the track with the bunched-up bass could be treated by adding a gentle 40Hz boost, combined with a little cut at around 120Hz. Every equaliser behaves differently, so there are no hard-and-fast figures – you'll just have to experiment.

- At the mid range and high end, a gentle boost applied at between 10kHz and 15kHz will add air and presence to a mix while cutting at between 1kHz and 3kHz will reduce harshness. Boxiness tends to occur between 150Hz and 400Hz. If you need to add top to a track that doesn't have any (as may be the case if you're working with an old analogue tape that's started to deteriorate), try a harmonic enhancer such as an Aphex Exciter, as applying high-end EQ boost in this situation will simply increase the hiss. Keep your EQ adjustments as subtle as possible because the more EQ you use, the more 'processed' the music is likely to sound. Pay particular attention to the timbre of the vocal and make sure that it stays natural. Finally, it's generally true that EQ cuts can be narrower than EQ boosts – boosting should always be as gentle as possible, while you can be more forceful when cutting to remove problem frequencies.

- To make a track sound louder when it's already peaking close to DFS (Digital Full Scale), use a digital limiter, either a software plug-in or one that comes as part of an external mastering processor. In most cases, you can increase the overall level

by up to 6dB or even higher before you can hear that the peaks have been processed in any way. Limiting can be applied after mastering compression, although in most cases you should apply any compression and EQing first and then use a normalising limiter, such as a Waves L1, to get the track sounding as loud as possible without compromising the sound quality. (In most cases, this means using the limiter to apply no more than 5–6dB of additional gain reduction to full-scale signals.) Once you've treated all of the tracks in this way, you can then balance the tracks with each other by reducing the levels of those that seem too loud. However, if you're using a limiter that also offers bit reduction with noise-shaped dithering (such as the Waves L1 Ultramaximiser plug-in), it's best to use it as the last process on track so that you can use the dither function to maintain the best possible dynamic range. Dithering must always be the last process that the audio data undergoes if it's to be effective, so get the tracks balanced with each other first if you plan to apply limiting and dithering in a single operation.

- Make sure you have a CD player and some reference material to hand and compare this with your own work regularly. Not only will this act as a reference point for your ears but it will also help you to compensate for any remaining inaccuracies in the monitoring system.

- Overall compression can add energy to a mix and will help to even out the performance, but it isn't mandatory; music needs some light and shade to provide dynamics. Often, full-band compression will change the apparent balance of a mix slightly, so you may need to use it in combination with EQ. Putting the equaliser before the compressor results in any boosted frequencies being compressed the most while putting it after the compressor allows you to equalise the compressed sound without affecting the compressor's operation. The best arrangement will depend on the material being treated, so try both.

A split-band compressor or dynamic equaliser

will give you more scope to change the spectral balance of a mix and will produce the least noticeable side-effects. I find that low thresholds (–20dB to –35dB) and low compression ratios (less than 1.3:1) work best for most material.

- One way of homogenising a mix that doesn't quite gel or sounds too dry is by adding reverb (usually an ambience setting) to the entire mix. This has to be done very carefully, however, as excess reverb tends to make things sound washy or cluttered, but I find ambience programs excellent for imbuing a mix with a sense of space and identity without making it sound processed. If the reverb is cluttering up the bass sounds, try rolling off the bass from the reverb send. I've used this technique on occasions when assembling albums from tracks recorded at different times and I've found that it can give them a similar sense of liveness, although you have to be very subtle in your approach.

- If you want to add a stereo-width-enhancing effect to a finished mix, there are two main things to consider: the balance of the mix and the mono compatibility of the end result. Most stereo-width enhancers tend to increase the levels of panned or stereo sounds while suppressing those in the centre slightly. This can sometimes be compensated for with judicious use of EQ, but being aware of the problem is half the battle. Stereo-width enhancement also tends to compromise the way in which a mono mix sounds, so always make sure that it still sounds acceptable with the Mono button in. While most serious listening equipment is stereo these days, a lot of TVs and portable radios are still mono, so mono compatibility is still important.

  Mastering processors such as the Drawmer 2476 make stereo enhancement easier as they provide it as a split-band process – in other words, you can leave the vulnerable low frequencies as they are (or even narrow them) and width-expand only the middle and high frequencies, if you want to.

- It's essential to listen to the finished master all the way through, preferably over headphones, as these

have the ability to show up small glitches and noises that loudspeakers may mask. Digital clicks occasionally appear in even the best systems, although using good-quality digital interconnects that are no longer than necessary always helps to reduce this risk.

- If the end product is destined to be a CD master, always try to work from a 44.1kHz master tape/file (or sample-rate-convert to 44.1kHz) at some stage in the proceedings. If you have to work from a 48kHz tape/file or a DAT with different tracks recorded at a different sample rates, you can use a stand-alone sample-rate converter as you transfer the material into the computer or use the analogue inputs. Some editing software will allow you to perform a conversion inside the computer, although this takes processing time.

  If your master is for commercial production rather than for making CD-Rs at home and you don't have any facility with which to convert sample rates, leave your master at 48kHz and inform the mastering house so that they can handle the conversion for you. (Also write the sample rate on the box in BIG LETTERS!) You may be charged extra for sample-rate conversion, so it's always better to handle it yourself if you can. You can always convert sample rates by using the analogue input of your mastering system, but unless the converters are of very high quality it may be best to stay digital and leave the sample-rate conversion to the mastering house.

- When transferring digital material into a computer, always make sure that the computer hardware is set to External Digital Sync when you're recording and Internal Sync when you play back. Double-check that your recorded sample rate matches the source sample rate – clients will often present you with DAT tapes either at the wrong sample rate or even with tracks at different sample rates. Making sure that you have a sample-rate converter permanently in line will prevent this situation from causing problems, although you should be aware that some hardware sample-rate converters won't work on 32kHz material, the sample rate used by

DAT machines in Long Play mode. This mode isn't generally used for music production because of its limited bandwidth, but on more than one occasion I've been sent 32kHz material to master.

- Digital de-noising programs are wonderful things, but they're not magic; even the best systems produce side-effects if the source material is excessively noisy. The simpler systems are effectively multiband expanders where the threshold of each band is set by first analysing a section of noise between tracks. For this reason, it's best not to try to clean up your original masters prior to editing, or there may be no noise samples left to work from. Used carefully, you can get a significant reduction in noise before the side-effects set in, but if you try to remove all of the noise from extremely noisy material, the noise may be modulated as individual expanders open and close, producing an unnatural 'chirping' sound. In this case, the more noise reduction you try to apply, the worse the chirping becomes, so it's best to use as little as you can get away with. A reasonably safe technique is to reduce the background noise as much as possible while leaving it high enough to mask any low-level chirping that occurs as a result.

- When editing individual tracks – for example, when compiling a version from the best sections of several mixes or recordings – try to make butt joins just before or just after a drum beat so that any discontinuities are masked by the beat. However, if you have to use a crossfade edit to smooth over a transition, try to avoid including a drum beat in the crossfade zone or you may hear a phasing or 'flamming' effect where the two beats overlap. As a rule, crossfades should be as short as possible in order to avoid producing a double-tracked effect during the fade zone. As little as between 10ms and 30ms is enough to avoid producing a click.

- On important projects, run off two copies of the final mastered DAT tape or CD-R (using one as a back-up) and mark these as 'Production Master' and 'Clone'. When using the CD-R format to produce a master that will itself be used for commercial CD production, the disk must be written in Disk-At-Once mode rather than a track at a time and the software must support Red Book PQ (Pause and Cue) coding. Check with your CD manufacturer to confirm that they can work from CD-R as a master and take note of any special requirements that they may have. Also, be sure to resist the temptation to use cheap blank CD-Rs, as these can produce significantly higher error rates than good-quality, branded disks.

- If you don't have a computer editing system, you can edit your master using a DAT player or MiniDisc recorder, although it's difficult to achieve any precision in this way and assembling sections of tracks is impossible. When making a digital transfer of your master from a DAT recorder to a CD recorder that can read DAT IDs, it's best to manually edit the DAT IDs first so that they occur around half a second before the start of the track and place the first ID two seconds before the start of the first song. This will mean that you won't risk part of the first note being missing when the track is accessed on a commercial CD player.

Mastering For Release

There are now numerous formats on which you can release a record if you include CD, MiniDisc, DVD and film or video soundtracks, and there are also various surround-sound formats currently emerging. The main consumer formats are CD, MiniDisc and the analogue compact cassette, although vinyl is still a viable option, especially for specialist dance and club music. DVD (Digital Versatile Disk) audio, with its various surround-sound formats, is clearly 'the next big thing', although surround mastering and DVD authoring are very specialised subjects and are largely beyond the remit of this book.

Once an original master recording has been made (by mixing the multitrack material to stereo), a production master must be made from it, because the original master (or masters) will contain out-takes and unwanted material, and the songs will probably be recorded in the wrong order and have gaps of incorrect lengths between them. It may also be necessary to adjust the relative levels of some of the tracks, and at this stage it's not uncommon to add further equalisation and/or compression. All of the stages that come between the original master tape and the production master fall under the umbrella of *mastering*.

When making a production master for vinyl or cassette, there must be a gap between the two sides, and the playing times of the two sides must also be as equal as possible. As a rule, side 1 of an analogue cassette is made slightly longer than side 2 so that, when the tape is turned over at the end of side one, side 2 is ready to play.

The total recording time of a C120 cassette can be a lot longer than that of a CD – most CDs offer a maximum recording time of 74 minutes, though it is possible to record up to 80 minutes. If you intend to exceed 74 minutes, you should discuss your requirements with the manufacturing company. In the case of other formats, including vinyl, you should consult the manufacturer before producing the production master tape in order to confirm the maximum playing time that can be accommodated. Creating mixed-media CDs – for example, those including video clips – will reduce the amount of time available for audio material, and again you should discuss any such requirements with the duplicating house.

For CD mastering, you can provide either a DAT or a CD-R, and providing the latter is often the easier option. Production master tapes should be arranged with no gap between the two sides of the album and a total playing time of less than 74 minutes, including gaps. The duplicating house may require a fully prepared CD master tape, which is most often handled by a specialist mastering facility and involves copying the production-master DAT to a U-Matic tape. This is PCM encoded, time-coded and has the necessary PQ (Pause and Cue) code information added in order to comply with the Red Book standard for CD manufacture. Fortunately, many companies are now equipped to work directly from a CD-R master, provided that it's Red Book compatible and has a low error rate.

The falling cost of low-volume CD-R duplication makes CD-R a viable alternative to conventional manufacture for small production runs – ie those of 250 disks or less. These may be made directly from a production master tape or from a Red Book CD-R. However, you should note that most *but not all* CD players will play CD-R disks, as the disks have a different optical characteristic to pressed CDs.

The CD Glass Master

When making commercial pressed CDs, the CD tape or CD-R master has to be played into a glass mastering machine in order to produce a 'glass master', so called because a glass disk is used to carry the photo-sensitive surface, which is then imprinted with digital data from a modulated laser. This is subsequently plated with nickel to make a mechanical stamper, similar in concept to those used to stamp out vinyl records. During manufacture, the reflective part of the CD is stamped out of aluminium and then sandwiched between layers of transparent plastic, which protect it and give it rigidity.

After manufacture, the disks are automatically loaded into plastic jewel cases along with an inlay card and booklet, so you'll also need to talk to the manufacturer about the practical details of providing artwork for the case and CD label. Although it's possible to produce your own CD artwork using a computer-graphics program and an inkjet printer, this is only cost-effective for very small runs, and fitting the inserts into the jewel cases can become very tedious!

17 3D SOUND

We are constantly being told that we stand on the threshold of a surround-sound revolution where every listener will have a properly set up, multi-speaker home-theatre system on which they can play back audio DVDs mixed in true surround sound. Indeed many people *do* now have some kind of surround playback system, which they use mainly for their TVs and DVD video players, but in my experience few are set up anything like well enough to entrust to audio, and I have yet to meet anyone who has bought an audio-only recording in one of the new surround formats. Maybe by the time this book is next updated everyone will be playing surround audio and we'll all have thrown out our hopelessly old-fashioned stereo CDs – and perhaps all pigs will be fully fuelled and ready to fly! Even if the surround formats do eventually enjoy a degree of commercial success, I expect stereo CDs to be the predominant music format for the next decade, and perhaps even beyond that.

Fortunately, there are techniques that can make even stereo recordings seem wider than the speakers over which they are replayed. Indeed, several devices (both hardware and software) that claim to create the illusion of three-dimensional sound from a standard two-speaker stereo system are available, where the term 'three dimensional' indicates that sounds in the mix can be made to appear to originate from a location outside the boundaries of the loudspeakers. Some processors, in particular Roland's RSS (Roland Sound Space), are able, under certain circumstances, to create the illusion that the sound source actually moves behind the listener. Bearing in mind that all of the sounds must emanate from two speakers in front of the listener, how is this possible?

3D Hearing

To understand how 3D sound systems work, it's necessary to know a little about how the human hearing system handles the directional nature of sounds. Indeed, a little understanding of this subject helps to position sounds in the normal stereo soundfield, so even if you have no intention of using a 3D processor, this section will be of value. Even so, I feel it's inevitable that low-cost 3D sound processors will soon be a common feature of even small recording studios.

Just as our two eyes give us stereoscopic vision by presenting two simultaneous viewpoints of the world, our two ears do the same for sound. Only if a sound is directly ahead of us or directly behind us (or somewhere on an imaginary line joining the two points) do both ears register the same sound. With the speed of sound being finite, it stands to reason that a sound originating directly from our right will arrive first at the right ear and then, some short time later, at the left. This time difference is noted by the brain and is just one of the means used to determine direction.

The sound arriving at the right ear will be unobstructed, while the sound arriving at the left ear will be masked by the head itself. This masking serves to reduce the level of the sound and also to modify its spectral content – high frequencies are more attenuated whereas low frequencies remain relatively unaffected because their wavelength is significantly greater than the dimensions of the head. So far, then, the human brain has three parameters to work with when analysing the input from a pair of ears: the time delay between the sound reaching first one and then the other ear; the difference in sound level occurring between the two ears; and the tonal change caused by the masking effect of the head. In contrast, a conventional pan pot simulates only one of these parameters: the level difference between the left and right ears.

Front Or Back?

Useful though the above explanation is, it doesn't tell us how it's possible to discriminate between a sound that's directly in front or directly behind because, in both cases, the signals arriving at both ears are identical. Similarly, if the sound originates at any point on the imaginary line drawn between these two extremes – such as directly over the head – the ears will still hear the same thing.

This is a very complex mechanism to comprehend, and it's thought that small, involuntary head movements help us to compare the signals arriving at both ears in the same way that we might move our heads to establish visual parallax between two objects that are otherwise ambiguous. The exact importance of this mechanism has not been confirmed, but there is another point to consider, which is far easier to quantify. Ears are not just biological microphones stuck onto the side of the head but are recessed and surrounded by the flaps of skin that form the outer ears – more correctly termed *pinnae*. This outer ear masks the inner ear from incoming sounds to a greater or lesser extent, depending on the direction of the sound, and measurements show that the effect of this masking is mainly spectral. In other words, the perceived tonal property of sound changes in accordance with the direction of the source relative to the head position.

Dummy-Head Recording

When Roland developed their 3D sound system, they took the logical approach of using a dummy head, complete with pinnae, to analyse sounds originating at different positions around the head. The inter-aural changes in level, time delays and spectral filtering effects were all noted and then used to control a set of computer-controlled filters, delays and level shifters which, in theory, would recreate the original sounds as perceived by a typical pair of ears. Indeed, they went further, making numerous measurements using volunteers with small microphones fitted into their ears to obtain a true average set of values.

The system so far allows (theoretically, at any rate) a mono sound to be processed so that, when it's monitored over a pair of good headphones, it can be positioned anywhere in front of, behind or above the listener using a couple of 360º pan pots, one for the horizontal plane and one for the vertical. However, such a system won't work effectively on loudspeakers because, when you listen to a conventional stereo system, some of the sound from the left speaker enters the right ear and vice versa, and this *crosstalk* completely undermines the validity of the effect. With this in mind, Roland went a stage further and measured this crosstalk in a typical listening room, then used the data to generate a crosstalk-cancelling signal. In other words, what you shouldn't be hearing in the left ear (from the right speaker) is synthesised and then reversed in phase before being added to the normal left signal, and vice versa for the right. Now, if you're listening to a properly set up stereo system in a decent listening room from a point equidistant between the two speakers, it should be possible to perceive the processed sound to be coming from wherever it's been positioned by the system.

There are an awful lot of ifs in this explanation, and the fact is that none of the 3D sound systems work perfectly for all material or on all stereo set-ups. Most systems will enable sounds to be placed noticeably outside the speaker boundaries, and the result is very convincing, but the success of any attempt to place the sound behind the listener depends on several factors, not least being the kind of sound being processed. In practice, the illusion of sound coming from behind the listener tends to break down unless the sound is moving; if it is panned from one side at the front, around the back of the listener's head and then back to the front opposite side, the result can be very convincing indeed, but any attempt to place a stationary sound behind the listener tends to fail. To confuse matters, different listeners respond to these effects in different ways.

In addition to Roland's RSS, there are two other major systems: Q Sound and Spatializer. All of these systems work on variations of the same principle, although there are fundamental differences in approach that mean each system has its own character.

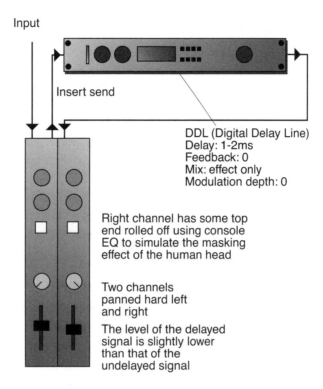

Input

Insert send

DDL (Digital Delay Line)
Delay: 1-2ms
Feedback: 0
Mix: effect only
Modulation depth: 0

Right channel has some top
end rolled off using console
EQ to simulate the masking
effect of the human head

Two channels
panned hard left
and right

The level of the delayed
signal is slightly lower
than that of the
undelayed signal

Figure 17.1: Stereo positioning using a DDL

Mono Compatibility

While it would appear that all of these systems offer a useful means of widening the available stereo image, and while some can be used in a gimmicky way to move sounds or effects right around the listener's head, their real downfall is in their lack of mono compatibility. This is inevitable, as real life can't be considered mono compatible, but as long as mono TV sound and mono radio receivers are with us, it has to be a cause for concern. The main problems are the phase and timbral changes that occur when the left and right signals are summed; the further the sound is panned outside the speakers by the 3D system, the more noticeable the side-effects become.

However, work is being done to improve the mono compatibility of these systems and to make their effects less dependent on the listener's position relative to the loudspeakers. Whether 3D systems will ever become fully effective is questionable at this stage, but the techniques that make these effects possible

are already being employed in various pieces of studio equipment as well as being built into some consumer audio playback equipment and TV sets. Some stereo sample-library material is prepared using 3D sound systems, and the technology has also been built into stereo effects units of different type – for example, it's used to widen the subjective sound of digital reverbs and delays.

Originally, 3D sound processors were very expensive items and were limited in the number of channels of audio that could be processed at any one time, but now that plug-in software versions are available at a much lower price anyone can experiment with these effects in their own productions. Their use requires no special skill, although knowing when to use them and when to leave the audio untreated does require a degree of experience. Whatever the limitations imposed by current processors of this type, their real beauty is that recordings need no decoding or special equipment at the user's end, and while in its present state 3D sound may be no substitute for true surround sound, it can be used to add interest to pop records and to enhance the special effects used in movie soundtracks.

Stereo Effects

Having learned how the human hearing system perceives sound direction, it's possible to employ a little studio trickery to exploit these effects without having to buy special equipment. For example, you now know that, in order to make a sound appear as though it's coming from one side or the other, you not only have to change the relative left/right balance but you also need to delay one of the signals slightly. The time it takes for sound to travel around the human head is a little under 1ms, so with this in mind you should be able to experiment with a DDL as shown in Figure 17.1. Here, the signal is being panned to make it appear as though it's coming from the right-hand side while a lower-level, delayed version is panned to the left. This creates a more solid directional image than using the pan pot alone, although it isn't perfect because no account has been taken of the crosstalk between the speakers. The effect can be made slightly more authentic by rolling some of the top off the delayed signal to simulate the effect of head masking. The delayed signal needs to be only 3dB or so lower in level than the undelayed signal, and varying the

delay time slightly shifts the perceived location of the sound source to some extent.

This principle is unwittingly employed when a sound is split and a direct version of the sound is panned to one extreme while a chorused or flanged version is panned to the other. The sense of depth and movement is due to the shifting delays between the processed and unprocessed signals, making this a very powerful processing technique, even though the chorus/flanger need only be a mono unit. Variations on this effect are used extensively to enrich synthesised string and pad keyboard sounds or to create pseudo-stereo guitar chorus effects. (These specific techniques are described in more depth in Chapter 15, 'Mixing').

Summary

Because of the inherent technical limitations, and the fact that the mix engineer has no control over the type of playback system employed by the end user, any type of 3D processing is bound to be a compromise and, in any event, it will never come close to providing the sense of direction and space that a true surround-sound recording does. Nevertheless, when used with care, it can make stereo recordings seem much more spacious and involving, although it may be wisest just to use it on those elements of the mix for which mono compatibility isn't vital – for example, sound effects and secondary percussion.

18 HEADPHONES

Have you ever wondered why people don't just mix all of their music over headphones? After all, it would reduce the amount of environmental noise considerably and would completely eliminate the need for acoustically treated control rooms. It sounds like the ideal solution. Unfortunately, headphones behave rather differently to loudspeakers in several key areas, and as most music is optimised for loudspeaker playback, relying solely on headphones can be very misleading.

Imaging

When stereophonic music is heard over a pair of conventional loudspeakers, the natural human hearing mechanism positions the soundstage in front of the listener, whereas with headphones there's little or no front-to-back information, which makes the sound appear to originate from either inside or above the listener's head. The problem of accurate stereo imaging is further compounded by the fact that, when listening via loudspeakers (or, indeed, to a sound in real life), some of the sound from the left speaker enters the right ear and vice versa. With headphones, there is a very high degree of separation between the signals presented to the two ears, which produces an artificially enhanced sensation of stereo imaging. While this makes it difficult to predict the effect of the same mix over loudspeakers, it can be helpful when you want to make sure that all the sounds are where you intended them to be and that any stereo effects sound properly balanced.

Tonal Imbalance

A more serious shortcoming of headphones is that each person who uses them will hear a different tonal balance, even though they're all using the same model

of headphone. This is particularly true at the low end of the audio spectrum, where factors such as the distance between the headphone diaphragm and the ear, and the effectiveness of the cushion seal will influence the amount of bass that the listener perceives. You can try this for yourself by listening via headphones and then pushing them closer to your ears; you should notice a dramatic increase in bass because the headphone diaphragm has moved closer to your ear and the proximity effect is causing a significant degree of bass lift.

The problem of maintaining an effective seal between the headphone and the area of head around the ear can be avoided by making the headphones acoustically open. On these models, instead of the headphone being in the form of a sealed enclosure that fits over the ears, the transducer is mounted in an acoustically transparent basket and spaced away from the head by means of padded cushions. Such open designs have the added advantage that the sound is less coloured than when confined by a sealed cavity, but the downside is that external sound is free to leak in and some of the sound from the headphones will leak out. This isn't a problem when monitoring while mixing, but it can be troublesome when a performer is using such headphones to listen to a backing track or click track as some of the spill from the headphones might leak back into the performer's microphone.

Although the sound quality of open headphones can be excellent and inconsistencies due to ineffective sealing can be largely eliminated, they still create some inconsistency in bass perception caused by variation in the distance between the headphone diaphragm and the ear, a distance that is dependent on the physical make-up of each individual ear. Where such headphones excel, however, is in their ability to discriminate fine detail within a musical mix, and traces of distortion that can go unnoticed when heard over a loudspeaker are more likely to be picked up. Ideally, a mix should be checked on both headphones and loudspeakers, although for the home recordist working in a noise-sensitive environment it's possible to do a considerable amount of work over headphones and to resort to loudspeakers only to check crucial stages of a mix for overall tonal balance.

Summary

Headphones are essential tools inasmuch as they can reveal recording flaws that may be missed on loudspeakers, but because of their imaging characteristics and their inconsistent bass reproduction they should be used to augment loudspeaker monitoring, not replace it.

Enclosed headphones are best for performance monitoring as they produce far less spill than partially open models, but be aware that many singers like to work with one headphone on and one off. In this case, the headphone not placed over the ears may still spill sound into the room, where it can be picked up by the vocal mic. The way to avoid problems is to choose a headphone amplifier on which one phone can be switched off, or even to make up a special headphone extension cable and leave one side of the phones disconnected.

19 MEDIA MATTERS

One of the less glamorous but nevertheless essential tasks in any studio is to ensure that all tapes and disks are properly labelled. To do otherwise risks confusion at best and, at worst, the erasure of an irreplaceable recording. This applies to analogue tape, digital tape, CD-Rs and removable hard drives. There is a standard tape labelling system devised by the APRS (Association of Professional Recording Studios), which sets out to reduce the potential for error. This was originally designed to cover both multitrack and stereo master tapes, copies, clones and DAT tapes, but it can also be used for disk-based media. Colour-coded labels are available via the APRS, but you can also print your own using an inkjet printer. Some media (such as professional DAT and ADAT tapes) also comes with a choice of AES-style labels, although as a last resort simply writing the correct term on the box will suffice.

Media should always be labelled with format details. In the case of analogue recordings, the tape speed, track format, noise-reduction format, EQ used and, of course, the title and date of the recording are essential. Digital tapes should be labelled with the sample rate employed and details of the type of machine used to make the recording. Open-reel tapes are traditionally stored 'tail out', as this reduces the degree of print-through when the tapes are stored for a long time. Tapes should be rewound before playing. CD-Rs may be labelled using an indelible pen designed for writing on the label side of the disk and removable hard drives usually have a space set aside for a label. Hard drives mounted in removable caddies can have labels stuck to the front of the caddies.

NB: The following descriptions were devised for tape-based media, but they can also apply to other storage media. Where test tones are discussed, digital tape and disk-based media can be treated in the same way.

Session Tapes

The first tape created during a project is a *session tape*. This is usually a multitrack tape and comprises the first-generation recordings made during a session. In other words, it's the working tape on which material is recorded and overdubbed, so consequently it may contain out-takes as well as wanted material. There may be several session tapes created during an album project, and they may be of any format and may be analogue or digital. Indeed, in the case of direct-to-stereo recording, the original recording is still known as the session tape. All relevant data should be recorded on the tape box or inlay card. The APRS label is solid blue and bears the words 'SESSION TAPE'.

Original Masters

When a multitrack tape is first mixed to stereo, the result is the *original master* tape. This is the earliest generation of the final stereo recording. This is not necessarily the tape used for production, as it may later be necessary to add EQ or to edit the material. The APRS label is solid red and bears the legend 'ORIGINAL MASTER'.

Production Masters

The *production master* is usually an edited copy of the original master on which the tracks have been placed in the correct running order and with correct spacing between the tracks. Often, the production master will be equalised, and as different versions may be required for different release formats, the production master should be marked with the desired format – CD, cassette, vinyl, DCC (Digital Compact Cassette) or MiniDisc. The standard APRS label is solid green with the legend 'PRODUCTION MASTER', while the label also includes space for release-format details.

For digital formats such as CD, DCC or MiniDisc, the production master will have to be transferred to Sony U-Matic format at the mastering stage, and you should be aware that test tones should not be recorded onto tapes destined for digital formats. Many production masters are now made on DAT, in which case a sampling rate of 44.1kHz is preferred, if the machine allows it.

Production Master Copy/Clone

This is copied from the production master to allow distribution of the tape for manufacturing purposes without having to release the original production master. A tape copied in the analogue domain from either a digital or analogue source is known as a *copy* while a digital duplication of a digital original is known as a *clone*. In theory, a clone will be identical to the original in every way. For this format, the APRS label is bright orange with the words 'PRODUCTION MASTER COPY/CLONE' printed on it. The appropriate copy or clone box should be ticked and the label should include all information relating to the production master.

Safety Copy/Clone

This is strictly a back-up copy or clone of another tape; the original from which it is taken should be clearly marked on the label, which is bright pink and bears the legend 'SAFETY COPY/CLONE'. The appropriate 'copy' or 'clone' box should be ticked and the label should include all information relating to the original.

Not For Production

This describes any tape produced in any format that must not be used as a source for media manufacture. The label is yellow and bears the words 'NOT FOR PRODUCTION'.

PQ-Encoded Master Tape

This is the final U-Matic tape ready for the manufacture of a digital-media release such as CD, DCC or MiniDisc and includes the coding information pertaining to

number of tracks, the playing time, a table of contents and so on. Each of the release formats requires the PQ-encoded master to be prepared in a specific way, so it's essential that the media required is identified on the label, which is grey and is branded 'PQ-ENCODED TAPE MASTER'. Tick boxes are provided for the various media formats required for release and to state whether the tape is an original or a clone. It's now increasingly likely that production houses will be able to work from a PQ-encoded CD-R master, which should also be labelled accordingly.

Media Version

This term describes a copy or clone made for a specific purpose, such as radio broadcast or film/video soundtrack work. If the tape is recorded with time code, this should be noted on the label, which is yellow and marked 'MEDIA VERSION', with tick boxes for the various options: radio, TV, film or video.

Analogue Tape Copying

When copying a tape, it's necessary to know the maximum recorded level on that tape. (This is not the case when making a digital clone, as the copy will be the same as the master tape in all respects.) Recordings are normally preceded by test tones, and the reference level of those tones should be marked on the tape box. Correctly recorded tones will be recorded with a burst in the left channel only at the start of the Tones section, so it should be possible to check that you haven't got the right and left channels transposed. It's also wise to do a few spot checks throughout the tape to ensure that the test tones do in fact relate to the recorded level.

If the tape has been produced as a production master for CD manufacture, or of some other digital format, there will be no test tones, in which case it may be necessary to play the material and establish the level at which the peaks have been recorded.

Test Tones

The standard format for test tones is five seconds of 1kHz tone on the left channel only, followed by around 30 seconds of the same tone on both channels. The tone should be recorded at 0VU and the level should be noted on the box. In terms of preserving alignment when the tape is played back on another machine, it also helps if a 100Hz, 0VU tone is recorded, followed by a 10kHz tone, the latter often recorded at around −10dB and the level again being noted on the box.

With digital tapes such as DAT, it is common practice for these to be recorded so that the peak levels come to around 2dB below the maximum meter reading or FS (Full Scale). It's always a good idea to record a couple of minutes of silence onto the start of the tape, as the very start of a tape is more prone to errors. If continuous test tones are required for calibration purposes, a nominal level of −14dB FS (1kHz) is considered acceptable, and this should be noted on the label. At the end of the copy, there should be at least 30 seconds of recorded silence before the tape is stopped.

Record, Tape And CD Manufacture

With the advent of MD (MiniDisc) and DCC (Digital Compact Cassette), there are now five potential record release formats, and this figure doesn't include film or video soundtracks. The main formats at the time of writing remain Compact Disc (CD) and the analogue compact cassette, although vinyl is still a viable option, especially for specialist dance and club music. What follows is an overview of the various processes that take place between completing a mix in the studio and the manufacture of a record from that recording.

Once the session tape (usually an analogue or digital multitrack) has been mixed down to stereo, the tape is designated the *original master* and it is from this tape that a *production master* must be made. In all probability, the original master (or masters) will contain out-takes and odd spuriae such as count-ins, and the material will probably be recorded in the wrong order with incorrect gap lengths between the songs. It may also be necessary to adjust the relative levels of some of the tracks, and it's not uncommon to add further equalisation.

Working With DAT

When mixing to DAT, it is important to record as close as possible to the digital peak shown on the recorder's meters and to use the 44.1kHz sampling rate setting if available. When working with a DAT machine that has a fixed 48kHz sampling rate, don't worry – if you're

planning to make CDs, the company who produce the CD master tape for you should be able to handle this. However, never mix the two sample rates on one tape (or set of tapes) – you could end up with part of your album playing back at the wrong speed!

When making DAT production masters, always set the Start ID function to On. Normally, playing a song cued using an ID recorded with the Auto ID is to risk clipping the first note, because the Auto ID function must sense the presence of the programme material before writing the ID. Because of this, it's wise to manually move all IDs back by half a second or so.

Avoid recording music on the first or last minute of tape and always record silence before and after the programme material – digital tapes contain subcode information and it is important that this starts before the recording and continues for a while after it. Don't simply run the tape in Play mode to create a gap as this will leave a section of tape with no subcode.

Hard-Disk Editing

While it's possible to make up a production master by compiling from one tape machine to another, a more precise option is to use a hard-disk editing system. These have the advantage that individual tracks can be 'topped and tailed' to ensure that they're clean up until the moment when the first note sounds and that all count-ins and other unwanted material are removed. The edited material is then copied from the hard-disk system to a stereo tape machine, ideally DAT, as the transfer can be made in the digital domain. This new tape is now the *production master*. Recording this on digital formats such as DAT gives you the advantage of being able to clone the material rather than having to copy it, making it possible to create back-ups and compiled production masters with no loss of quality.

Preparing A Production Master

When making the production master, a decision must be made as to whether the release will be on vinyl, cassette or some digital format. If it's to be on cassette, there must be a gap between the two sides and the playing times of the two sides must be calculated to be as equal as possible. As a rule, side 1 is made slightly longer than side 2 so that, when the tape is turned over at the end of side 1, side 2 is ready to play.

Careful listening is required to ascertain whether any of the tracks need to be adjusted in either level or EQ. The gaps between songs should also be auditioned, and although most will be around four seconds, the length must be determined by ear; if the preceding song fades out, the required gap may be shorter than if the song finishes abruptly. Essentially, if the gap feels right, it is right.

A full listing of the songs by title, start time (Start IDs) and playing time must accompany the production master, and this list should also include full details of the recording format, such as sampling rate and, ideally, the type and model of machine that was used.

When compiling to analogue tape on an open-reel machine, the gaps are created by splicing either blank tape or leader tape between the songs. The lengths of blank tape required can be calculated from the running speed of the recorder.

The total time on a cassette can be a lot longer than on CD – most CDs offer a maximum recording time of 74 minutes. However, most commercial CDs are under 60 minutes in duration, so this should present no problems. In the case of other formats, including vinyl, before producing the production master tape, it's best to consult the manufacturer to find out the maximum playing time that can be accommodated.

What Comes Next?

If you're planning to release your material only on analogue cassette, a copy or clone of the production master may be all you need. Of course, you'll also have to think about artwork, but that subject will be covered shortly.

Unfortunately, the production master isn't the end of the line if you're aiming for a CD release – there are two more stages you'll need to negotiate: the CD master tape and the glass master. Similarly, if you're going to add MiniDisc to your release formats, you'll need to speak to the manufacturers to find out their requirements. The main difference between MD and the established formats is that MD uses a form of data compression to reduce the amount of digital data to around one-fifth of that needed by a conventional CD or DAT tape. Furthermore, MD has the ability to store text, which can be used to display such things as the song titles on those machines equipped with display windows.

CD Mastering

For CD mastering, the production master tape will be arranged with no gap between the two sides of the album and will have a total playing time (including gaps) of less than 74 minutes. The factory will require a fully prepared CD master tape, which is most often handled by a specialist mastering facility and involves cloning or copying the production master to a U-Matic Tape. This is PCM encoded, time coded and has the necessary PQ (Pause and Cue) code information added. This information is then used to create the TOC (Table Of Contents) on the finished CD so that a CD player can locate the tracks. A sheet listing the titles and times of the tracks will also be produced at this time for use by the CD manufacturers, usually by the company that produces the CD master tape.

Some mastering facilities can make a reference CD from the CD tape master. This is relatively inexpensive, and the small outlay is worth it for the peace of mind it gives you in knowing that the finished product will turn out as you expected it. If a proper reference CD is unavailable, a one-off CD-R disk is better than nothing, although on these the start times of the track may not accurately reflect those on the finished product.

It's now increasingly popular for CD production masters to be recorded onto CD-R, usually after the mastering process (carried out either by the user or by a dedicated mastering facility). Provided that the master CD-R is recorded in Disk-At-Once mode using software designed to handle PQ encoding (the so-called Red Book standard), it should be usable as a production master, but be aware that some cheap media and some CD-R writers generate higher error rates than are acceptable by the production houses. Unfortunately, you won't know what the error rate is until you submit your CD-R, so it's best to use only good-quality, branded media for serious work and ensure that the disk's surface is absolutely free from dust before you record it.

While on the subject, the falling cost of low-volume CD-R duplication makes CD-R a viable alternative to conventional manufacture for small-quantity runs of 250 disks or less, although you should be aware that a few commercial players refuse to play CD-R. This is not deliberate but simply a result of the playing surface of CD-Rs having a different reflectivity to that of a pressed CD. CD-Rs may be made directly from a production master tape or audio CD-R, thus saving the cost of having to have a CD master tape produced. Many companies can print colour artwork directly onto the label side of a CD-R, making the finished product look very professional.

Glass Masters

At the CD plant, the CD tape master (or audio CD-R master) is played into a glass mastering machine, which reads the PQ data from the master to create a table of contents. After the data has been transferred to the glass master (so called because a glass disc is used to carry the photosensitive surface, which is imprinted with digital data from a modulated laser), the glass master is plated with nickel to make a mechanical stamper, similar in concept to that used to stamp out vinyl records.

During manufacture, the reflective part of the CD is stamped out of aluminium and then sandwiched between layers of transparent plastic, which protect it and give it rigidity. Labels are printed directly onto the pressed CD using a special quick-drying ink and may be in single or multiple colours. The manufacturer should be consulted when it comes to deciding the exact form that the artwork should take.

After manufacture, the discs are automatically loaded into jewel cases along with inlay cards and booklets, which must be provided by the client prior to manufacture. Few CD pressing plants handle their own inlay-card printing, but most will be able to recommend a company that can do this for you or arrange printing on your behalf. However, if you don't arrange the printing yourself, there are going to be at least two other businesses in the chain, which increases the possibility of error. Although it's always possible to produce your own inlays using an inkjet printer, cutting them and inserting them is a tedious business,

and unless you're producing only a very small quantity, it's probably a more cost-effective option to have them printed professionally.

Brokers

An common approach to CD production is to negotiate a package price with a broker who will handle all the aspects of record or CD production, including the various mastering stages, printing and packaging. However, don't assume that, just because you've hired a broker, everything will proceed smoothly – check how things are going at every stage, if at all possible. You should also make sure that there no hidden costs; companies quoting attractive prices for CD manufacture often don't include essential services such as producing the CD master tape, glass mastering and producing printed material, and these are often priced as extras. Realistically, a minimum practical production run of CDs is 500, with 1,000 or more being even more cost-effective. For lower quantities, CD-R production is the most affordable option.

Try to find a broker recommended to you by someone you know, if at all possible, because, as in all areas of business, there's a vast difference in quality between the best and worst companies offering what is ostensibly the same service.

Vinyl

Vinyl records are produced using metal stampers, which, in turn, start life as a pair of lacquer masters, one for each side of the record. These are cut from blanks using a record-cutting lathe and then taken to the record-manufacturing plant, where the stampers are made. The stampers (or factory masters) are formed onto the lacquers using an electroplating process.

The actual record labels are printed on paper using special heat-resistant inks, and most record plants have the facility to arrange the manufacture of these. The fixing of the labels is achieved during the pressing process, and once the records have been trimmed of waste material and inspected, they are placed in sleeves. Inner sleeves are often optional, so you should discuss sleeve requirements with the factory when discussing cost. As with CDs, the minimum practical quantity for manufacture is several hundred.

Compact Cassette
High-Speed Copying

Cassettes may be made from a production master tape(ideally in DAT format). In the case of high-speed copying, the production master will normally be copied onto a special analogue machine designed to work at high speeds. The recording will then be made onto cassette tape stored on large reels (or 'pancakes'), which will be wound into empty cassette shells after recording. This procedure offers the advantage that the tape can be cut exactly to the required length and the copying process isn't compromised by the mechanics of the cassette shells.

As a rule, both sides of the tape will be copied at the same time, and unless you state otherwise, the recordings will be made using Dolby B noise reduction. Depending on your budget, there is a choice of standard Fe tape or Type II tape, also known as 'chrome equivalent'. Standard cassette shells will be available in black or white.

Solid-state memory stores have now replaced high-speed tape for mastering purposes in some duplicating plants and, in theory, these produce less degradation in audio quality. Essentially, the whole album is loaded into a large digital memory in real time and then clocked out at high speed during the copying process.

Real-Time Copying

Real-time copies may be made directly from a DAT source, and the destination cassettes are usually pre-loaded with tape. This procedure gives less flexibility when it comes to controlling the playing time of the final product, but it gives the advantage that low-production runs are economically viable.

High-Speed Cassette-To-Cassette Copying

The least satisfactory method of cassette duplication is the high-speed system, which works from a cassette master and records onto pre-loaded blank cassettes. The tape guides in cassette shells don't work well at high speeds and this leads to inconsistent recording quality. The fact that the production master must be copied to cassette also introduces another generation of quality loss into the duplication process.

Labelling

When labelling a cassette, it's possible to either stick printed paper labels onto the case or to print directly onto the shell itself. This latter process must be done during the duplication process and is only cost-effective for runs of several hundred tapes or more due to the cost of making the special printing plates. As a rule, paper labels allow you more scope in the use of colour and design.

Packaging

Cassettes are normally delivered in transparent library boxes and the folded inlay cards are generally printed separately. For small runs, these may be inserted by hand. In the case of very small runs, it may be worth using a colour photocopy bureau to produce copies of the original artwork.

Media And Machine Care

While analogue multitrack machines are now something of a rarity, there are still many open-reel machines in service, and these must be cleaned and serviced on a regular basis if they are to remain reliable. More important, perhaps, is that a badly maintained machine could damage your tape. To clean an open-reel machine or analogue cassette deck, you'll need a pack of cotton buds and a bottle of pure isopropyl alcohol.

Cleaning Analogue Recorders

The cleaning procedure for open reel and cassette machines is essentially the same, the only real difference being that the heads and guides on cassette decks aren't as easily accessible as they are on an open-reel recorder. Particles of oxide shed from the playing surface of the tape eventually build up to form a hard, dark-brown layer on the heads, causing a loss of high-end reproduction, but oxide also builds up on the tape guides, where it can interfere with the smooth passage of the tape over the heads.

Using a cotton bud soaked in isopropyl alcohol, clean the record head, the playback head, the capstan and all of the guides until no further oxide comes off on the cotton bud. Repeat the process using a new cotton bud. If this comes away clean, you're done. Clean all of the other parts of the tape path (ie the parts touched by the tape) in the same way, except for rubber rollers, which should be cleaned with a weak detergent/water solution. Be sure not to allow excess alcohol to run into bearings, as it will dissolve the grease. Once everything is clean, wipe off any excess alcohol with a dry cotton bud and wait a few minutes before playing a tape to ensure everything is properly dried out.

You should clean the heads before every important recording project and visually check the heads, capstan and pinch roller for oxide build-up regularly.

Demagnetisation

Analogue tape recorders (both cassette and open-reel models) contain lots of ferric metal parts that may eventually become magnetised, resulting in a loss of playback quality, and in serious cases you may even damage tape played back on the machine. Exposure to magnetism causes a partial erasure, most evident at high frequencies, and this is irreversible. All of the heads and guides should be demagnetised on a monthly basis as a preventative measure.

For open-reel machines, use a hand-held demagnetiser and follow the instructions precisely. Switch off the tape machine, then switch on the demagnetiser well away from the tape heads. Bring the demagnetiser slowly towards the machine, pass it gradually over the heads and guides and then slowly withdraw it to a safe distance of a metre or more before switching it off. Slow movements ensure a gradual build up and reduction of the alternating demagnetising field, which is necessary to demagnetise the recorder.

Open-reel tape demagnetisers may also be used on a cassette deck, although battery-powered, automatic demagnetisers are available that may be more convenient to use.

Analogue Tape Machine Alignment

Aligning a cassette machine isn't really a job for the end user, but these days few people use cassette machines for anything other than casual listening, so accurate alignment is less important than perhaps it once was. However, it's possible to align your own open-reel analogue machine with the aid of a test tape and a CD of test tones. If you've never done this before, it's advisable to have someone on hand to take you

through the process before you try, even though your tape machine manual should contain detailed alignment instructions. If you're not confident about doing this yourself, it's best to have your machine checked over every few months by a service centre, as careless alignment can render a machine unusable.

Recorder Mechanics

Analogue tape recorders need occasional lubrication, and parts such as rubber drive belts and brake pads will need to be replaced from time to time. Eventually, the heads will also need to be replaced, although the precise life of heads depends on the design of the head, the abrasive properties of the brand of tape being used and the regularity with which the heads are cleaned. Excessive wear of mechanical parts or heads will be picked up during a routine service, but servicing can be expensive, especially when it comes to replacing heads, so never buy a used open-reel machine unless you know that the heads are in good condition.

Analogue Tape

All brands and types of analogue tape exhibit different magnetic characteristics, so your machine will have to be set up to work with a specific brand. The record bias, record/playback levels and record/playback EQ all have to be adjusted to give a flat frequency and to calibrate the maximum recording level to the headroom of the tape itself. This can be done for you when you have the machine serviced, although, as I mentioned earlier, you can do it yourself with the aid of a test tape (a tape on which is recorded a set of standard tones at specific levels). If you intend to use a brand of tape other than that for which your machine was set up, you should have your machine realigned to suit the new tape. Cassette decks are also optimised for certain types of tape, but with a little trial and error you should be able to find a brand that gives a reasonably accurate result with your machine.

Analogue Tape Care

Even if you don't plan to service your own analogue recorder, you will need to take special care of the tapes. Magnetic tape hates extremes of temperature, dust or humidity. Normal room temperature is fine for storage, but try to pick a dry place where the temperature stays stable, such as a bedroom drawer. Keep tapes out of direct sunlight and wind them through before use.

Cleaning Digital Tape Machines

Most digital tape machines use a rotating-head system rather like that used by a video recorder. Dry-cleaning tapes are available, and these are usually OK for routine cleaning, but specialist wet cleaning should be carried out whenever the machine is serviced. Access to the heads is usually a matter of removing the top cover, but cotton buds must never be used on digital machines as the fibres become jammed in the gaps between the heads and will ruin them. A purpose-designed cleaning cloth is available for digital machines, made from something that looks a little like heavy silk, and a special cleaning fluid should be used instead of simple isopropyl alcohol. If you'd like to clean your own heads, get an engineer to take you through the process first, as it's very easy to cause expensive damage inside these machines, especially stereo DAT machines, as everything is so small.

Sticky-Shed Syndrome

It's well known that analogue tapes deteriorate in storage, and many master tapes produced during the '70s are virtually unplayable (due to technical problems with the binder materials at this time) unless they are first 'baked' at a controlled temperature of around 50ºC for several hours to drive off the moisture they've absorbed over the years. Even this cure is only temporary, and it's advisable that digital copies of all valuable old material are made as soon as possible. It's easy to tell if a tape has this problem as oxide sheds at an alarming rate and sticks to the heads and tape guides. You'll probably also notice a physical

screeching noise as the tape passes over the heads or guides.

Tape doesn't last forever, of course, but storing it properly makes a big difference. If you do have to leave tapes in the studio building, consider using a dehumidifier to prevent moisture from building up.

Digital Data Integrity

Digital audio and MIDI sequencing involves storing data on a number of different media, including floppy disks, fixed and removable hard drives, removable magneto-optical drives, tapes, RAM cartridges and CD-Rs. If any of this data becomes corrupted, you may lose important work, so digital media needs to be stored just as carefully as analogue media. What's more, although analogue-media deterioration is progressive, digital media always seems perfect until the day it fails, so you really have no safe way of assessing its quality. The moral here is that you should back up anything important.

WARNING: Never try to splice damaged DAT, ADAT or DA88 videotapes as the splice will almost certainly damage the rotary head.

CD-Rs are useful for backing up computer audio data that doesn't subsequently need to be changed or updated, and they tend to be reasonably robust, as long as they're shielded from sunlight and not subjected to scratching. To ensure a long life for CD-Rs, keep them in a disk-storage unit or jewel case when not in use and exclude all unnecessary light. Because of the low cost and high capacity of CD-R, it's a useful medium for backing up MIDI sequences for individual songs, along with their audio files, once the composition has been completed. Because the audio data is stored in the same way as other computer data, rather than as 16-bit audio, any audio format can be backed up, from 16-bit/44.1kHz audio to 24-bit/96kHz surround files.

20 SURROUND-SOUND CONCEPTS

Ever since the stereo vinyl record was introduced into the consumer audio market in the 1960s, stereo has been the standard release format for the vast majority of commercial music. When the compact disc superseded vinyl, the stereo format remained the standard. However, surround-sound audio has been used for the replay of cinema soundtracks for many years, and there was even an unsuccessful push to establish the quadraphonic (four-speaker) surround format in the consumer audio marketplace over 30 years ago. There are many explanations for the failure of the quadraphonic format, but the relatively large size of loudspeakers and the technical inadequacies of the system, combined with a limited amount of quadraphonic material, must have been major contributing factors.

Multiple Speakers

Perhaps the main point to note about surround sound is that it relates to audio reproduction using more than the two speakers required for conventional stereo reproduction. Although there are some systems based on psychoacoustic processing that claim to provide a surround experience from only two speakers (as described in the Chapter 17, '3D Sound'), true surround requires four or more loudspeakers positioned around the listening position at specifically defined locations. Even now, there is a lot of domestic resistance to the use of multiple speakers to reproduce surround sound, but the fact that today's speakers systems can be made physically much smaller than their predecessors, coupled with the huge success story of DVD-video home cinema, has helped make surround systems more acceptable.

Cinema Sound

Commercial surround sound has its origins in the movie industry, and even today it could be argued that we wouldn't be discussing surround audio at all if it weren't for the uptake of home cinema. The first true incarnation of surround sound is accredited to Walt Disney's animated film *Fantasia*, for which the soundtrack was conceived from the start as surrounding the audience rather than being played from the front, as had been done previously. Apparently, some fairly innovative technology was needed to take this surround audio show on the road, but the introduction of magnetic film soundtracks, and subsequently optical soundtracks, made the whole process a lot more doable, from a technical standpoint.

Matrixing systems such as Dolby Pro Logic were developed as a way to compact multiple audio steams into just two streams (for delivery using systems originally designed to carry only stereo audio tracks), and there are some ingenious methods used to minimise the inevitable effects of crosstalk caused by poor channel separation, but for really high-quality surround-audio playback you can't beat using discrete audio channels. Poor channel separation may go unnoticed when your eyes are glued to the screen watching an adventure movie, but your unaided ears are less forgiving when you're listening to music with no visual distractions.

Quadraphonics

The ill-fated quadraphonic system was based on locating a conventional stereo pair of loudspeakers at the front and another at the rear, with all four speakers being at 90º to each other. In contrast, conventional stereo requires the loudspeakers to be positioned 30º either side of centre, as this produces the best compromise between stereo width and stability of image. Moving the speakers to larger angles than this causes the phantom centre image to collapse if you move only slightly from the ideal listening position between the speakers, and quadraphonic systems suffered from exactly this problem. In other words, instead of the sound appearing to originate from locations all around the listener, it always seemed to be coming only from the four speakers. For some people, this was novelty enough, but it's my guess that the old 'You're not leaving those great big boxes there!' domestic dispute did the most to kill off the concept.

While tape machines could be constructed with four tracks to reproduce quadraphonic sound as discrete tracks (the original TEAC 3340S four-track machine that launched the home-recording revolution was originally conceived as a quadraphonic tape recorder), this wasn't possible using vinyl. Instead, 'matrixing' was used to cram four channels of information into two audio channels in such a way that the recording could be replayed in mono, stereo or quadraphonic with a reasonable degree of compatibility. To achieve this, the four audio channels are encoded into two (using all kinds of ingenious sum-and-difference matrixing circuits) during the recording process and decoded into four channels again during replay. If this sounds impossible, to some extent it is, as the inter-channel separation achieved by matrixing is pretty poor. Today's Dolby Pro Logic works with a similar matrixing system but includes a lot of technical enhancements to improve separation.

Dolby And Surround

Dolby Laboratories originally made their name in audio noise-reduction systems for use with analogue tape recorders but went on to become perhaps the biggest name in cinema sound reproduction. Using their existing expertise in audio processing, Dolby developed a four-channel analogue audio encode/decode system that could be used to recreate the surround effects now associated with films of that genre while still using only the original stereo soundtrack to carry the audio information. Rather than try to recreate quadraphonics, Dolby used most of its

resources to get the 'front' sound right by providing conventional stereo plus a centre speaker for dialogue. The remaining channel of audio provides the surround component and is traditionally fed to multiple speakers at the rear and sides of the theatre. The four-channel 'stem' is known as *LCRS*, standing for Left, Centre, Right and Surround, and is encoded using a matrixing system at the recording stage so that it can be carried by a two-channel (stereo) delivery format (film or video stereo soundtrack). In the context of film and video, the centre speaker was introduced to pin the main dialogue to the centre of the screen, regardless of where in the theatre members of the audience were sitting, but in music mixing it can also play an important role and offers an alternative to creating central 'phantom' images by the usual method of feeding equal amounts of the same signal to the front left and right speakers. (Note that the rear surround speakers are all fed from the same signal and therefore contain no left/right information.)

Separating the four audio tracks on replay requires a matrix-type decoder, but unless additional processing is used, most of the original separation is lost. Delay and filtering are used to enhance what separation can be salvaged from the process, not least the bandpass filtering that limits the surround channel to 100Hz–7kHz. For domestic systems, this has the advantage that the rear speakers can be physically small, as they aren't required to reproduce much low end, and in budget systems they can even be manufactured without tweeters without too much loss of effect because of the 7kHz limit on the signal feeding them.

Dolby Encoding

A Dolby surround encoder takes the left and right channels and mixes them with a modified version of the centre and surround channels in order to reduce what was originally four channels of information to two channels. Additionally, the surround channel is filtered below 100Hz and above 7kHz.

Finally, the surround signal is split into in two and the resulting components shifted by +90º and −90º before being summed back into the left and right signals. (This phase shift is what makes it possible to separate the signals to a useful extent when decoding.)

The matrix-encoded Dolby signal, which can be recorded onto any form of two channel audio recorder, is referred to as Lt and Rt (left and right 'total'). Note that any phase errors in the recording/replay chain will worsen the already limited channel separation that can be achieved, as well as causing image shifts. Unfortunately, this is exactly what you get from low-budget VCRs, as their analogue-audio record/replay system is notoriously unsophisticated!

Dolby Decoding

The Dolby decoding process (which in home theatre takes place in your domestic Dolby decoder) is largely the reverse of the encoding process, but delay is also used to minimise the psychoacoustic effect of any crosstalk that bleeds through to the surround channel. While the front signals can be recovered with a reasonable degree of accuracy, there's barely 3dB of separation between the front and surround channels.

When films were first released on VHS video with Dolby-encoded soundtracks, the separation provided by early generations of Dolby decoder (using passive-matrixing electronics) were, at the very least, disappointing. The later Dolby Pro Logic improved on this, and recently a Pro Logic II version was announced, ostensibly to provide even better decoding while still being compatible with existing Dolby-encoded media. However, Dolby Pro Logic is not the direction that high-quality surround music is likely to take in the future as there are now better alternatives that obviate the need to cram multiple tracks of audio into a delivery format intended for stereo. This is not to demean the achievements of Dolby in any way, as they went a long way towards making the impossible possible, but the restriction of having to shoehorn multiple channels of audio onto a stereo soundtrack have now been largely removed.

The main reason for mentioning Dolby Pro Logic at all in a book on music production is that most domestic home-theatre systems based on DVD players can also play regular audio CDs. If this is done with the Dolby Pro Logic decoder left switched on, parts of the mix occasionally appear in the rear channel, giving rise to an unplanned surround effect. This is caused by elements within the mix being phase-shifted with respect to each other. There are techniques using mixing consoles that allow you to exploit this effect by creating deliberate phase shifts to push parts of your mix into the surround channel, but a simpler method is to use an effects processor such as the Lexicon PCM 90/91 that includes a number of phase-shifting options to create intentional surround-sound effects. Because using a Dolby Pro Logic mix is not a precise science, it's essential to monitor the mix via a Dolby decoder when adding surround elements in this way, but with a little care some worthwhile results can be achieved. Even the simple act of adding some reverb to the surround channel as well as to the front speakers provides a convincing impression of listening in a large, reflective environment.

Current Formats

Modern films and DVDs employ a more advanced type of digital surround reproduction that provides five discrete channels of audio plus a sub-bass channel (this is the 5.1 format) for low-frequency sound effects, such as earthquakes and explosions. More elaborate cinema installations may also use 7.1 systems, which provide separate surround channels for the sides and rear of the auditorium, but the 7.1 system has had little impact on music recording so far. The term '5.1' will turn up quite often in this section, but in essence the '5' part refers to the three front speakers and two rear speakers (ie Left, Centre, Front, Left Surround and Right Surround) while the '.1' refers to the audio channel feeding the LFE (Low-Frequency Effects) sub-bass speaker. Thus 5.1 audio requires six discrete audio channels.

It's perfectly possible to use just the audio capabilities of DVD video to provide music in a surround format, but now that the final specifications for DVD audio-only discs (DVD-A) have been agreed and suitable players are being built, there is also the opportunity to enjoy a higher-quality, audio-only format. DVD-Audio is a quite different format to that used for DVD-V and is based upon 24-bit/96kHz uncompressed audio with options for 192 and even 384kHz sample rates. The benefits of the 96kHz sample rate are questionable, as far as the typical consumer is concerned, so I can't see many music producers going to the expense of upgrading their systems to record and mix at 192kHz, or even twice that. What's more, I anticipate that a lot of DVD releases will be remastered from original multitrack recordings originally made for stereo release, or even 'folded out' from existing stereo masters, so the ultra-high-sample-rate argument is largely academic.

The problem with new standards is that they are so good that everybody wants one, so along with DVD-V and DVD-A there are competing (and mutually incompatible) systems such as Digital Theater Systems' DTS and Sony's Super-Audio CD (SACD). Furthermore, 5.1 film soundtracks may be included in the Dolby Digital or DTS formats. Many commercial DVD players are designed to play DTS-format recordings as well as DVD-V (although most output the DTS data via their digital outputs and require an extra DTS encoder to extract the surround information), but we're some way from having one player that can accommodate all of the competing formats. At the time of writing, very few DVD players can handle SACD discs or provide full DVD-A compatibility, although it's expected that universal players capable of replaying all formats will soon become available. Once a significant number of consumers are geared up to replay music mixed in surround rather than simple stereo, there will be pressure upon music producers to mix songs in surround, probably in addition to stereo. Indeed, this is already happening, even where the surround-sound version of the record isn't planned to be released until some unspecified time in the future. Even Microsoft has joined the format battle with its WMA format, supported by some commercial DVD players.

Surround In Music

For the music producer, surround provides both technical and artistic challenges, but on the other hand it opens up creative possibilities that could never be fully explored in stereo. On the technical side, it means employing a multispeaker surround monitoring system and having access to mixing facilities that can handle surround and not just stereo. Then there's the question of which recording format to use for the multichannel surround master, followed by the technical issues involved in producing a playable surround-sound DVD. As you might imagine, the authoring issues concerning DVD production are rather more complex than those presently faced in stereo mastering and CD master production.

Why Bother With Surround At All?

Conventional CD players are already being superseded by DVD players, the majority of which can play back 5.1 audio as well as your old CDs, at the very least. Then there's the Sony-Philips Super-Audio CD (SACD) format which, although only supported by some DVD players at this time, also has stand-alone audio players. All new Sony DVD players are able to replay SACD discs, and of course DVD-A is out of the starting gate.

Whether or not you think surround sound is a good thing, either commercially or artistically, the record companies, film producers, television producers, computer-games developers and so on are increasingly expected to provide surround-audio tracks as a matter of course, even though they may not be needed for release in that format, initially. Furthermore, although the public demand for surround audio may be small at the moment, it will almost certainly increase on the back of the home-movie-theatre revolution.

More About Formats

The 5.1 loudspeaker arrangement used in home-theatre systems and cinemas comprises three speakers in front of the listener and two behind, all of which are capable of handling full-range audio. These are augmented by a sub-woofer fed from the LFE (Low-Frequency Effects) channel. As stated, 5.1 simply means that the system comprises five full-range speakers (ideally 20Hz and 20kHz) plus an LFE channel feeding a sub-woofer. A 7.1 system would comprise seven full-range speakers plus an LFE channel. Where there isn't space for full-range speakers, 'bass management' is used to feed the 'missing' bass from smaller satellite speakers to the LFE speaker.

In order to guarantee accurate playback, the speakers in a 5.1 system must be placed at precise locations around the listener in order to reproduce the intended listening experience (although we all know that most owners of home-theatre systems put the speakers wherever they'll fit!). The LFE channel isn't strictly necessary for musical use, as music rarely contains very-low-frequency special effects, and many surround-sound mixing engineers argue as to whether it should be employed or not. My own view is that most home cinemas are set up with the LFE channel far too loud so as to make explosions on film more impressive, so if the LFE channel was used for important musical information, the mix could end up sounding ridiculously bass-heavy.

Data Compression

In all probability, commercial surround material will be mastered by a specialist mastering facility, but it's inevitable that surround-sound authoring software will become more readily available to the home studio owner. It's when you look into this that a number of potentially confusing issues arise, not least being the use of data compression to make all that audio fit onto a DVD and still leave room for the picture.

Dolby Digital is a term often associated with 5.1 surround film releases, but in this case Dolby are responsible for only the data-reduction system being used. In fact, both Dolby Digital and DTS are different types of multichannel audio data-reduction systems commonly used in both film work and DVD, where Dolby Digital can support anything from mono to 7.1 surround.

These two systems – the most popular cinema-sound data-compression systems currently used – have made the transition to DVD in order to make the most effective use of the available data-storage capacity. Dolby Digital is the best-known format and relies on a type of encoding known as *AC3*, a perceptual coding system that effectively leaves out parts of the audio signal that would normally be inaudible to a human listener because of masking by stronger components (in principle, not unlike the ATRAC system used on MiniDisc or .mp3). The resulting data stream is compact enough to be able to be fitted between the sprocket holes on a cine film, where they can be read by a specially designed optical reading system.

DTS (Digital Theatre Systems) is a fairly common format these days, and I believe that it was first used on the original *Jurassic Park* movie, where the audio was played back from a separate CD-ROM played in sync with the film. I'm particularly hopeful about DTS as a music format for the project studio, as it can be recorded onto a regular CD-R, as opposed to the more expensive DVD-R, and yet it can still be played back by the majority of DVD players. Note, though, that the DVD-V specification only includes Dolby Digital (AC3) coding and MPEG, leaving DTS as an optional format. Although some players can decode DTS directly, most simply provide a data feed via their digital outputs for use with an external DTS encoder.

DVD-A

DVD-Audio was devised as a means of using the whole considerable storage capacity of DVD as a means of providing high-quality, multichannel audio playback at up to 24-bit/96kHz resolution, or higher. Unlike sound used with video, DVD-A doesn't have to employ the same lossy data-compression techniques because there are no pictures to find room for.

The 5.1 Speaker Layout

Although 5.1 isn't the only surround-sound format, it's likely to be the most commercially popular for some time, and so is the monitoring arrangement that's most useful to the musician wanting to mix 5.1 music in the recording studio.

The physical positioning of the loudspeakers in a 5.1 system is defined by the ITU (International Telecommunications Union) and states that the front three speakers should be arranged with the angle between the left/right and centre speakers set at 30°, as shown in Figure 20.1. Some cinema systems deviate from this for practical reasons to do with screen size, but the ITU system prevails for music playback. Note that the left and right speakers in the ITU set-up are also correctly placed for playing stereo mixes so that the same monitoring system can be used for stereo and 5.1 simply by routing audio to the required speakers.

The three front speakers should be positioned in an arc centred at the listening position so that all are equidistant from the listener. In a professional installation where it isn't practical to set back the centre speaker by an adequate amount, a small centre-speaker delay (usually no more than a couple of milliseconds) is applied to compensate, effectively making the speaker behave as though it's further away.

The rear speakers are also positioned at points on

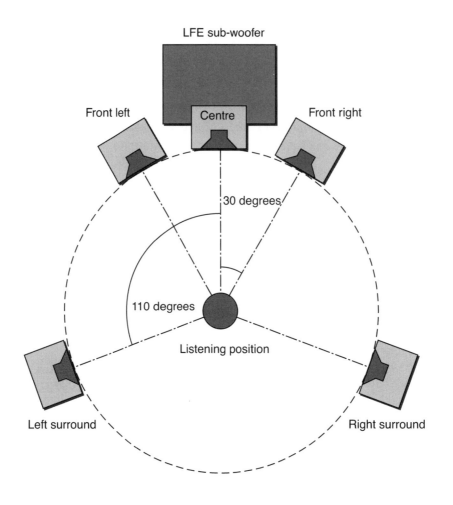

Figure 20.1: Using a surround amplifier as a controller

an imaginary circle drawn around the listener, as shown in Figure 20.1. These are set up at an angle of 110° from the centre front speaker, though a leeway of +/- 10° is allowed. Some surround amplifiers are equipped with variable rear speaker delay, which permits the speakers to be mounted closer to the listening position than the ITU recommended alignment while maintaining the correct time alignment. The rear speakers are known as *surrounds* and are generally abbreviated to as *Ls* and *Rs*.

Positioning of the LFE speaker is less critical because of the low frequencies involved, but some experimentation may be required to find a position that gives a nominally even level of bass in any given room, as unfortunate positioning that coincides with room mode dimensions or multiples thereof can result in some notes being too loud and others too quiet. Starting with the LFE beneath the centre speaker is probably a good starting point, but always follow the speaker manufacturer's guidelines in this respect.

To achieve accurate monitoring for film mixing, standard playback levels are used, although when it comes to mixing music, this is less likely to be observed. The main criteria is that all five full-range speakers are set up to produce exactly the same level for the same magnitude of input signal. A commercial surround amplifier will have a built-in calibration system for achieving this, usually by emitting sequenced bursts of pink noise around the speakers in a special set-up test mode.

Practical Systems

Although full-range speakers are specified for the five main speakers in a 5.1 playback system, this is clearly impractical in a domestic situation, and the number of systems available with tiny speakers indicates that there must be an alternative. The practical solution is to use smaller speakers with a limited low-frequency range and then to feed the missing low end to the sub-woofer, along with the genuine LFE information. This is known as *bass management*. If taken to extremes, it will compromise spatial accuracy at mid and low frequencies, but it's an acceptable compromise for consumer systems and (when implemented carefully) a practical solution for the smaller studio, too. In a typical studio system, it's unlikely that frequencies above 80Hz would be diverted from the main speakers into the sub-woofer.

The cut-off frequency of the LFE channel is defined specifically as 120Hz for film mixing, although some engineers have been known to set a lower value – 80Hz, say – for music-only applications in order to minimise the overlap between the LFE channel and the full-range speakers.

Calibrating the replay level of the sub-woofer is more difficult than calibrating the five main speakers as you can't use the same noise burst because of the restricted bandwidth of the LFE channel. Where bass management is being used, you may be able to get away with playing known material through the system while adjusting the LFE level by ear until you get a comfortable balance of bass to the rest of the mix. However, if you buy the speakers and surround amplifier as a complete matched package, there may also be a calibrated setting to provide the optimum main/LFE balance.

Choosing A 5.1 Monitoring System

The simplest way of setting up surround monitoring in the smaller studio is to use a powerful, commercial surround-sound amplifier combined with passive speakers. (Unfortunately, it's rather more difficult to control the level of an active surround system than a passive one as most project-studio mixing desks don't include dedicated surround-monitoring capabilities, even those that may cater for surround mixing.) It's vital that all five main loudspeakers are matched, in terms of their main characteristics, and the best solution is to use five identical speakers. Where this isn't possible, some manufacturers provide smaller speakers from the same family and with the same general characteristics (other than bass extension) that can be used as surrounds instead. Additionally, they may also produce a centre speaker that can be used horizontally rather than vertically, which can be useful when trying to maintain a line of sight through a control-room window.

Where active speakers are employed, these must be used either with a mixer that provides surround-monitoring control or be used with a separate surround-monitoring controller. Currently, these tend to be expensive, so a cheaper option may be to buy a commercial surround amplifier that provides line-level outputs (after the volume control) as well as amplified feeds for passive speakers. The signal output from your mixer must then be split to feed both the multitrack recorder used to record the six discrete channels of the surround mix and to feed the controller/surround amplifier.

Summary

Setting up a surround-monitoring system need not be difficult or expensive, although finding a suitable controller for active surround monitors connected to a mixer with no dedicated surround monitoring facilities (or to run directly from a sequencer's audio interface) can be difficult. Often, using a suitable surround amplifier with line level outputs is the cheapest solution. Given that most MIDI-plus-audio sequencers now include the ability to handle surround mixing (often with automatable parameters), it's relatively easy to experiment with surround mixing once a suitable monitoring system has been set up.

As you may have gathered from the brief explanations of the different surround formats in common usage, authoring any form of surround material to create a production master involves a lot of specialist knowledge and mistakes can be very expensive as some faults may not show up until you've had a batch of discs manufactured. I'm sure that more software will appear to make this task easier, but at the time of writing it's probably best to mix your surround material onto six tracks of an ADAT or DA88, or to save them as discrete audio files on CD-ROM and then employ the services of a competent mastering house to create the master for you. One possible exception is the DTS format, where software for systems such as Pro Tools and Digital Performer is already available. DTS has the attraction that it can be recorded onto regular CD-R, but the downside is that many DVD players will only play back DTS discs in stereo, unless a dedicated DTS decoder is connected.

The next chapter will look at some of the artistic issues raised by the possibilities of surround mixing.

21 SURROUND SOUND IN PRACTICE

The previous chapter was mainly theoretical, but it seems inevitable that surround recording and mixing will become a significant part of the project studio in the near future. Until now, most musicians have bought equipment designed to produce finished tracks in stereo, so some additional expenditure is inevitable when moving up to surround. Additionally, producing surround-sound recordings means there's a host of new factors to consider at all stages of the music-making process.

Advantages Of Surround Sound

When live music is played in ambient surroundings, the majority of what we hear is in fact reflected sound coming from all of the surfaces of the venue, not just from the musicians in front of us. When working in stereo, digital reverberation is used to try to create a sense of spaciousness, but it's always played back from speakers in front of the listener and so fails to create a convincing sense of envelopment. The attraction of surround sound is that it helps the studio engineer to escape from the boundaries of stereo and to create music that really does surround the listener, but that doesn't mean you have to use gimmicks such as placing instruments behind the listener.

As you may already know from working in stereo, individual musical elements may be in either mono or stereo, and in the case of mono, panning and effects are used to give the sound a sense of stereo width or placement. Surround productions can incorporate mono, stereo and full surround elements, the latter usually furnished by surround mic systems such as the Soundfield (coincident point source) or an array of numerous discrete mics roughly analogous to the surround version of a stereo spaced pair. However, you don't have to buy a Soundfield mic or extra mics to work in surround any more than you have to employ stereo-miking techniques to create stereo records. It's more likely – in pop-music production, at any rate – that working with mono and stereo sources most of the time will suffice. Positional information is then added by the use of 3D panning and effects such as reverberation placed in the surround speakers.

Surround Mixing

Mixing in surround means having access to the surround equivalent of a pan pot that can move signals from front to back as well as from left to right, while a further width control is also useful when working with stereo sources. Many of the better sequencers now include surround mixing as standard by providing multiple mix busses, virtual-joystick surround-positioning controls and separate sends for each mixer channel in order to feed the surround LFE channel. There also needs to be a way of deciding whether centre-panned signals should be reproduced from only the left and right speakers (as in conventional stereo) or from the centre speaker as well. In this respect, a variable control to set the phantom/centre balance (sometimes called 'divergence') is the ideal solution.

The main mixer-control requirements for surround panning are the abilities to pan from front to back as well as from left to right and to adjust the width of stereo source material. If your sequencer offers surround mixing, this is a great help, but if you're working with more traditional hardware that offers no surround support, you may need to improvise a little. Even the affordable hardware digital mixers offering surround support tend to be less flexible than their software equivalents (and seldom offer surround-monitoring facilities), so the alternative is to find ways of getting the job done using equipment originally designed for stereo work.

A surround mixer, or a stereo mixer being used for surround mixing, must have at least six busses that can be used to carry the six elements of the surround mix, and at the channel level some way must be found of panning the signal left and right and between the front and rear busses. Many stereo mixers designed for multitrack recording have enough busses, but obviously they're not fitted with surround pan controls. One possible solution is to use two

channels fed from the same source and to route one to the front left/right busses and the other to the rear (surround) left/right busses. Conventional panning can then be used to move the signals to the left or right in the mix, while adjusting the relative levels of the signal sent to the front and rear busses provides a means of front/rear positioning. This doesn't address the issue of the centre speaker or the LFE channel, but this is easily catered for by using two pre-fade sends, one to feed the signal to the LFE channel and one to feed some of the signal to the centre speaker, as shown in Figure 21.1.

Positioning a sound within the surround mix in this way is cumbersome, but it can be done. However,

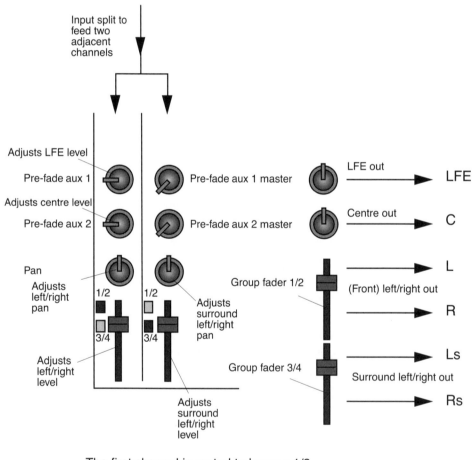

The first channel is routed to busses 1/2 while the second channel is routed to busses 3/4. Note that aux sends are not used (turned down) on the second channel

Figure 21.1: Using stereo mixer channels for surround mixing

things get more difficult when you want to move a sound around in real time, as you end up having to adjust several controls at once. With this being the case, unless you're planning to keep most elements static in the surround mix, you're better off buying a mixer with some basic surround-mixing capabilities – for example, Yamaha's 03D and 02R digital consoles include a Surround mode in which automatic panning is possible based on preset patterns, such as arcs and circles, and adjustable pan rates.

Although these are useful for some effects, they're not nearly as flexible as having a joystick that can position sounds anywhere within the surround mix by a single movement. When positioning a sound manually on a console not capable of surround panning, you generally need to operate at least two separate controls, and that's without considering what happens to the centre channel, so it's important to understand that, while you can make a perfectly acceptable surround mix using a multibuss stereo mixer with enough input channels, you'll face a number of practical limitations that will render some mixing techniques extremely difficult or even impossible. At least if you have mix automation you can fine-tune some of the more impossible multicontrol moves until they sound right. However, audio software with virtual pan pots often provides far more comprehensive surround-mixing capabilities than hardware mixers.

Surround Effects

There are already exotic surround processors available, such as TCWorks' System 6000, which can handle dynamics and surround reverb (amongst other things), but a number of professional engineers are using entire processors designed for stereo without finding too many limitations. For example, if you want to create surround reverb, you can either use a single stereo reverb and use surround panning to position it midway between the front and rear speakers, or you can use two different stereo reverbs, one feeding the front left and right speakers and the other the left and right surrounds. Adding a little delay to the rear reverb or using a reverb algorithm with a slower reflection build-up can create a very convincing sense of spatial envelopment.

Software And Surround

The typical project studio combines an audio-plus-MIDI sequencer with external MIDI hardware, and while some of the lateral thinking described earlier must be used to create surround panning effects from external stereo sound modules, it's much easier to deal with sounds generated within the sequencer (via audio tracks and virtual instruments), as these can be treated by using the surround capabilities of the internal virtual mixer before they're fed into the external mixer to be merged with the hardware-generated sounds. MIDI sources that need to be handled in surround can be recorded into the sequencer as audio tracks. On a conventional mixer, six mono channels would be needed to route the six surround feeds from the computer soundcard or interface to the six mixer busses being used to handle the surround mix. Figure 21.2 shows a software surround mixer.

Using automation to effect changes in level and surround panning is straightforward in a software environment, and although most processing plug-ins are still designed for stereo use, there are some surround plug-ins appearing that offer interesting creative possibilities. It's also likely that affordable surround-sound CD-R and DVD-R software will be available to project-studio users before any hardware equivalent becomes affordable, although at the time of writing surround-authoring software was relatively expensive and supported only by specific hardware or software platforms.

Interfacing

In order to work as I've described here, you'll need an audio output card or interface with at least six outputs, and if you're working with a digital mixer that can accept an ADAT or other standard digital multichannel audio interface card, it makes things much simper if you choose a computer-audio interface with a compatible multichannel digital output.

If you want to use external MIDI synths as well as virtual ones, you'll need to add either a surround mixer or a conventional hardware mixer with plenty of inputs and at least four output busses, plus a couple of pre-fade send busses to feed the six surround streams to your mastering recorder. However,

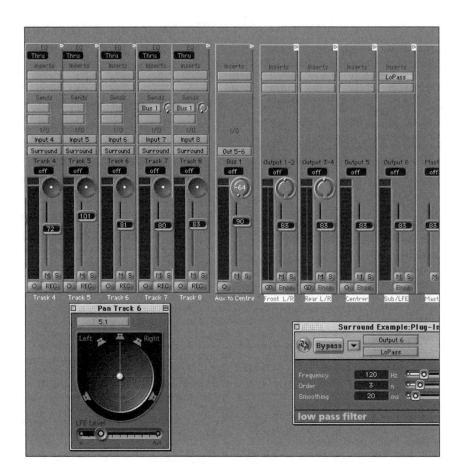

Figure 21.2: Achieving surround with a virtual computer mixer

the most practical alternative may be to record the external synth parts into the computer as separate audio tracks so that they can be processed via the sequencer software's virtual surround mixer. This approach has the advantage that your surround mix can be recorded into the computer and saved on the hard drive, thus avoiding the need for an external multitrack mastering recorder. This is particularly relevant if you want to make use of the higher sample rates that may not be supported by some older hardware multitrack recorders.

Surround Monitoring

As I explained in the last chapter, a surround monitoring system comprises six speakers, one of which is a sub-bass or LFE unit handling low-frequency effects below 120Hz. Finding space for surround

monitoring in a small studio can be a problem, but if you don't have room for five full-range speakers, you can use smaller speakers with a restricted low-frequency range and use the sub-bass speaker to reproduce the missing bottom end as well as the LFE. This requires a surround amplifier with a bass-management system so that the low-frequency energy from the main speakers can be redirected to the sub-bass speaker.

One of my pet complaints is that very few of the project-studio mixers currently available cater for surround monitoring. They may have the buss outputs to feed your multitrack master recorder and they may have some form of surround panning, but there's nowhere to connect your surround-monitoring system and no Master Volume knob that lets you turn the overall monitoring level up or down. Even the bigger mixers with assignable outputs that could be used to feed your monitors don't provide an adequate means of overall level control.

If you decide to use passive monitors, the solution is simple and straightforward: buy a reasonably powerful domestic surround amplifier/decoder with separate analogue inputs for all six surround components. You can connect your master surround output busses to these inputs, using split cables if necessary to allow you to feed a multitrack recorder at the same time. The amplifier's volume control is used to control the level of your surround mix and the monitor-switching function means that you can play back your stereo mixes or CDs through the same system without repatching.

Active Monitoring

Things are less simple if you use active speakers, although there are commercial surround decoder/amplifiers available that have individual line-level ins and outs that you can use in much the same way as that described for passive speakers. Alternatively, there are specialist surround-monitoring controllers that will do the job, but most cost far more than a suitable surround amplifier.

One compromise is to plug the multiple buss outs from your surround mixer or audio interface directly into the mastering recorder (for example, an ADAT or DA88) and then feed your active monitors from the output of the recorder. The limitation with this solution is that, when the optimum recording level is being fed into the recorder, the monitors will play back at a fixed level, determined by how you set the gain pots on their back panels. It's easy enough to set this up for a sensible monitoring level, but there are always occasions when you'll need to check the mix at a different level or turn down the monitors to answer the phone.

When you're at the tracking stage, you can turn down the (physical or virtual) mixer-buss outs to reduce the feed to the multitrack recorder, and Figure 21.3 over the page shows this arrangement. The problem is, when you're actually mixing, your monitoring level is effectively fixed, determined by the optimum record level.

Surround Mastering

The surround-mix recorder can be any high quality recorder capable of recording six tracks simultaneously, ideally at 20-bit resolution or higher. Six spare sequencer tracks in a software-based set-up, or a stand-alone ADAT/DA88 machine will do the job well enough (be sure to use a standard system so you know which part of the surround mix is on which tape track), but you can only replay your surround mix from this master. It's not like stereo, when you can burn a CD and play it back on your friend's hi-fi system – at least, not without some very specialised software

To create a disc that can be played back on a home-theatre system, you need to decide on the surround format on which you want to release your work and then transfer your work onto DVD (or DTS-encoded CD-R). This part of the process requires specialist hardware and/or authoring software to create the necessary AC3 files (for Dolby Surround) or DTS files and to add the metadata (all of the additional 'invisible' data that DVDs require that we didn't have to deal with when working with stereo CDs). Dolby Digital AC3- and DTS-encoding software is already available for use with systems such as Digidesign's Pro Tools and Mark Of The Unicorn's Digital Performer software, but that isn't the whole story – you then have to burn that information onto a DVD using compatible 'burning' software.

Although DVD burners and the media that they employ have fallen in price dramatically since their introduction, they are still far more costly than the stereo CD-R equivalent and unforeseen complications often arise when trying to burn audio DVDs. Hopefully, this will become simpler, as well as cheaper, as time passes, but currently the most painless way of getting a DVD master (other than financially, of course!) is to have a commercial mastering house do the job for you. If you're a professional producer, this is probably the route you'd take anyway. However, it can be frustrating not to be able to create listening copies straight after mixing, so the situation won't be an entirely happy one until cheaper and simpler means of mastering surround material to DVD are available to the project-studio owner.

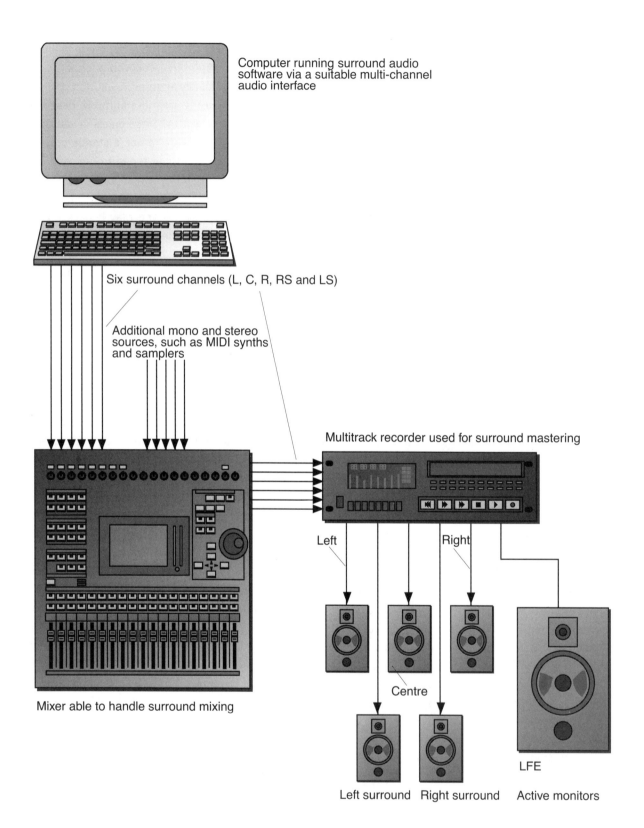

Computer running surround audio software via a suitable multi-channel audio interface

Six surround channels (L, C, R, RS and LS)

Additional mono and stereo sources, such as MIDI synths and samplers

Multitrack recorder used for surround mastering

Left

Right

Mixer able to handle surround mixing

Centre

Left surround   Right surround

LFE

Active monitors

Figure 21.3: Monitoring the multitrack output

Artistic Considerations

I've spoken to a number of engineers already involved in surround mixing, and I've been surprised by the number of differing views on what is and what isn't artistically acceptable. The whole point – indeed, the only point – of working with surround audio is to present the listener with a more interesting or more involving listening experience, so in one sense there are no rules, but even so, there are 'considerations'. Creating surround music is still a relatively new art form, and at least one element of the debate centres around whether or not we want guitar solos coming from behind the sofa, or whether it's better to leave all the instruments at the front and use the surrounds to add ambience and depth. Another concern is more practical and involves the use of the centre speaker.

The centre speaker in a film theatre generally carries the dialogue and other sounds that need to be keyed to the centre of the visual image (ie the screen) while the left and right speakers carry the stereo elements of the soundtrack. Because of our exposure to conventional stereo systems, we're used to hearing stereo with no centre speaker, so mixing with all of the mono components coming from a centre speaker sounds different to what we're used to (the stereo effect seems less pronounced, for one thing), and because of the axial response of the human ear, it also makes the signal sound tonally different.

Some producers and engineers think it best to put the voice and solo instruments in the centre channel while others prefer not to use the centre channel in this way and instead stick with the phantom centre image we've all got used to from listening to two-speaker stereo systems. Locating centred sounds in the centre speaker means that their position is less ambiguous if the listener isn't sitting exactly in the sweet spot between the speakers, but in my experience it also makes the stereo soundstage appear narrower, in some way, than the usual two-speaker approach, possibly because the only sound that comes from the front left and front right speakers comprises the stereo components of the sound and not the mono components normally needed to build a phantom centre image.

A number of producers like to exploit the difference between the centre speaker and the conventional phantom centre image by using both in a mix. For example, a double-tracked vocal might appear once in the centre speaker with the second version panned to the centre of the left and right speakers. The version in the centre speaker usually seems to sit slightly in front of the phantom image, an effect that can be exploited when you want to push lead vocals to the front and backing vocals to the rear. Simply put the lead vocal in the centre speaker only and the backing vocals in the left and right speakers only.

My main concern over using the centre speaker is that domestic playback systems are often very poorly set up, and while the stereo left/right balance may be OK, there's a good chance that the centre speaker level will be a decibel or two too loud or too quiet and that the LFE channel will be much too loud.

If on playback the centre channel is a few decibels adrift of its correct level balance, a carefully crafted mix could end up with the vocals, bass guitar, kick drum and any other centre-panned sounds noticeably too high or low in the mix, and of course the consumer will assume that he's listening to a poorly mixed record, not a poorly set up sound system.

The LFE (Low-Frequency Effects) channel (the '.1' part of the system's description) is not mandatory in all surround formats, and not all home systems will have a proper LFE speaker so you can never be certain that something you place in the LFE channel will be heard by the listener. Normal bass will be reproduced, even when small satellite speakers are being used, as a bass speaker and bass-management system is always provided as part of a serious domestic system. For mixing in surround format, it's probably safest to ensure that your mix sounds good when heard on just the full-range speakers and never to put anything into the LFE channel that you can't afford to lose.

Dynamics In Surround

When compressing a stereo mix, it's usual to employ a stereo compressor that has the ability to link its side chains so that both channels always undergo exactly the same degree of gain reduction, regardless of the relative balance of the two channels at any one time. The reason for doing this is that, by applying the same gain reduction to both channels, there will be no unwanted image shifts that might otherwise occur if a peak in one channel were to result in significantly activating more gain reduction on that channel than on the other.

Strictly speaking, a surround mix should be treated in the same way, using five channels of compression with linked side chains, and this is one facility provided (digitally) by TCWorks' System 6000 processor. Nevertheless, I've spoken to a number of surround mixing engineers who have tried both linked side chains and independent stereo compressors for the front and rear left/right signals plus a regular mono compressor for the centre channel. Clearly, using an independent compressor for the centre channel isn't going to cause any left/right image shifting, and similarly using linked stereo compressors for the front left/right and surround left/right channels will also avoid left/right image shifts. However, because the front and rear compressors are working independently, it's conceivable that front/rear image shifts could occur, although in typical mix situations this problem appears not to arise to any significant extent.

The Surround Element

So far, the discussion has related to the reproduction of stereo via three front speakers rather than the usual two, but what should you feed into the surround speakers? The answer to this question is mainly down to artistic judgement rather than science, but again there are 'considerations'. For acoustic recordings, the acoustics of the room (or simulated acoustics) can be used to provide the listener with a best-seat-in-the-house listening experience, where the music still comes mainly from the front and the reverberant field comes from both the front and the surround speakers. The next step up from this is to push some elements of the mix slightly towards the surrounds to increase the apparent width of the mix but still to keep the sound coming predominantly from the front.

Anything more dramatic than this can be distracting, especially if the music is accompanying a video and the action is on a screen in front of the listener, but there's no reason at all not to conceive music where different sounds come from different directions, effectively placing the listener in the middle of the performance rather than in the audience. More conservative producers may decide to play safe and move just some of the effects or incidental instrument parts out to the sides or even to the rear while others may place a different instrument in each corner of the room. As with the introduction of stereo, I expect there to be some horrendous excesses before a general consensus of good taste is arrived at, so don't go spinning sound sources around in 360° all the time as you'll only make your listeners feel ill. Having said that, there will always be room for the occasional dramatic effect, used in context, and for more subtle surround effects such as panning delays that move around the speakers.

Processing Back Catalogue

When the CD format was launched, a lot of marketing energy was put into remastering back-catalogue material for the new format, and DVD surround audio seems to be going the same way. Wherever possible, engineers will go back to the original multitrack tapes and remix these for surround-sound in as artistically sympathetic a manner as possible, but sometimes the master multitrack tapes are no longer available or there's no budget available for extensive remixing. In these cases, a lot can be done simply by processing an existing stereo master, although there is a limit to what can be achieved with one of these.

Mastering engineers routinely split a stereo signal into its mid and side components (using a mixer or other specialised hardware to derive sum and difference signals) so that they can process the (centre-panned) mono components of a mix differently to the left/right (difference) information. For example, they may wish to EQ or compress the vocals and other centre-panned elements of the mix without changing the sound of the rest of the mix, or conversely they may want to add extra reverb to the stereo elements of a mix without affecting the lead vocal.

Once the middle and/or side elements have been processed, they can be recombined – once again by deriving sum and difference signals – in order to provide a proper stereo mix with all of the desired modifications in place. This technique of splitting a stereo mix into its middle and side components and then recombining it is obviously very useful when processing stereo mixes for surround purposes, as various techniques can be used to wrap the side components around the room while leaving the centre sounds intact. Also, because the centre sounds can be extracted, they can be sent to the centre channel, if required.

One technique used to 'unwrap' the sound is to feed some of the side signals into surround channels and also to add artificially generated 'rear of room' reflections, creating a more convincing sense of space.

Recording In Surround

In many instances, surround recording can be undertaken using any of the familiar mono or stereo mic arrangements, and the recording can then be positioned at the mixing stage, with or without additional processing (such as applying reverberation). However, the result of this isn't true surround any more than panned mono recordings are true stereo. Of course, this isn't often an issue, especially if the mix is being assembled from numerous multitracked components, but when you're recording a complete live event or attempting to capture natural events for use in film soundtracks, true surround-miking is often preferable. One extremely successful method is based on the established ambisonic recording principle established over a quarter of a century ago.

Ambisonics

In an ideal world, a limited number of loudspeakers would be able to reproduce a surround-audio experience identical to that enjoyed by a person present at the original recording. The process known as *ambisonics* was devised with this aim in mind, and on a technical level it was surprisingly successful, even though it never made a big commercial impact.

Perhaps the best established method of making ambisonic recordings is to use a technique involving coincident microphones, and surround recording using multiple coincident mics is analogous to using a pair of coincident stereo mics for stereo-recording purposes. The ambisonic principle is based on research carried out in the 1930s by Alan Blumlein, arguably the pioneer of stereo miking, and although you may never encounter ambisonics as a commercial format, it has enough technical advantages that it's worth learning a little about it. Indeed, some of the recording techniques involved in ambisonics translate well into more conventional surround formats.

Ambisonic Recording

Ambisonic material is recorded using a special multicapsule microphone or multimic array, with the British-built Drawmer Soundfield microphone probably being the best-known commercial example of such a mic. Although ideally suited to purist ambisonic recording, this microphone may also be used for other forms of surround and stereo recording.

The main point about Ambisonic miking using a Soundfield mic is that the sound is captured at a single point in space using coincident mics, rather as coincident middle-and-side microphones are used to capture stereo recordings. To achieve this, the Soundfield uses four directional microphone capsules arranged as a regular tetrahedron and spaced very closely together. Delay circuitry is then used to make the four closely spaced capsules combine their signals as though they were all located at the same point (at a virtual point in the centre of the actual array). A processor is then used to convert the outputs from the capsules into a four-channel signal (known as the *B format*), which can then be used to reconstruct the original soundfield when played back over a four-speaker system via a suitable ambisonics decoder. The best way to describe the B format is as three sets of signals corresponding to three pairs of M&S (Middle and Side) mics covering the three axes and where each of the figure-of-eight mics shares the same omni microphone as its 'middle' mic. So, the B format may later be recombined in different ways to reconstruct any desired mic pattern or to reconstruct the original three-dimensional sound.

The B-format signals may be recorded directly to four tracks of an audio recorder, if desired, in order to allow for the greatest possible flexibility during post-production. Replaying these B-format audio tracks through a suitable ambisonic decoder using speakers that are positioned correctly recreates the original ambisonic soundstage, although it is not possible to extract height information when using a conventional surround speaker layout as all of the speakers are arranged in the same plane.

Decoding from a B-format recording relies on the recording being phase-coherent, but this isn't difficult to achieve with modern digital-recording systems.

Soundfield Advantages

A microphone such as the Soundfield has the advantage that only four audio channels are needed to capture a signal that can then be processed to work with any of the current surround-playback loudspeaker formats and will also be compatible with any future formats. Furthermore, the ability to extract stereo and mono signals from the B-format recording is not compromised by time or phase differences between the elements in the microphone as they are all effectively at the same point in space. Although I anticipate that much surround material will be created using surround panning from mono or stereo sources (just as we produce stereo by panning mono sources), microphones such as the Soundfield are very powerful tools for capturing surround events that exist in a real acoustic environment.

True ambisonic playback requires a decoder that uses psychoacoustic processing to get as close to the original soundfield as possible, but I think that a more likely procedure in today's commercial environment is to process the B-format signal for replay over conventional 5.1 surround-speaker systems. One way of achieving this is by using the Soundfield SP451 Surround Processor, a dedicated decoder that accepts B-format input signals and generates discrete outputs appropriate to a regular 5.1 loudspeaker arrangement. Using this system, ambisonically recorded material can be reformatted for playback within a 5.1 production without the need for an ambisonics decoder.

Multimic Surround Sound

If a 5.1 speaker system has to have the speakers set up at precise angles to each other, it therefore follows that it ought to be possible to capture a surround recording using five discrete mics, each angled to pick up the signal appropriate for each of those five speakers. These mics could be coincident or spaced, and just as with stereo, opinions differ amongst those making 5.1

surround recordings as to which approach is better. Point-source coincident systems used by mics such as the Soundfield have the advantage of offering extremely good mono and stereo compatibility, although with these systems sometimes the impression of surround can be more dramatically created by using spaced mics, albeit at the sacrifice of perfect mono or stereo compatibility.

Spaced stereo-miking set-ups can employ either omnidirectional or cardioid mics, placed some distance apart in order to capture timing differences between the two channels that occur when sounds arrive from any direction other than directly on the axis between the microphones. However, the coincident-mic array works only when using directional mics, as it relies entirely on differences in amplitude. In addition to using a Soundfield mic, it's also possible to adapt the conventional M&S mic technique for surround purposes by using two cardioid mid mics, one facing backwards and one facing forwards. Using a sum-and-difference matrix between the figure-of-eight side mic and the forward-pointing cardioid provides what is in effect a front stereo signal, while doing the same thing with the rear-facing cardioid provides the rear-channel information. When all this information is combined via a four-speaker system, the result is true surround-sound playback. Furthermore, the forward-facing mic signal may also be used to feed the centre speaker in a 5.1 system, and by adjusting the M&S balance the ratio of centre signal appearing in the left and right channels can be increased or decreased accordingly.

Spaced Arrays

The most common spaced-mic arrangement for 5.1 recording is based on a modified 'Decca Tree' arrangement, which was originally developed for stereo recording (although there are several variations on this theme) and comprises five spaced cardioid microphone capsules fixed to a frame comprising a central hub with five arms fixed to it on the horizontal plane. A typical arrangement of this kind of set-up is shown in Figure 21.4. The front three microphones are arranged quite close together while the two rear mics are located about 60cm behind the hub and angled at 60º angles to the axis. I know of at least one commercial system that uses this approach but offers the ability to switch

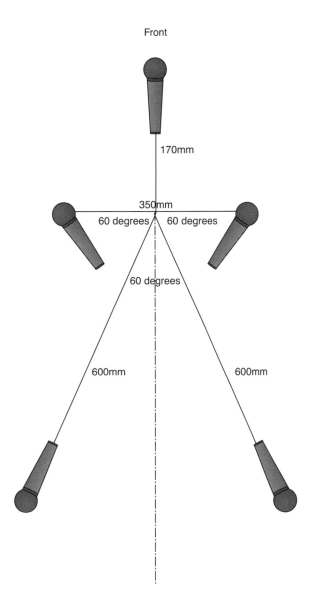

Front

170mm

350mm

60 degrees   60 degrees

60 degrees

600mm   600mm

Figure 21.4: 'Decca Tree' mic array

microphone patterns for situations where other patterns might be considered more appropriate. Given that there is no one definitive surround-miking technique, this degree of flexibility is welcome.

As when working with stereo, using any spaced surround-mic technique means that you have to pay special attention to creating mono- and stereo-compatible 'fold-down' mixes, as the physical spacing and the consequent inter-mic delays give rise to phase problems when the signals are combined. The greater the separation between the mics, the more serious this problem is likely to be, although you always have the option of using only some of the mic outputs in order to create the mono and stereo down-mixes.

22 SUMMING UP

Today's engineers and producers have to possess both technical and musical skills as well as the ability to handle people in what can be a stressful working environment. To add to these responsibilities, decisions also have to be made when a project needs to be moved between two or more recording facilities, as the issue of equipment and media/format compatibility then becomes very important. At the very least, it pays to have a reasonable degree of familiarity with modern sequencing programs and of course the Digidesign Pro Tools platform, which is very much an industry standard when it comes to tapeless recording and editing. It's also useful to know how work made on an ADAT multitrack tape machine (for example) can be transferred into a computer system and vice versa, which means that you have to know about the various audio-file formats and interface standards. Furthermore, because of budgetary restraints, it's important for a commercial producer to build up a list of contacts, both musical and technical, including session players, CD-duplication companies, mastering houses, engineers with specialist software skills and so on.

Behind The Technology

Perhaps the most important skill of all is the ability to look beyond the mass of technical options to decide on a practical strategy for completing each project based on its needs and the available budget. For example, a well-rehearsed live band may still work best in a traditional tape-based studio, whereas artists who make extensive use of MIDI and sampling may be able to do a lot of pre-production work in a relatively modest computer suite before moving somewhere better equipped for mixing or overdubbing vocals.

Collaborations

Technology can also help make the most of budgets by allowing artists from different parts of the world to work together without leaving their home countries. Sadly, the limitations imposed by the speed of light will always prevent real-time collaboration between very remote locations, as the monitoring delay would be enough to throw the timing of the performers, but audio tracks may be sent via ISDN lines, ADSL or some other wide-bandwidth connection, enabling a singer, for example, to sing along to a rough mix and then send his vocals back to the co-ordinating studio, where they could be integrated into the final project. A company called Rocket Networks, Inc, have devised an even more streamlined way of handling such remote collaborations. Essentially, the music files – which are generally data-compressed in order to speed up transfer – are stored on a central server where any of the participating artists can access them, copying them to their own machines or adding new files of their own. Where the music software being used supports Rocket Networks technology, this method of moving files around becomes relatively fast and intuitive, and although real-time operation is still an impossibility, a vocalist could be adding a harmony only minutes after the lead vocalist working on a different continent has laid down the main vocal.

It's also common for mobile recording gear to be used to record artists *in situ*, enabling them to collaborate in a musical project while on tour. One recent example of this was a Mick Jagger album for which U2's Bono added his vocal parts in a hotel room using a Yamaha 4416 hard-disk workstation while U2 were on a European tour. The recordings where then taken back to the UK and transferred to the system on which the various parts of the project were being assembled. In fact, computer-based systems such as Pro Tools or Nuendo are ideal for this kind of assembly work. An important factor in this kind of work is that more audio software is now adding support for OMF, a standard file-interchange format that allows audio files and their time-stamping information (ie the time at which they start playing within a song) to be moved between different platforms.

Email Or Snail Mail?

Of course there's always the low tech option of sending your collaborator (let's say the guitarist for your global band) a CD-R containing a rough mix of the backing track via the postal system. Here, the guitarist receives the CD-R, imports it directly into his audio program and then records his part on a spare track. When he's happy with the track, he records the guitar part only onto one track of a fresh CD-R, puts the guide mix in mono on the other track and sends it back. Because digital equipment is so stable, it's possible to run quite long sections of audio in sync, provided that they start at the right time, and so dropping in a couple of dozen bars of guitar solo shouldn't be a problem. You'll still have the rough mix on the other track to use as a positioning guide, and if sync problems do become evident with longer sections, it's usually possible to break them into shorter sections and (manually) synchronise their start points individually.

Of course, if the various collaborators in the project use the same audio software (or software with OMF support), it's even easier because, instead of posting simple audio recordings to each other, they can instead send CD-Rs containing the song data and audio files to be used in the project (mixing multiple parts to form guide tracks still makes sense for larger projects, as CD-Rs have a limited capacity), thus enabling the session to be worked on without running into synchronisation problems.

Personally, I feel that this kind of remote working should be used only as a last resort because musicians invariably spark off each other and come up with better ideas when they work together in real time, but it does provide a practical means of getting jobs done in circumstances where conventional studio recording just isn't possible, and it also means that you can add to or replace parts of a project after the performers have separated. It also provides a means for home studio owners and composers to collaborate where physically working together would be impractical.

Our Changing World

As technology becomes ever more sophisticated, it will become even more important that both engineers and producers keep abreast of current developments and are aware of what is achievable, even if they aren't experts in using the equipment or software in question. After all, as audio recording diversifies into more and more specialist areas, it would be unreasonable to expect anyone to be an expert in all of them, but knowing what's possible and where to contact the people that can help bring your project to fruition is a big part of what being a producer is all about in the 21st century.

The Plug-in Revolution

Since the first edition of this book was published, the music world has seen the introduction of VST and other plug-in standards for software effects and virtual-instrument plug-ins, which I feel has made a great difference to the way in which people now work. In the main, the production techniques that apply to plug-ins are little different to those used in traditional methods, but they make certain jobs much easier, specifically the automation of parameters. Furthermore, plug-in settings can be saved within a song, so it's now much easier to revisit old projects and continue from where you left off as, when you load up a song, everything comes back exactly the way you left it, even down to the samples loaded into virtual samplers. In the context of remote collaboration, this also makes it easier to send complete project files between locations – although, because of the size of uncompressed audio files, posting CD-Rs may still be more appropriate in some cases than using the internet. Hopefully, internet bandwidth will continue to increase so that, by the next time this book is updated, the suggestion of posting CD-Rs will seem a little quaint. At the moment, though, it's the best option for any long files.

One point to bear in mind when exchanging projects that use plug-ins is that both parties need to use compatible software, either the same type or programs that support a common file-transfer protocol, and they must also have the same plug-ins installed. There's no use sending somebody a song with plug-in settings if they don't have that plug-in! Similarly, the audio and program files associated with any samples used by a plug-in sampler must also be sent along with the song.

While progress brings with it complexity, it also opens up possibilities that were previously denied to the studio musician, so both professional producers and project-studio owners (who tend to double as engineers and producers) can take advantage of things like plug-in effects, software automation, software instruments and an almost unlimited number of audio recording tracks at much less than the cost of the traditional tape-based alternative. The future promises to be an interesting time, but the best producer will still be the one with the best ideas and the most focused approach. No amount of technology can change that.

GLOSSARY

AC

Abbreviation for Alternating Current.

A/D Converter

Abbreviation of Analogue-To-Digital Converter, a circuit for converting analogue waveforms into a series of values represented by binary numbers. The more 'bits' a converter has, the greater the resolution of the sampling process. Current effects units are generally 16 bits or more with the better models being of either 20- or 24-bit resolution.

Active

Term that describes a circuit containing transistors, ICs, tubes and other devices that require power in order to operate and are capable of amplification.

Additive Synthesis

System for generating waveforms or sounds by combining basic waveforms or sampled sounds prior to further processing with filters and envelope shapers.

ADSR

Envelope generator with Attack, Decay, Sustain and Release parameters. This is a simple type of envelope generator and was first used on early analogue synths. This form of envelope generator continues to be popular on modern instruments. See *Decay* for more details.

Active Sensing

System used to verify that a MIDI connection is working and involves the sending device sending frequent short messages to the receiving device in order to reassure it that all is well. If these active-sensing messages stop for any reason, the receiving device will recognise a fault condition and switch off all notes. Few current MIDI devices support active sensing.

AES/EBU

Digital interface protocol for stereo audio signals at sample rates of up to 48kHz using balanced cable, normally connected via a standard three-pin XLR connector. Systems for delivering audio at sample rates of up to 96kHz have been devices using a pair of AES/EBU cables. Certain consumer 'flags' are not recognised by AES/EBU, including SCMS copy-protection data and DAT track-start IDs.

AFL

Abbreviation of After-Fade Listen, a system used within mixing consoles to allow specific signals to be monitored at the level set by their faders or level-control knobs. Aux sends are generally monitored AFL rather than PFL (see *PFL*).

Aftertouch

A means of generating a control signal based on how much pressure is applied to the keys of a MIDI keyboard. Most instruments that support this do not have independent pressure sensing for all keys but rather detect the overall pressure by means of a sensing strip running beneath the keys. Aftertouch may be used to control such functions as vibrato depth, filter brightness, loudness and so on.

.AIFF

Audio file format often used by Mac-based audio systems.

Algorithm

Computer program designed to perform a specific task. With effects units, the term describes a software building block designed to create a specific effect or combination of effects.

Aliasing

When an analogue signal is sampled for conversion into a digital data stream, the sampling frequency must be at least twice that of the highest frequency component of the input signal. If this rule is disobeyed, the sampling process becomes ambiguous as there are insufficient points to define each cycle of the waveform, resulting in enharmonic frequencies being added to the audible signal.

Ambience

The result of sound reflections in a confined space being added to the original source sound. Ambience may also be created electronically by some digital reverb units. The primary difference between ambience and reverberation is that ambience doesn't have the characteristic long delay times that are characteristic of reverberation – the reflections mainly give the sound a sense of space.

Ambisonic

Sophisticated system for recording 'surround' audio for replay over multiple speakers via an ambisonic decoder. Uses a 'point' surround mic, such as the Drawmer Soundfield.

Amp

Abbreviation of *ampère*, the SI unit of electrical current.

Amplifier

Device that increases the level of an electrical signal.

Amplitude

Another word for level. Can refer to sound levels or electrical signal levels.

Analogue

Term used to describe circuitry that uses a continually changing voltage or current to represent a signal.

The origin of the term is that the electrical signal can be thought of as being analogous to the original signal.

Analogue Synthesis

System for synthesising sounds by means of analogue circuitry, usually by filtering simple repeating waveforms.

Attenuate

To make lower in level.

Anti-Aliasing Filter

Filter used to limit the frequency range of an analogue signal prior to A/D conversion so that the maximum frequency does not exceed half the sampling rate.

Application

Alternative term for computer program.

Arpeggiator

Device that allows a MIDI instrument to sequence around any notes currently being played. Most arpeggiators also allow the sound to be sequenced over several octaves so that holding down a simple chord can result in an impressive repeating sequence of notes.

ASCII

Abbreviation of American Standard Code for Information Interchange, a standard code for representing computer-keyboard characters in binary data.

ASIO

Standard of software driver developed by Steinberg to allow compatible soundcards/audio interfaces and software to work together effectively and with low latency. ASIO II also provides the option for source monitoring with compatible hardware in an effort to avoid the effects of latency when recording or overdubbing.

ATRAC

Data-compression system used in commercial MiniDisc recorders.

Attack

Term used to describe the time it takes for a sound to achieve its maximum amplitude. Drums have a fast attack, for instance, whereas bowed strings have a slow attack time. In compressors and gates, the attack time equates to how quickly the processor can change its gain.

Audio Frequency

Signals in the human audio range, nominally 20Hz–20kHz.

Auto-Locator

Feature of a tape machine or other recording device that enables specific locations to be stored. Then, some later time, these locations within the recording may be recalled. For example, you may store the start of a verse as a locate point so that you can get the tape machine to wind back the start of the verse after you've recorded an overdub.

Auto-Tune

Device designed by AnTares to correct vocal-pitching problems by forcing notes to the nearest correct note in a selected musical scale. Released in both hardware and software formats.

Aux

Abbreviation of *auxiliary*, a control on a mixing console designed to route a proportion of the channel signal to the effects or cue-mix outputs (see *Aux Send*).

Aux Send

Physical output from a mixer aux send buss.

Aux Return

Mixer inputs used to add effects to a mix.

Azimuth

Alignment co-ordinate of a tape head that references the head gap to the true vertical relative to the tape path.

Back-up

Safety copy of software or other digital data.

Balance

This word has several meanings in recording. It may refer to the relative levels of the left and right channels of a stereo recording, or it may be used to describe the relative levels of the various instruments and voices within a mix.

Balanced Wiring

Wiring system that uses two out-of-phase conductors and a common screen to reduce the effect of interference. For balancing to be effective, both the sending and receiving device must have balanced output and input stages respectively.

Bandpass Filter

Filter that removes or attenuates frequencies above and below the frequency at which it is set. Frequencies within the band are emphasised. Bandpass filters are often used in synthesisers as tone-shaping elements.

Bandwidth

Term used to describe a means of specifying the range of frequencies passed by an electronic circuit, such as an amplifier, mixer or filter. The frequency range is usually measured at the points where the level drops by 3dB relative to the maximum level.

Beta Version

Software that is not fully tested and may include bugs.

Bias

High-frequency signal used in analogue recording to improve the accuracy of the recorded signal and to drive the erase head. Bias is generated by a bias oscillator.

Binary

Counting system using only two numbers:1s and 0s.

bios

Part of a computer operating system held on ROM rather than on disk, handling basic routines such as accessing the disk drive.

Bit

Abbreviation of *binary digit*, which may be either 1 or 0.

Boost/Cut Control

Single control that allows the range of frequencies passing through a filter to be either amplified or attenuated. The centre position is usually the 'flat' or 'no effect' position.

Bouncing

Process of mixing two or more tracks together and re-recording them onto another track.

BPM

Abbreviation of Beats Per Minute.

Breath Controller

Device that converts breath pressure into MIDI controller data.

Buffer

Circuit designed to isolate the output of a source device from loading effects due to the input impedance of the destination device.

Buffer Memory

Temporary RAM used in some computer operations, sometimes to prevent a break in the data stream when the computer is interrupted to perform another task. All audio software employs buffer memory to ensure a continuous stream of audio. The greater the buffer size, the less likely it is that glitches or other problems will occur, but at the same time a larger buffer size increases the system latency. (See also *RAM*.)

Bug

Slang term for software fault or equipment design problem.

Buss

Common electrical signal path along which signals may travel. In a mixer, there are several busses carrying the stereo mix, the groups, the PFL signal, the aux sends and so on. Power supplies are also fed along busses.

Byte

Piece of digital data comprising eight bits.

Cardioid

Describes the polar response of a unidirectional mic. The term itself means 'heart-shaped'.

CD-R

Recordable type of compact disc that can be used to record only once – it cannot be erased and reused.

CD-R Burner

Device capable of recording data onto blank CD-R discs.

CV

Abbreviation of Control Voltage, used to control the pitch of an oscillator or filter frequency in an analogue synthesiser. Most analogue synths follow a one-volt-per-octave convention, although there are exceptions. To use a pre-MIDI analogue synthesiser under MIDI control, a MIDI-to-CV converter is required.

Capacitance

Property of an electrical component able to store electrostatic charge.

Capacitor

Electrical component exhibiting capacitance. Capacitor mics are often abbreviated to capacitors.

Capacitor Microphone

Microphone that operates on the principle of measuring the change in electrical charge across a capacitor where one of the electrodes is a thin conductive membrane that flexes in response to sound pressure.

Channel

On a mixing console, a single strip of controls relating to either a single input or a pair of main/monitor inputs.

Channel

In MIDI, one of 16 possible data channels over which MIDI data may be sent. The organisation of data by channels means that up to 16 different MIDI instruments or parts may be addressed using a single cable.

Chase

Term used to describe the process whereby a slave

device attempts to synchronise itself with a master device. In the context of a MIDI sequence, the term may also be used to refer to the action of chasing events – ie, looking back to earlier positions in a particular song to determine if there are any program changes or other events that need to be acted upon.

Chip
Integrated circuit.

Chord
Three or more different musical notes played at the same time.

Chorus
Variety of effect that is created by doubling a signal and adding delay and pitch modulation.

Chromatic
Scale of pitches rising in semitone steps.

Click Track
Metronome pulse that helps musicians to play in time.

Clipping
Severe form of distortion that occurs when a signal attempts to exceed the maximum level that a piece of equipment can handle.

Clone
Exact duplicate. Often refers to digital copies of digital tapes.

Common-Mode Rejection
Measure of how well a balanced circuit rejects a signal that is common to both inputs.

Compander
Device that compresses a signal while encoding it and then expands it when decoding it.

(Dynamic) Compressor
Device designed to reduce the dynamic range of audio signals by reducing the level of high signals or by increasing the level of low signals.

(Data) Compression
See *Data Compression*.

Computer
Device for storing and processing digital data.

Conductor
Material that provides a low resistance path for an electrical current.

Console
Alternative term for mixer.

Contact Enhancer
Compound designed to increase the electrical conductivity of electrical contacts such as plugs, sockets and edge connectors.

Continuous Controller
Type of MIDI message used to translate continuous change, such as those from a pedal, wheel or breath-control device.

Copy Protection
Method used by software manufacturers to prevent unauthorised copying.

Crash
Slang term relating to the malfunctioning of a computer program.

Cut-And-Paste Editing
Copying or moving sections of a recording to new locations.

Cutoff Frequency
Frequency above or below which attenuation begins in a filter circuit.

Cycle
One complete vibration of a sound source or its electrical equivalent. One cycle per second is expressed as 1Hz (Hertz).

CV

Abbreviation of Control Voltage, used in analogue synthesisers to control oscillator or filter frequency.

Damping

In the context of reverberation, damping refers to the rate at which the reverberant energy is absorbed by the various surfaces in the environment.

Daisy Chain

Term used to describe a serial electrical connection between devices or modules.

DAT

Abbreviation of Digital Audio Tape. The commonly used DAT machines are more correctly known as R-DAT because they use a rotating head similar to a video recorder. Digital recorders using fixed or stationary heads (such as DCC) are known as S-DAT machines.

Data

Information stored on and used by a computer.

Data Compression

System used to reduce the amount of data needed to represent an audio signal, usually by discarding audio information that is being masked by more prominent sounds. Data-compression algorithms are based on psychoacoustic principles designed to ensure that only components that cannot be heard are lost, although in practice heavy compression does compromise the subjective audio quality. Both MiniDisc audio and .mp3 files use a type of data compression.

dB

Abbreviation of Decibel, the SI unit used to express the relative levels of two electrical voltages, powers or sounds.

dBm

Variation on dB, referenced to 0dB = 1mW into 600 ohms.

dBv

Variation on dB, referenced to 0dB = 0.775 volts.

dBV

Variation on dB, referenced to 0dB = 1 volt.

dB Per Octave

Means of measuring the slope of a filter. The more decibels per octave, the sharper the filter slope.

DC

Abbreviation of Direct Current.

DCC

Stationary-head digital-recorder format developed by Philips. Uses a data-compression system to reduce the amount of data that needs to be stored.

DBX

Commercial encode/decode tape-noise-reduction system that compresses the signal during recording and expands it by an identical amount on playback.

DCO

Abbreviation of Digitally Controlled Oscillator.

DDL

Abbreviation of Digital Delay Line.

De-esser

Device for reducing the effect of sibilance in vocal signals.

Deoxidising Compound

Substance formulated to remove oxides from electrical contacts.

Decay

The progressive reduction in amplitude of a sound or electrical signal over time. In the context of an ADSR envelope shaper, the Decay phase starts as soon as the Attack phase has reached its maximum level. In the Decay phase, the signal level drops until it reaches the Sustain level set by the user. The signal then remains at this level until the key is released, at which point the Release phase is entered.

Defragmenting

The process of rearranging the files on a hard disk so

that all of the files are as contiguous as possible and that the remaining free space is also contiguous.

Detent

Physical click-stop in the centre of a control such as a pan or EQ cut/boost knob.

DI

Abbreviation of Direct Injection, where a signal is plugged directly into an audio chain without the aid of a microphone.

DI Box

Device used to match the signal-level impedance of a source to a tape machine or mixer input.

Digital

Term used to describe an electronic system that represents data and signals in the form of codes comprising 1s and 0s.

Digital Delay

Digital processor for generating delay and echo effects.

Digital Reverb

Digital processor used for simulating reverberation.

DIN connector

Consumer multipin signal-connection format, also used for MIDI cabling. Various pin configurations are available.

Direct Coupling

Means of connecting two electrical circuits so that both AC and DC signals may be passed between them.

Dithering

System of adding low-level noise to a digitised audio signal in such a way as to extend the signal's low-level resolution at the expense of a slight deterioration in noise performance.

Disc

Term used to describe vinyl discs, CDs and MiniDiscs.

Disk

Abbreviation of diskette, now used to describe computer floppy, hard and removable disks.

DMA

Abbreviation of Direct Memory Access, part of a computer operating system that allows peripheral devices to communicate directly with the computer memory without going via the CPU (Central Processing Unit).

Dolby Noise Reduction

Encode/decode tape-noise-reduction system that amplifies low-level, high-frequency signals during recording and then reverses this process during playback. There are several different Dolby systems in use: types B, C and S for domestic and semi-professional machines, and types A and SR for professional machines. Recordings made using one of these systems must also be replayed via the same system.

Dolby Surround

Means of encoding a two-channel signal so that information can be extracted to drive rear speakers as well as stereo front speakers and sometimes a front mid speaker. Many consumer TV systems now include the Dolby Pro Logic system.

DOS

Abbreviation of Disk-Operating System, part of the operating system of PC and IBM-compatible computers

DSP

Abbreviation of Digital Signal Processor, a powerful microchip used to process digital signals.

Driver

Piece of software that handles communications between the main program and a hardware peripheral, such as a soundcard, printer or scanner.

Drum Pad

Synthetic playing surface that produces electronic trigger signals in response to being hit with drum sticks.

Dry

Term used to describe a signal that has had no effects added.

Dubbing

Process of adding further material to an existing recording. This process is also known as *overdubbing*.

Ducking

System for controlling the level of one audio signal with another. For example, background music can be made to duck whenever there's a voice-over.

Dump

To transfer digital data from one device to another. A sysex (system-exclusive) dump is a means of transmitting information about a particular instrument or module over MIDI, and may be used to store sound patches, parameter settings and so on.

Dynamic Microphone

Type of microphone that works on the electric-generator principle, whereby a diaphragm moves a coil of wire within a magnetic field.

Dynamic Range

Range in decibels between the highest signal that can be handled by a piece of equipment and the level at which small signals disappear into the noise floor.

Dynamics

Way of describing the relative levels within a piece of music.

EASI

Proprietary audio driver format developed by Emagic for use with compatible soundcards.

Early Reflections

First sound reflections from walls, floors and ceilings following a sound created in an acoustically reflective environment.

effect

Device used to treat an audio signal in order to change it in some creative way. Effects often involve the use of delay circuits, and include such treatments as reverb and echo.

EIDE

Sometimes known as Ultra DMA, this is a type of hard-drive interface used within both PC and all recent Mac computers. It is not as fast as SCSI, but it is much cheaper.

Effects Loop

Connection system that allows an external signal processor to be connected in an audio chain.

Effects Return

Additional mixer input designed to accommodate the output from an effects unit.

Electret Microphone

Type of capacitor microphone utilising a permanently charged capsule.

Encode/Decode

Describes a system that requires a signal to be processed prior to recording, which is then reversed during playback.

Enhancer

Device designed to brighten audio material using techniques such as dynamic equalisation, phase shifting and harmonic generation.

Envelope

Term used to describe the way in which the level of a sound or a signal varies over time.

Envelope Generator

Circuit capable of generating a control signal, which represents the envelope of the sound you want to recreate. This may then be used to control the level of an oscillator or other sound source, although envelopes may also be used to control filter or modulation settings. The most common example is the ADSR generator.

Equaliser

Device that selectively cuts or boosts frequencies that occur in various parts of the audio spectrum.

Erase

To remove recorded material from an analogue tape, or to remove digital data from any form of storage media.

Event

In MIDI terms, an event is a single unit of MIDI data, such as a note being turned on or off, a piece of controller information, a program-change message and so on.

Exciter

Enhancer that works by synthesising new high-frequency harmonics.

Expander

Device designed to decrease the levels of low-level signals and increase those of high-level signals, thus increasing the dynamic range of the signal.

Expander Module

Synthesiser without a keyboard, often rack-mountable or in some other compact format.

Fader

Sliding potentiometer control used in mixers and other processors.

Ferric

Term used to describe a type of magnetic tape coating that uses iron oxide.

FET

Abbreviation of Field-Effect Transistor.

Figure Of Eight

Term used to describe the polar response of a microphone that is equally sensitive to both the front and the rear and yet rejects sounds coming from the sides.

File

Meaningful list of data stored in digital form. A Standard MIDI File is a specific type of file designed to allow sequence information to be interchanged between different types of sequencer.

Filter

Electronic circuit designed to emphasise or attenuate frequencies falling within a specific range.

Flanging

Type of modulated delay effect that uses feedback to create a dramatic, sweeping sound.

Floppy Disk

Computer disk that uses a flexible magnetic medium encased in a protective plastic sleeve. The maximum capacity of a standard high-density disk is 1.44Mb. Earlier double-density disks held only around half the amount of data.

Flutter Echo

Resonant echo that occurs when sound reflects back and forth between two parallel, reflective surfaces.

Foldback

System for feeding one or more separate mixes to the performers for use while recording and overdubbing. Also known as a *cue mix*.

Formant

Frequency component or resonance of an instrument or voice sound that doesn't change with the pitch of the note being played or sung. For example, the body resonance of an acoustic guitar remains constant, regardless of the note being played.

Format

To make a computer disk ready for use. Formatting organises the disk's surface into a series of electronic pigeonholes into which data can be stored. Different computers often use different formatting systems.

Fragmentation

Process by which the available space on a disk drive gets split up into small sections due to the storing and erasing of files. See *Defragmentation*.

Frequency

Indication of how many cycles of a repetitive waveform occur in one second. A waveform that has a repetition cycle of once per second has a frequency of 1Hz (hertz).

Frequency Response

Measurement of the frequency range that can be handled by a specific piece of electrical equipment or loudspeaker.

FSK

Abbreviation of Frequency Shift Keying, a method of recording a sync clock signal onto tape by representing it as two alternating tones.

Fundamental

Any sound comprises a fundamental or basic frequency plus harmonics and partials at higher frequencies.

FX

Abbreviation of *effects*.

Gain

Amount by which a circuit amplifies a signal.

Gate

Electrical signal that is generated whenever a key is depressed on an electronic keyboard. This is used to trigger envelope generators and other events that need to be sync'd to key action.

Gate

Electronic device designed to mute low-level signals so as to improve noise performance during pauses in the wanted material.

General MIDI

Addition to the basic MIDI specification to assure a minimum level of compatibility when playing back GM-format song files on different devices to those on which they were recorded. The specification covers type and program number of sounds, minimum levels of polyphony and multitimbrality, response to controller information and so on.

Glitch

Term used to describe an unwanted short-term corruption of a signal, or the unexplained short-term malfunction of a piece of equipment. For example, an inexplicable click on a DAT tape would be termed a glitch.

GM Reset

Universal sysex (system-exclusive) command that activates the General MIDI mode on a GM instrument. The same command also sets all controllers to their default values and switches off any notes still playing by means of an All Notes Off message.

Graphic Equaliser

Equaliser whereby several narrow segments of the audio spectrum are controlled by individual cut/boost faders. The name comes from the fact that the fader positions provide a graphic representation of the EQ curve.

Ground

Electrical earth, or 0 volts. In mains wiring, the ground cable is physically connected to the ground via a long, conductive metal spike.

Ground Loop

Wiring problem whereby multiple ground connections are causing audible mains hum to be picked up. Also known as *earth loops*.

Group

Collection of signals within a mixer that are mixed and then routed through a separate fader in order to provide overall control. In a multitrack mixer, several groups are provided to feed the various recorder track inputs.

GS

Roland's own extension to the General MIDI protocol.

Hard Disk

High-capacity computer storage device based on a rotating, rigid disk with a magnetic coating onto which data may be recorded.

Harmonic

High-frequency component of a complex waveform.

Harmonic Distortion

Addition of harmonics that were not present in an original signal.

Head

Part of a tape machine or disk drive that reads/writes data to and from the storage medium.

Headroom

Safety margin (measured in decibels) between the highest peak signal being passed by a piece of equipment and the absolute maximum level that the equipment can handle.

High-Pass Filter

Filter that attenuates frequencies below its cut-off frequency.

Hiss

Noise caused by random electrical fluctuations.

Hum

Signal contamination caused by the addition of low frequencies, usually related to the mains power frequency.

Hz

Abbreviation of *Hertz*, the unit of frequency.

IC

Abbreviation of Integrated Circuit.

Impedance

Can be visualised as the 'AC resistance' of a circuit that contains both resistive and reactive components.

Inductor

Reactive component that presents an increasing impedance with frequency.

Initialise

To automatically restore a piece of equipment to its factory-default settings.

Insert Point

Connector that allows an external processor to be patched into a signal path so that the signal flows through the external processor.

Insulator

Material that does not conduct electricity.

Interface

Device that acts as an intermediary to two or more other pieces of equipment. For example, a MIDI interface enables a computer to communicate with MIDI instruments and keyboards.

Intermittent

Term usually used to describe a fault that appears only occasionally.

Intermodulation Distortion

Distortion that introduces frequencies not present in the original signal. These are invariably based on the sum-and-difference products of the original frequencies.

I/O

Abbreviation of In/Out, used to describe the part of a system that handles (usually digital) inputs and outputs.

IPS

Abbreviation of Inches Per Second, a measure of tape speed.

IRQ

Abbreviation of Interrupt Request, part of a computer operating system that allows a connected device to request attention from the processor in order to transfer data to it or from it.

Isopropyl Alcohol

Type of alcohol commonly used for cleaning and de-greasing tape-machine heads and guides.

Jack

Commonly used audio connector, either mono or stereo.

k

Abbreviation for 1,000 (kilo). Used as a prefix to other values to indicate magnitude.

LED

Abbreviation of Light-Emitting Diode, a solid-state lamp.

LCD

Abbreviation of Liquid-Crystal Display.

LFO

Abbreviation of Low-Frequency Oscillator, an oscillator used as a modulation source, usually below 20Hz. The most common LFO waveshape is the sine wave, though there is often a choice of sine, square, triangular and sawtooth waveforms.

Limiter

Device that controls the gain of a signal so as to prevent it from ever exceeding a preset level. A limiter is essentially a fast-acting compressor with an infinite compression ratio.

Linear

Used to describe a device where the output is a direct multiple of the input.

Line Level

Nominal signal level that is around −10dBV for semi-pro equipment and +4dBu for professional equipment.

Load

Electrical circuit that draws power from another circuit or power supply. Also describes the action of reading data into a computer.

Local On/Off

Function that allows the keyboard and sound-generating section of a keyboard synthesiser to be used independently of each other.

Logic

Type of electronic circuitry used for processing binary signals comprising two discrete voltage levels.

Loop

Circuit in which the output is connected back to the input.

Low-Pass Filter

Filter that attenuates frequencies above its cut-off frequency.

LSB

Abbreviation of Least-Significant Byte. If a piece of data has to be conveyed as two bytes, one byte represents high-value numbers and the other represents low-value numbers, much in the same way as tens and units function in the decimal system. The high value, or the most significant part of the message, is referred to as the MSB(Most Significant Byte).

mA

Abbreviation of milliamp (one-thousandth of an amp).

Mega

Abbreviation for 1,000,000.

MDM

Abbreviation of Modular Digital Multitrack, a variety of digital recorder that can be used in multiples to provide a greater number of synchronised tracks than a single machine.

Machine Head

Term used to describe the tuning mechanism of a guitar.

Memory

Computer's RAM used to store programs and data. This data is lost when the computer is switched off and so must be stored to disk or other suitable media.

Menu

List of choices presented by a computer program or a device with a display window.

Mic Level

Low-level signal generated by a microphone. This must be amplified many times to increase it to line level.

Microprocessor

Specialised microchip at the heart of a computer. It is here that instructions are read and acted upon.

MIDI

Abbreviation of Musical Instrument Digital Interface.

MIDI Analyser

Device that gives a visual readout of MIDI activity when connected between two pieces of MIDI equipment.

MTC

Abbreviation of MIDI Time Code, a MIDI sync implementation based on SMPTE time code.

MIDI Bank Change

Type of controller message used to select alternate banks of MIDI programs where access to more than 128 programs is required.

MIDI Control Change

Also known as MIDI Controllers or Controller Data, these messages convey positional information relating to performance controls such as wheels, pedals, switches and other devices. This information can be used to control functions such as vibrato depth, brightness, portamento, effects levels, and many other parameters.

MIDI Controller

Term used to describe the physical interface over which a musician plays a MIDI synth or other sound generator, such as keyboards, drum pads and wind synths.

(Standard) MIDI File

Standard file format for storing song data recorded on a MIDI sequencer in such as way as to allow it to be read by other makes or model of MIDI sequencer.

MIDI Implementation Chart

Chart usually found in MIDI product manuals providing information concerning which MIDI features are supported. Supported features are marked with a o while unsupported feature are marked with an X. Additional information may be provided such as the exact form of the Bank Change message.

MIDI Merge

Device or sequencer function that enables two or more streams of MIDI data to be combined.

MIDI Module

Sound-generating device with no integral keyboard.

Multitimbral Module

MIDI sound source capable of producing several different sounds at the same time and capable of being controlled on different MIDI channels.

MIDI Mode

MIDI information can be interpreted by the receiving MIDI instrument in a number of ways, the most common being polyphonically on a single MIDI channel (Poly/Omni-Off mode). Omni mode enables a MIDI instrument to play all incoming data regardless of channel.

MIDI Note Number

Every key on a MIDI keyboard has its own note number ranging from 0 to 127, where the number 60 represents middle C. Some systems use C3 as middle C while others use C4.

MIDI Note Off

Message sent when a key is released.

MIDI Note On

MIDI message sent when a note is played (key pressed).

MIDI Port

MIDI connections of a MIDI-compatible device. In the context of a MIDI interface, a multiport is a device with multiple MIDI output sockets, each capable of carrying data relating to a different set of 16 MIDI channels. Multiports are the only means of exceeding the limitations imposed by 16 MIDI channels.

MIDI Program Change

Type of MIDI message used to change sound patches on a remote module or the effects patch on a MIDI effects unit.

MIDI Splitter

Alternative term for a MIDI thru box.

MIDI Thru Box

Device that splits the MIDI Out signal of a master

instrument or sequencer to avoid daisy-chaining. Powered circuitry is used to buffer the outputs in order to prevent problems when many pieces of equipment are driven from a single MIDI output.

MIDI Sync

Description of the synchronisation systems available to MIDI users: MIDI clock and MIDI time code.

Mixer

Device used to combine two or more audio signals.

Monitor

Reference loudspeaker used for mixing.

Monitor

Action of listening to a mix or a specific audio signal.

Monitor

Computer VDU (Visual Display Unit).

Monophonic

Describes the practice of playing one note at a time.

Motherboard

Main circuit board within a computer into which all other components connect or are plugged.

.mp3

Form of data compression used to minimise the size of mono or stereo audio files for transmission over the internet or for use in a portable .mp3 player. Various levels of compression are available depending on how much quality can be sacrificed for the sake of small file size, but a typical .mp3 file takes up around 10 per cent of the size of the uncompressed 16-bit/44.1kHz file.

.mp3 Player

Term used to describe either a hardware playback device for .mp3 audio or a piece of software allowing .mp3 audio to be replayed via the soundcard of a computer. The latter can usually be downloaded free of charge, although the software needed to create .mp3 files normally isn't.

Multisampling

Creation of several samples, each covering a limited musical range, the idea being to produce a more natural range of sounds across the range of the instrument being sampled. For example, a piano may need to be sampled every two or three semitones in order to sound convincing.

Multiport MIDI Interface

Device with multiple MIDI output sockets, each capable of carrying data relating to a different set of 16 MIDI channels. Multiports are the only means of exceeding the limitations imposed by 16 MIDI channels when controlling external hardware synths.

Multitimbral

Term used to describe a synthesiser, sampler or module that can play several parts at the same time, each under the control of a different MIDI channel.

Multitrack

Recording device capable of recording several 'parallel' parts or tracks, which may then be mixed or re-recorded independently.

Near Field

Term used to describe a loudspeaker system designed to be used close to the listener. The advantage is that the listener hears more of the direct sound from the speakers and less of the reflected sound from the room. Some people prefer the term 'close field'.

Noise Reduction

System for reducing analogue tape noise or for reducing the level of hiss present in a recording.

Noise Shaping

System for creating digital dither so that any added noise is shifted into those parts of the audio spectrum where the human ear is least sensitive.

Non-Registered Parameter Number

Addition to the basic MIDI spec that allows controllers 98 and 99 to be used to control non-standard parameters relating to particular models of synthesiser.

This is an alternative to using sysex (system-exclusive) data to achieve the same ends. NRPNs tend to be used mainly by Yamaha and Roland instruments.

Non-Linear Recording

Describes digital recording systems that allow any parts of the recording to be played back in any order with no gaps. Conventional tape is referred to as *linear* because the material can be played back only in the order in which it was recorded.

Normalising

A socket is said to be normalised when it is wired so that the original signal path is maintained unless a plug is inserted into the socket. The most common examples of normalised connectors are the insert points on a mixing console.

Nyquist Theorem

Rule which states that a digital sampling system must have a sample rate at least twice as high as that of the highest frequency being sampled in order to avoid aliasing. Because anti-aliasing filters aren't perfect, the sampling frequency usually has to be made more than twice that of the maximum input frequency.

Nut

Slotted plastic or bone component at the headstock end of a guitar neck used to guide the strings over the fingerboard and to space the strings above the frets.

Octave

When a frequency or pitch is transposed up by one octave, its frequency is doubled.

Offline

Term used to describe a process carried out while a recording is not playing. For example, some computer-based processes have to be carried out offline as the computer isn't fast enough to carry out the process in real time.

Ohm

Unit of electrical resistance.

OMF

Abbreviation of Open Media Framework, a protocol developed by Digidesign to allow the transfer of time-stamped audio files between different software platforms.

Omni

Refers to a microphone that is equally sensitive in all directions or to the MIDI mode where data on all channels is recognised.

OMS

Abbreviation for Opcode's Open MIDI System, Macintosh-based software that links a multiport MIDI interface with OMS-compliant host software.

Open Circuit

Break in an electrical circuit that prevents current from flowing.

Open Reel

Tape machine on which the tape is wound on spools rather than sealed in a cassette shell.

Operating System

Basic software that enables a computer to load and run other programs.

Opto-Electronic Device

Device in which some electrical parameter changes in response to a variation in the intensity of light. Variable photo-resistors are sometimes used as gain-control elements in compressors where the side-chain signal modulates the light intensity.

Oscillator

Circuit designed to generate a periodic electrical waveform.

Overdub

To add another part to a multitrack recording or to replace one of the already existing parts.

Overload

To exceed the operating capacity of an electronic or electrical circuit.

Pad

Resistive circuit used for reducing signal levels.

Pan Pot

Control enabling the user of a mixer to move the signal to any point in the stereo soundstage by varying the relative levels fed to the left and right stereo outputs.

Parallel

Term used to describe a way of connecting two or more circuits together so that their inputs are connected together and their outputs are all connected together.

Parameter

Variable value that affects some aspect of a device's performance.

Parametric

Term used to describe an equaliser with separate controls for changing frequency, bandwidth and cut/boost.

Passive

Term used to describe a circuit with no active elements.

Patch

Alternative term for *program*, referring to a single programmed sound within a synthesiser that can be called up using Program Change commands. MIDI effects units and samplers also have patches.

Patch Bay

System of panel-mounted connectors used to bring inputs and outputs to a central point from where they can be routed using plug-in patch cords.

Patch Cord

Short cable used to connect up a patch bay.

Peak

Maximum instantaneous level of a signal.

PFL

Abbreviation of Pre-Fade Listen, a system used within a mixing console to allow the operator to listen in on a selected signal, regardless of the position of the fader controlling that signal.

Phantom Power

48V DC supply for capacitor mics, transmitted along the signal cores of a balanced mic cable.

Phase

Timing difference between two electrical waveforms, expressed in degrees, where 360° corresponds to a delay of exactly one cycle.

Phaser

Effect that combines a signal with a phase-shifted version of itself to produce creative filtering effects. Most phasers are controlled by means of a low-frequency oscillator.

Phono Plug

Hi-fi connector developed by RCA and used extensively on semi-pro, unbalanced equipment.

Pick-up

Part of a guitar that converts the string vibrations to electrical signals.

Pitch

Musical interpretation of an audio frequency.

Pitch Bend

Special MIDI control message specifically designed to produce a change in pitch in response to the movement of a pitch-bend wheel or lever. Pitch-bend data can be recorded and edited, just like any other MIDI controller data, even though it isn't part of the controller message group.

Pitch Shifter

Device for changing the pitch of an audio signal without changing it's duration.

Polyphony

Ability of an instrument to play two or more notes simultaneously. An instrument which can play only one note at a time is described as *monophonic*.

Poly Mode

Most common MIDI mode, allowing MIDI instruments to respond to multiple simultaneous notes transmitted on a single MIDI channel.

Port

Connection for the input or output of data.

Portamento

Gliding effect that allows a sound to change pitch at a gradual rate, rather than abruptly, when a new key is pressed or MIDI note sent.

Post-Production

Term used to describe work done to a stereo recording after mixing is complete.

Post-Fade

Aux signal taken from after the channel fader so that the aux send level follows any channel fader changes. Normally used for feeding effects devices.

Power Supply

Unit designed to convert mains electricity to the voltages necessary to power an electronic circuit or device.

PPM

Abbreviation of Peak Programme Meter, a meter designed to register signal peaks rather than the average level.

PPQN

Abbreviation of Pulse Per Quarter Note. Used in the context of MIDI Clock-derived sync signals.

Pre-Emphasis

System for applying high-frequency boost to a sound before processing in order to reduce the effect of noise. A corresponding de-emphasis process is required on playback so as to restore the original signal and to attenuate any high-frequency noise contributed by the recording process.

Pre-Fade

Aux signal taken from before the channel fader so that the channel fader has no effect on the aux send level. Normally used for creating foldback or cue mixes.

Preset

Effects unit or synth patch that cannot be altered by the user.

Print-Through

Magnetic information from a recorded analogue tape that becomes imprinted onto an adjacent layer. This can produce low-level pre- or post-echoes.

Processor

Device designed to treat an audio signal by changing its dynamics or frequency content. Examples of processors include compressors, gates and equalisers.

Program Change

MIDI message designed to change instrument or effects unit patches.

Pulse Wave

Similar to a square wave but non-symmetrical. Pulse waves sound brighter and thinner than square waves, making them useful in the synthesis of reed instruments. The timbre changes according to the mark/space ratio of the waveform.

Pulse-Width Modulation

Means of modulating the duty cycle (mark/space ratio) of a pulse wave to change the timbre of the basic tone. LFO modulation of pulse width can be used to produce a pseudo-chorus effect.

Punching In

Action of placing an already recorded track into record at the correct time during playback so that the existing material may be extended or replaced.

Punching Out

Action of switching a tape machine (or other recording device) out of record after executing a punch-in. With most multitrack machines, both punching in and punching out can be accomplished without stopping the tape.

PQ Encoding

Process for adding pause, cue and other subcode information to a digital master tape in preparation for CD manufacture.

PZM

Abbreviation of Pressure Zone Microphone, a type of boundary microphone designed to reject out-of-phase sounds reflected from surfaces within the recording environment.

Q

Measure of the resonant properties of a filter. The higher the Q, the more resonant the filter and the narrower the range of frequencies that are allowed to pass.

Quantising

Means of moving notes recorded in a MIDI sequencer so that they line up with user defined subdivisions of a musical bar – for example, 16ths. The facility may be used to correct timing errors, but over-quantising can remove the human feel from a performance.

RAM

Abbreviation of Random Access Memory, a type of memory used by computers for the temporary storage of programs and data. All RAM data is lost when the power is turned off. For that reason, work needs to be saved to disk if it is not to be lost.

R-BUS

Roland proprietary audio data format for interconnecting R-Bus-compatible equipment. The interface supports eight audio channels but may be used in multiples.

R-DAT

Digital tape machine using a rotating head system.

Real Time

Term used to describe an audio process that can be carried out as a signal is being recorded or played back. The opposite is *offline*, where the signal is processed in non-real time.

Release

The time taken for a level or gain to return to normal. Often used to describe the rate at which a synthesised sound reduces in level after a key has been released.

Resistance

Opposition to the flow of electrical current, measured in ohms.

Resolution

Accuracy with which an analogue signal is represented by a digitising system. The more bits are used, the more accurately the amplitude of each sample can be measured, but there are other elements of converter design that also affect accuracy. High conversion accuracy is known as *high resolution*.

Resonance

Same as *Q*.

Reverb

Acoustic ambience created by multiple reflections that are produced in a confined space.

ReWire

Audio-routing software protocol developed by Propellerhead that allows multiple channels of audio to be routed between different programs in real time.

RF

Abbreviation of Radio Frequency.

RF Interference

Interference significantly above the range of human hearing.

Ribbon Microphone

Microphone in which the sound capturing element is a thin metal ribbon suspended in a magnetic field. When sound causes the ribbon to vibrate, a small electrical current is generated within the ribbon.

Roll-off

Rate at which a filter attenuates a signal once it has passed beyond the filter cut-off point.

ROM

Abbreviation of Read-Only Memory, a permanent or non-volatile type of memory containing data that can't be changed. Operating systems are often stored on ROM as the memory remains intact when the power is removed.

E-PROM

Abbreviation of Erasable Programmable Read-Only Memory. Similar to ROM, but the information on the chip can be erased and replaced using special equipment.

Release

Rate at which a signal amplitude decays once a key has been released.

Resonance

Characteristic of a filter that allows it to selectively pass a narrow range of frequencies. See *Q*.

Ring Modulator

Device that accepts and processes two input signals in a particular way. The output signal does not contain any of the original input signal but instead comprises new frequencies based on the sum and difference of the input signals' frequency components. The best known application of ring modulation is the creation of the voices of the Daleks in the sci-fi series *Dr Who*, but it may also be used to create dramatic instrumental textures. Depending on the relationships between the input signals, the results may either be musical or extremely dissonant – for example, ring modulation can be used to create bell-like tones. (The term *ring* is used here because the original circuit that produced the effect used a ring of diodes.)

RMS

Abbreviation of Root Mean Square, a means of specifying the behaviour of a piece of electrical equipment under continuous sine-wave-testing conditions.

Safety Copy

Copy or clone of an original tape for use in case of loss or damage to the original.

Sampling

Process carried out by an A/D converter where the instantaneous amplitude of a signal is measured many times per second (44.1kHz in the case of CD).

Sample

Digitised sound used as a musical sound source in a sampler or additive synthesiser.

Sample Rate

Measurement of the number of times an A/D converter samples a waveform each second.

Sample And Hold

Usually refers to a feature whereby random values are generated at regular intervals and then used to control another function, such as pitch or filter frequency. Sample-and-hold circuits were also used in old analogue synthesisers to 'remember' the note being played after a key had been released.

Sawtooth Wave

Waveform that resembling the serrated teeth of a saw, containing both odd and even harmonics.

SCMS

Abbreviation of Serial Copycode Management System, a system of data flags carried by the S/PDIF digital-audio interface that indicates whether the source material may be copied for one generation, unlimited generations or not at all. The SCMS code is generated by some consumer DAT machines as an anti-piracy measure. However, transferring the material to any system via an AES/EBU interface will ignore the SCMS flags. SCMS is not transferred via analogue connections.

SCMS Stripper

Hardware or software device used to reset the SCMS flags in order to allow unlimited copying. The stripper is connected between the source and destination devices when the data to be stripped is transferred.

SCSI

Abbreviation of Small Computer System Interface and pronounced 'skuzzi'. SCSI is an interfacing system for connecting hard drives, scanners, CD-ROM drives and similar peripherals to computer. Each SCSI device has its own ID number and no two SCSI devices in the same chain must be set to the same number. The last SCSI device in the chain should be terminated, either via an internal terminator (where provided) or via a plug-in terminator fitted to a free SCSI socket.

SDII

Originally a Digidesign software editor called Sound Designer II, though it is no longer in production. The SDII file format is still supported by a number of Mac-based software packages and has become a professional standard.

Session Tape

Original tape made during a recording session.

Sequencer

Device for recording and replaying MIDI data, usually in a multitrack format, allowing complex compositions to be built up a part at a time.

Short Circuit

Low-resistance path that allows electrical current to flow. The term is usually used to describe a current path that exists through a fault.

Sibilance

High-frequency whistling or lisping sound that affects vocal recordings, due either to poor mic technique or excessive equalisation.

Side Chain

Part of a circuit that splits off a proportion of the main signal so that it can be processed in some way. Compressors use the side-chain signal to derive their control signals.

Signal

Electrical representation of an input such as sound.

Signal Chain

Route taken by a signal from the input of a system to its output.

Signal-To-Noise Ratio

Ratio of the maximum signal level to the residual noise, expressed in decibels.

Sine Wave

Waveform of a pure tone with no harmonics.

Single-Ended Noise Reduction

Method of removing or attenuating the noise component of a signal that doesn't require previous coding, as in the case of Dolby or DBX.

Slave

Device under the control of a master device.

SMPTE

Time code developed for the film industry but now extensively used in music and recording. SMPTE is a real-time code and is related to hours, minutes, seconds and film or video frames rather than to musical tempo.

S/PDIF

Stereo digital audio interconnection format developed jointly by Philips and Sony for the interconnection of digital audio equipment. The connections may either be co-axial (with phono connectors) or optical. The data stream includes flags to indicate copy-code status (SCMS) and track start IDs.

SPL

Abbreviation of Sound Pressure Level, measured in decibels.

SPP

Abbreviation of MIDI Song Position Pointer.

Standard MIDI File

Standard file format that allows MIDI files to be transferred between different sequencers.

Step Time

System for programming a sequencer in non-real time.

Stereo

Two-channel system feeding left and right loudspeakers.

Sticky-Shed Syndrome

Problem affecting some brands of analogue tape after a long time in storage. A breakdown of the binder causes the oxide to shed and the tape tends to adhere to the tape heads and guides when played. A short-term cure can be achieved by baking the affected tape for several hours at 50ºC.

Stripe

To record time code onto one track of a multitrack tape machine.

Square Wave

Symmetrical rectangular waveform. Square waves contain a series of odd harmonics.

Sub-Bass

Frequencies below the range of typical monitor loudspeakers. Some people define sub-bass as frequencies that can be felt rather than heard.

Sub-Woofer

Loudspeaker that handles only very low frequencies.

Subcode

Hidden data within the CD and DAT format that includes such information as the absolute time location, number of tracks, total running time and so on.

Subtractive Synthesis

Process of creating a new sound by filtering and shaping a raw, harmonically complex waveform.

Surge

Sudden increase in mains voltage.

Surround

Audio replay system designed to reproduce 3D sound over multiple loudspeakers.

Sustain

Part of the ADSR envelope that determines the level to which the sound will settle when a key is held down. Once the key is released, the sound decays at a rate determined by the Release parameter. Also refers to a guitar's ability to hold notes that decay very slowly.

Sweet Spot

Optimum position for a microphone, or for a listener in relation to a set of monitor loudspeakers.

Switching Power Supply

Type of power supply that uses a high-frequency oscillator before the transformer so that a smaller, lighter transformer may be used. These power supplies are commonly used in computers and some synthesiser modules.

Sync

Abbreviation of *synchronisation*, a system of making two or more pieces of equipment run in synchronism with each other.

Synthesiser

Electronic musical instrument designed to create a wide range of sounds, both imitative and abstract.

Tape Head

Part of a tape machine that transfers magnetic energy to the tape during recording or reads it during playback.

TDIF

Audio interfacing standard handling up to eight channels per connection developed by Tascam. Connection is via a multipin connector.

Toslink

Standard optical interface used by the S/PDIF and ADAT interfaces.

Tempo

Rate of the 'beat' of a piece of music measured in beats per minute.

Test Tone

Steady, fixed-level tone recorded onto a multitrack or stereo recording to act as a reference when matching levels.

THD

Abbreviation of Total Harmonic Distortion.

Thru

MIDI connector that passes on the signal received at the MIDI In socket.

Timbre

Tonal 'colour' of a sound.

Track

Term that dates back to multitrack tape, on which the tracks are physical stripes of recorded material, located side-by-side along the length of the tape.

Tracking

System whereby one device follows another. Tracking is often discussed in the context of MIDI guitar synthesisers or controllers where the MIDI output attempts to track the pitch of the guitar strings.

Transparent

Subjective term used to describe audio quality where the high-frequency detail is clear and individual sounds are easy to identify and separate.

Tremolo

Term used to describe the modulation of the amplitude of a sound using a low-frequency oscillator.

Transducer

Device for converting one form of energy to another. A microphone is a good example of a transducer as it converts mechanical energy to electrical energy.

Transpose

To shift a musical signal by a fixed number of semitones.

Triangle Wave

Symmetrical, triangular wave containing odd harmonics only but with a lower harmonic content than a square wave.

TRS jack

Stereo-type jack with Tip, Ring and Sleeve connections.

Truss Rod

Metal bar within the neck of a guitar, tensioned so as to counteract the tendency for the neck to bend under the pull of the strings.

Unbalanced

Term used to describe a two-wire electrical signal connection where the inner or hot (or positive) conductor is usually surrounded by the cold (or negative) conductor, forming a screen against interference.

Unison

Term to describe the same melody being used by two or more different instruments or voices.

Valve

Vacuum-tube amplification component, also known as a tube.

Velocity

Rate at which a key is depressed. This may be used to control loudness (to simulate the response of instruments such as pianos) or other parameters on later synthesisers.

Vocoder

Signal processor that imposes a changing spectral filter on a sound based on the frequency characteristics of a second sound. By taking the spectral content of a human voice and imposing it on a musical instrument, talking-instrument effects can be created.

Voice

Term used to describe the capacity of a synthesiser to play a single musical note. An instrument capable of playing 16 simultaneous notes is said to be a 16-voice instrument.

Vibrato

Pitch modulation using an LFO to modulate a VCO.

VST

Abbreviation of Virtual Studio Technology, a Steinberg-originated standard for plug-in design for use with their Cubase VST software. It is now supported by other leading sequencers, including Emagic's Logic Audio.

VST Effect

Plug-in effect or processor written to the VST standard that may be used within any VST-compliant music-software package. Both Mac and PC versions of many VST products are available. VST II-compliant plug-ins can receive MIDI data, which makes automation possible.

VST Instrument

Plug-in MIDI instrument, such as a synth, sampler or drum machine written to the VST standard that may be used within any VST-compliant music software package. Both Mac and PC versions are available for many VST products. VST instruments are played like any other MIDI instrument and most have comprehensive parameter automation.

VU Meter

Meter designed to interpret signal levels in roughly the same way as the human ear, which responds more closely to the average levels of sounds rather than to the peak levels.

Wah-Wah Pedal

Guitar effects device that uses changes in frequency of a bandpass filter as a means of pedal control.

Watt

SI Unit of electrical power.

Warmth

Subjective term used to describe sound where the bass and low-mid frequencies have depth and where the high frequencies sound smooth rather than aggressive or fatiguing. Warm-sounding tube equipment may also exhibit some of the aspects of compression.

.WAV

Type of audio-file format first used for PC audio programs but now also supported by Macintoshes.

Waveform

Graphic representation of the way in which a sound wave or electrical wave varies with time.

White Noise

Random signal with an energy distribution that produces the same amount of noise power per hertz.

Write

To save data to a digital storage medium, such as a hard drive.

XG

Yamaha's alternative to Roland's GS system for enhancing the General MIDI protocol so as to provide additional banks of patches and further editing facilities.

Y-Lead

Lead split so that one source can feed two destinations. Y-leads can also be used in console insert points, in which case a stereo jack plug at one end of the lead is split into two monos at the other.

Zenith

Parameter of tape-head alignment relating to whether or not the head is perpendicular to the tape path and aligned so as to be in the same plane.

Zero-Crossing Point

The point at which a signal waveform crosses from being positive to negative or vice versa.

Zipper Noise

Audible steps that occur when a parameter is being changed in a digital audio processor.